Complex and Archetype

"This dynamic book showcases a new generation of scholars as they extend the Jungian concepts of complexes and archetypes. By engaging some of the cutting edges of contemporary culture with 21st century models of these concepts they invite us to reimagine the Zeitgeist. A rewarding read for anyone looking to expand their psychological view of our modern world."

—Joe Cambray, PhD, Past-President/CEO, *Pacifica Graduate Institute*

"Not only is the book about the ways complexes and archetypes work together to convey compensatory messages from the unconscious (thereby conspiring to bring individuals and communities to where they need to be), but a timely contribution that extends what it means to *do* Jungian, psycho-social research. What I value most is the fearlessness with which potentially sensitive topics are engaged."

—Kevin Lu, PhD, *Professor of Applied Psychoanalysis, Royal Central School of Speech and Drama, University of London*

"This is an outstanding collection by a group of writers from both academic and therapeutic backgrounds which seeks to explore the contribution that Jungian ideas – and specifically archetype and complex – can make to understanding contemporary social and cultural issues. The contributors deal with a wide range of topics – which include, among others, video-gaming, romantic love, parenting, and the modern academy. However, this refreshingly outward-facing approach is coupled with and underpinned by an impressively rigorous scholarly understanding of all the ideas that are employed, such that a whole gamut of Jungian and post-Jungian notions receives a thorough contemporary re-working. Throughout, insights are provided with elegance, clarity and lightness of touch and the book as a whole leaves us with no doubt that a depth-psychological approach can shed genuinely new light on psychosocial questions. A rich and enjoyable collection that will be of interest to students, clinicians and lay readers."

—Mark Saban PhD, *Jungian analyst and Director of the MA in Jungian and post-Jungian Studies at the University of Essex*

"This volume provides a much-needed clarification about two key principles of Carl Jung's that often are misunderstood in and/or omitted from today's psychology curriculum. As our global society currently grapples with numerous interrelated challenges, uncertainties, and existential threats, the authors clearly demonstrate the contemporary relevance of Jung's psychology in myriad contexts—from polarization, populism, and cancel culture to some younger people's decision to forego marriage and/or having children to video games, gender, and spirituality. As a former graduate student of Jim Dillon's, I can say with confidence that this collection of essays emanating from his classroom and reading group offers a fly-on-the-wall view of his phenomenal teaching."

—Andrew Bland, PhD, LP, *Associate Professor of Psychology, Millersville University*

James J. Dillon
Editor

Complex and Archetype

Exploring the Forces which Animate Our Lives

palgrave
macmillan

Editor
James J. Dillon
School of Social Sciences
University of West Georgia
Carrollton, GA, USA

ISBN 978-3-032-02608-8 ISBN 978-3-032-02609-5 (eBook)
https://doi.org/10.1007/978-3-032-02609-5

Cover illustration: Bob Garner

This Palgrave Macmillan imprint is published by the registered company Springer Nature Switzerland AG.
The registered company address is: Gewerbestrasse 11, 6330 Cham, Switzerland

Foreword

In October 2024, I was simultaneously astonished and delighted to hear from Ben Swogger, a fellow presenter at Northeastern University's *Psychology & the Other* conference, that a paper I had co-authored with Dr Ann Yeoman had been introduced to a reading group to which he belonged. The article in question is "Jungian Psycho-Social Studies: *Akira*, Greta Thunberg and Archetypal Thematic Analysis (ATA)," published in the *International Journal of Jungian Studies* (2024). I was gratified to learn that the piece, so soon after its publication, had a considerable impact on the discussions of Ben's group and on the realisation of the group's research objectives. And now, we have the publication of a significant volume of essays, *Complex and Archetype: Exploring the Forces Which Animate Our Lives*, edited by Prof James J. Dillon. A number of the essays in this volume feature ATA, the methodology proffered by Dr Yeoman and me in our paper, and I am delighted that Ben and his reading group invited me to contribute a Foreword introducing Archetypal Thematic Analysis. I will briefly outline ATA's 'story'—its genesis, and development, what it is, what its goals are, what its future direction might be. Above all, both Dr Yeoman and I hope that ATA will be questioned, utilised and, in the process, enhanced by others working in Jungian and post-Jungian Studies and the field of psycho-social studies.

The Past

My deep respect for the discipline of history was cultivated by Prof Timothy Brook, who taught an undergraduate course (HIS104, *Ten Days that Shook the World*) I completed at the University of Toronto. Although clearly taking its inspiration from John Reed's book of the same name, the course served as an introduction to global history. Through the autumn semester of my freshman year, Tim took us on a journey through ten seemingly unconnected events, having started and stopped our expedition in the same location—Salt Spring Island, British Columbia, Canada. He challenged a linear understanding of the past and encouraged us to reflect on the relationship between time, history, and the practice of historical writing. On the last day, the threads that Tim had been weaving throughout the semester emerged as a complex tapestry for our undergraduate eyes to behold—he connected each and every event, and showed us how they all led back to Salt Spring Island. I was astounded by Tim's care, craft, research skills, and storytelling abilities. In that moment, I had felt an overwhelming sense of meaning, that the intertwining stories mattered and needed to be told. By the following year, I was Tim's research assistant, helping him with the completion of writing projects that included *The Chinese State in Ming Society* (Brook, 2005b), *Collaboration* (Brook, 2005a), and *Death by a Thousand Cuts* (Brook et al., 2008). But it is his 2008 book, *Vermeer's Hat* (Brook, 2008), that best captures the approach that captivated me. There, 'keyhole moments' or objects are chosen as the starting point to investigating wider trends and patterns; they serve as a springboard to ask more in-depth and complex questions, but also as occasions to appreciate and understand the interconnectedness of human activity and the relationships that bind individuals and communities together.

My undergraduate studies also afforded an opportunity to rekindle (and ignite) earlier interests. In my third year, I discovered the Jungian Studies courses led by Dr Ann Yeoman that were offered as part of my Minor in Humanism (later renamed a Minor in Paradigms & Archetypes). Several of these courses involved the application of analytical psychological theory to disciplines as diverse as religion, ethnology, literature, film and the arts. Through my undergraduate studies, I came to appreciate the necessary interdisciplinarity of research into human behaviour; the complexity of who we are and how we define ourselves is a negotiation and constant conversation between our interiority and the influence of our external environment. This understanding was cultivated and deepened through my MA and PhD, where my focus turned to Jung's theory of *synchronicity* which, in hindsight, neatly captured and encapsulated the various strands of my burgeoning research interest—the inner, psychological world, its relationship to the outer, and a search for meaning in a time-bound (at least on the surface) existence.

Those who have read and engaged with the 2024 paper will, I hope, recognise some of the continuities that find expression and refinement in the development of ATA. First, there is a stylistic and hermeneutic choice of locating 'keyhole moments,' those opportunities when we are afforded a glimpse—through a keyhole—of that which lies beyond a closed door but, once opened, can radically shift what and how we see.

Second, ATA takes, as its starting point, the inseparability of the inner and outer worlds and seeks to bring into greater dialogue the 'inner' and 'outer' worlds, the latter epitomised by disciplines such as history, sociology and anthropology. In outlining our rationale for using the hyphen in psycho-social, Yeoman and I suggest that the hyphen may "most usefully be seen to function as a *bridge*, linking rather than separating inner and outer. In this way, the hyphen serves as a metaphor for an on-going conscious relationship and evolving dialogue between the psychological and social spheres of human experience; it also recognises that inner and outer continually shape and condition each other" (2024, p. 81). We interpret the hyphen in psycho-social not merely as a link but a "creative *interface*" between inner and outer (p. 81). Crucially, the hyphen frames our pursuit of knowledge "as a two-way exchange that is on-going and open, as well as, necessarily, nuanced and rigorous," avoiding a search for universal truths that has been, often, a hallmark of earlier Jungian research (p. 81). Since my undergraduate studies, I have been gripped by the idea that our psychological interiority is inevitably shaped by the 'outer,' as much as the 'inner' moulds our understanding of the external world and the collective life we share in groups. This interest stems from Jung's observation that the "psyche expresses itself in all the activities and achievements of the human mind" and that, accordingly, "we can nowhere grasp the nature of the psyche *per se*" but that we meet and study it in its diverse manifestations—in life, art, history and humanistic enquiry (Jung, 1930/1966, p. 85).

Third, using an 'event' or object as the 'keyhole moment' provides an opportunity to question if 'patterns on the surface' may well be interconnected with patterns (archetypal energies) operating at a level of 'depth'—that is, unconsciously. In other words, archetypal patterns, themes or energies may well constitute the invisible thread connecting seemingly unconnected events happening relatively close in time, and may then constellate in the keyhole moments identified. What seems, on the surface, to be either a minor or insignificant event resigned to fade from collective memory is injected with new significance that is psychological in scope. ATA as a methodology highlights Jung's assertion that the unconscious has a 'logic' of its own; it takes patience, openness, courage, consciousness and, as Yeoman and I argue, a psycho-social approach to research to recognise the myriad ways the unconscious communicates its compensatory messages to consciousness.

Fourth, because of the impact of HIS104 and encountering Jung's theory of *synchronicity*, I am fascinated by the concept of time. In Jung's articulation of synchronicity, notions of time and space seemingly collapse when we pose questions of meaning from the perspective of a deep and dynamic unconscious. Space and time, as Jung argues, are "elastic" when assessed from the perspective of the psyche "and can apparently be reduced almost to a vanishing point, as though they were dependent on psychic conditions and did not exist in themselves but were only 'postulated' by the conscious mind" (Jung, 1952/1960, p. 435). In developing ATA, I was keen to integrate synchronicity as a valuable contribution to the way we think about, look at, and *do* research. In many ways, synchronicity's emphasis on acausal, meaningful connections resonated with—rightly or wrongly—some of the principles I valued in learning about global history. What is, on the surface, ostensibly unconnected may actually be linked in a myriad of ways; unearthing these connections could be meaningful not only for the researcher, but those who have to live with the resonances and repercussions of these interdependencies, whether they are aware of it or not.

The Present

While I have provided a description of archetypal thematic analysis's (ATA's) intellectual roots, the approach is equally my response to a question often asked by students: how do you 'prove' the existence of an archetype? When the question was posed, I found myself responding in typical ways:

(a) An emphasis on *archetypal images* and their occurrence/reoccurrence (often across mythologies, cultures, and as dream images) would support an assertion that archetypal patterns are evident.
(b) That some things cannot be known beyond a shadow of a doubt, and 'unknowing' (tolerating uncertainty) and holding the resulting tension is an important skill to learn.
(c) One also needs to query the nature of evidence, and what constitutes 'sufficient' evidence to prove an assertion to be compelling and potentially true. This largely depends on the contingent context, as well as the intended audience being addressed.

Yet despite the profound importance of Christian Roesler's (2013) empirical studies—which established a firm foundation for more qualitative and quantitative research in Jungian and Post-Jungian Studies, particularly in articulating the long-term efficacy of Jungian psychotherapy—the fundamental question of the validity of Jungian therapy's underlying ideas, especially Jung's archetypal hypothesis, still remained unanswered. I could not dismiss my students' compelling reflections, and the task was not so much definitively proving the existence of archetypes *per se* as to establish a methodology, a way of questioning, seeing and understanding to demonstrate the constellation of archetypal energy through an examination of the archetypal imagery that this energy generates and presents to consciousness. Emotions, reactions and feelings are also forms of archetypal imagery and point to the existence of some *thing*, power or energy called an 'archetype.'

As Ann Yeoman and I argue in our paper, archetypal thematic analysis (ATA) is, then, a methodology (still in need of development and constructive criticism) that may be utilised to enhance qualitative research in the field of psycho-social studies, as well as other disciplines. ATA constitutes what we hope is a rigorous approach to research which uses thematic analysis as its starting point, together with the inner- and outer-world focus of Jung's psychology, and Jung's archetypal hypothesis; it uses Jung's description of specific archetypal imagery (imagery that points to the activation of the *child* archetype, the archetype of the *hero* or *shadow*, etc.) to establish an *a priori* code manual in order to test, validate or refute the proposition that an archetype has been constellated in real world events as presented in a particular dataset. Yeoman and I argue that ATA may be used productively not only for the selection of data and in codifying practices but to enrich the interpretation of datasets (Lu & Yeoman, 2024, p. 108). We anticipate that ATA will support the development of code manuals and the analysis of datasets in a holistic and robust practice that utilises all of the 'functions' of consciousness that Jung identified in his typology (thinking, feeling [valuing], intuition and sensation)—and their *introverted* or *extroverted* direction—to reinforce and realise a truly psycho-social approach. Best practice in thematic analysis—which suggests that datasets are analysed independently by two or more researchers—already lays the framework for such a method.

Moving forward, Yeoman and I hope that the limitations of ATA will be critiqued and the ATA methodology fine-tuned accordingly. Jung's analytical psychology remains a product of the Global North and we anticipate ATA being developed by researchers form the Global South to provide necessary correctives which give voice to marginalised perspectives, experiences and histories. Also, while ATA attempts to ground analytical psychology in empirical, psycho-social dialogue, the development of further safeguards and 'checks and balances' is essential to prevent intellectual slippage or spurious, ungrounded claims. ATA can most certainly learn from researchers in other qualitative disciplines to enhance its validity and reliability. We hope that the reflexivity we have worked to adopt—together with our commitment to dialogue and inter-coder reliability—constitute an effective starting point. We welcome continued debate and the vigilance and critique of others to ensure ATA's intellectual integrity and viability.

The Future

From the outset, Yeoman and I have framed the publication of our 2024 article as an opportunity to deepen an appreciation of method and methodology and its utility within Jungian and Post-Jungian Studies. We will continue to encourage debate on ATA's potential limitations and advocate for proactive steps to be taken to strengthen it. The intent remains for others to question, apply and test the method so that together, a community of scholars and practitioners can supplement the important hermeneutic and philosophical work already being done with a robust, qualitative scaffolding for future research. ATA introduces a more systematic and structured way of working that consciously addresses the need to justify what it is we do—not only *why* we do it, but *how* we do it (Lu, 2013).

In this vein, James J. Dillon's edited volume, *Complex and Archetype*, judiciously continues the conversation by exploring the intricate relationship between *complex* and *archetype* in Jung's thinking. The possibilities of meaning latent in the unconscious are not only found in the very depths of our psychological existence, but in the everyday. The book constitutes an in-depth exploration of how the personal, cultural and collective strata of the unconscious influence our lives, resulting in a distinctive, Jungian contribution to psycho-social studies. A fine balance is struck between theoretical contributions and practical applications. In Part I, James J. Dillon identifies *complexes* as the conceptual bridge connecting the psyche and the social. Indeed, a detailed and nuanced understanding of Jung's theory of complexes is the groundwork for a more secure, Jungian contribution to psycho-social studies. Michael V. Steder insightfully articulates the centrality of complexes in grasping the advancement of self-knowledge in three stages or movements: *impression*, *naming* and *integration*. The final chapter of Part I, authored by Ben Swogger, presents a Post-Jungian reflection on the tensions and opportunities that exist between multiple strands of Jungian and Post-Jungian thought: complexes, the science of complexity, and Jung's archetypal hypothesis. While connections can be made between complexes and complexity, the latter seems to be at odds with the notion of an *a priori* archetype. Swogger confidently guides the reader through this conundrum and ends the section by suggesting new areas of development that would amplify our thinking around Jung's archetypal hypothesis.

Part II presents several applications of Jungian theory to develop the case for a distinctly Jungian contribution to psycho-social studies. Noah Cochran, utilising the framework of ATA, analyses the figures of Kim Kardashian and Elon Musk as the constellation of 'lover' and 'creator' archetypes, respectively, in American popular culture. Louisa Grann rightly intuits gaming as a modern site for the facilitation and expression of *individuation*. Utilising ATA, Grann contends that Nintendo's *Legend of Zelda* franchise is a poignant example of the hero's journey, while judiciously mobilising autoethnographic reflections to deepen her analysis of the array of archetypal images constellated within this digital world.

What purpose does marriage now serve in contemporary, western society, and to what extent are our fantasies of romantic love informed by the stories we consume in diverse media and forms? These are the very questions that Andrea Stover addresses; with shifting values and relationship styles that challenge the 'traditional' structures and arrangements of Jung's time, do analytical psychological concepts such as *anima* and *animus* remain relevant? Stover's contribution is beautifully juxtaposed with Ben

Swogger's astute historical overview of Jung's contrasexual archetype, which aims to penetrate to the root of these notions in Jung's own thought. In Chap. 9, Andrea Stover and James J. Dillon explore individuation in the context of childlessness. Although Jung reflected extensively on the psychological role of children (both positive and negative) within a family dynamic, Stover and Dillon extend the conversation to challenge Jung's conceptualisation of individuation itself, as so much of it hinges on preconceived notions of the psycho-social impact of the nuclear family on one's development. Alternative sublimations are explored, with practical reflections on how to avoid one-sidedness when consciously activating complexes and archetypal energies typically associated with having and raising children. Mark Rich examines, in Chap. 10, how a yearning for meaning finds expression in *sacred practices.* Rich distinguishes four ways the collective unconscious appears in these practices, while highlighting the proclivity to project the sacred onto and into our geographical surroundings. In the penultimate chapter of this section, James J. Dillon mobilises ATA to critique the state of modern academia. He argues for the constellation of three separate yet interconnected archetypal energies: a *negative father complex*, a *positive mother complex*, and a *Prometheus complex.* Ways to move beyond these complexes are presented, with an emphasis on universities becoming, once more, sites devoted to the exploration of truth.

Not only is the book about the ways complexes and archetypes work together to convey compensatory messages from the unconscious (thereby conspiring to bring individuals and communities to where they need to be), but a timely contribution that extends what it means to *do* Jungian, psycho-social research. What I value most is the fearlessness with which potentially sensitive topics are engaged. Psychological depth and insight are always foregrounded, with academic debate and conversation the main course in an enviable feast that is likely to satisfy as much as it is to raise further challenging questions. The 'gold' of the volume is not to be found in the moments of agreement, but at junctures where opinions divide—a tension of opposites unfolds and produces the very conditions necessary for an emergence of new knowledge.

What we write is unequivocally shaped by the context in which we write. I cannot help but be reminded of the global tensions, intense political polarisation and economic uncertainties that currently define our collective existence. Indeed, these are the very areas where ATA may usefully be applied to interrogate, debate and deepen research. In these challenging times, I find strength in the friendship of academic colleagues who continue to support one another. They uphold the primacy of intellectual exchange based on critical engagement and driven by principles of best ethical practice, which include honesty, equity, transparency, open communication, care, respect, humility and accountability. To James, Noah, Louise, Mark, Michael, Andrea and Ben, my sincere congratulations for envisioning and bringing to life such an important contribution, for critically engaging with ATA, and for the camaraderie that unites and overcomes division.

University of London, Royal Central School of Speech and Drama
Toronto, Canada
April 2025

Kevin Lu

References

Brook, T. (2005a). *Collaboration: Japanese agents and local elites in wartime China*. Harvard University Press.

Brook, Timothy. (2005b). *The Chinese state in Ming society*. RoutledgeCurzon.

Brook, T. (2008). *Vermeer's hat: The seventeenth century and the dawn of the global world*. Bloomsbury Press.

Brook, T., Bourgon, J., & Blue, G. (Eds.). (2008). *Death by a thousand cuts*. Harvard University Press.

Jung, C. G. (1960). Synchronicity: An acausal connecting principle (R. F. C. Hull, Trans.). In H. Read, M. Fordham, G. Adler, & W. McGuire (Eds.), *The collected Works of C.G. Jung: Vol. 8. The structure and dynamics of the psyche* (pp. 418–519). Routledge & Kegan Paul. (Original work published 1952).

Jung, C. G. (1966). Psychology and literature (R. F. C. Hull, Trans.). In H. Read, et al., (Eds.), *The collected works of C. G. Jung: Vol. 15. The spirit in man, art, and literature* (pp. 84–105). Princeton University Press. (Original work published 1930).

Lu, K. (2013). Can individual psychology explain social phenomena? An appraisal of the theory of cultural complexes. *Psychoanalysis, Culture & Society, 18*: 386–404.

Lu, K., & Yeoman, A. (2024). Jungian psycho-social studies: Akira, Greta Thunberg, and archetypal thematic analysis (ATA). *International Journal of Jungian Studies, 16*, pp. 77–112.

Roesler, C. (2013). Evidence for the effectiveness of Jungian psychotherapy: A review of empirical studies. *Behavioral Sciences, 3*, pp. 562–575.

Contents

List of Contributors

Noah W. Cochran University of West Georgia, School of Social Sciences, Carrollton, GA, USA

James J. Dillon School of Social Sciences, University of West Georgia, Carrollton, GA, USA

Louise Grann University of West Georgia, School of Social Sciences, Carrollton, GA, USA

Mark S. Rich Independent Scholar, Bowdon, GA, USA

Michael V. Steder University of West Georgia, School of Social Sciences, Carrollton, GA, USA

Andrea M. Stover Licensed Marriage & Family Therapist, Kansas City, MO, USA

Benjamin J. Swogger University of West Georgia, School of Social Sciences, Carrollton, GA, USA

List of Figures

CHAPTER 1

Confronting Archetypes Through the Complex

James J. Dillon

This collection of essays springs from a bi-monthly reading group formed at the University of West Georgia in 2018, which continues to meet today. To provide a bit of history, I offered several theory-heavy courses on C.G. Jung's psychology to master's and doctoral students. Given the large number of faculty in our program, I was only able to offer a graduate class about every academic year or so. Several students approached me after each class ended wanting more regular contact with Jung than we were able to offer through our regular course offerings. This led to the eventual formation of our bi-monthly Jung study group. It was a way for these students who were deeply interested in Jung to dive more deeply into his work. Each semester after our founding, we brainstormed psychological themes we wanted to explore and identified the volumes of the *Collected Works* which would help us do it. Most semesters we set ourselves the task of exploring a single theme in one volume. If the book were just too big, we would split it into two semesters of work. Sometimes we devoted a semester to explore a theme related to secondary sources such as Giegerich, Hillman, or Goethe.

J. J. Dillon (✉)
School of Social Sciences, University of West Georgia, Carrollton, GA, USA

J. J. Dillon (ed.), *Complex and Archetype*,
https://doi.org/10.1007/978-3-032-02609-5_1

The group was composed of serious scholars dedicated to exploring the mysteries of the psyche under Jung's tutelage. Some members remained in the group after graduating from our program and starting their own careers in therapy, academia, and other venues. The contributors to the present volume have all been in the group between five and seven total years. Among the many lessons we learned from working together over this time was how to have deep and serious academic discussions. Looking at it now, our process had several notable features: profound interpersonal respect, genuine curiosity, avoidance of name-dropping, academic jargon, political posturing, and the other vices which unfortunately plague today's graduate classrooms. Participants were well-prepared before each meeting, drove discussions with guiding questions about the reading selection, and offered answers by pointing to the details and logic of the text on the table and to the growing corpus of work we gradually came to read together. The group has been one of the most rewarding experiences of my 33-year teaching career.

In addition to learning how to learn in an academic group, we discovered important things about how to read Jung's texts. Jung's written work is immensely vivid, stimulating, at times frustrating, but highly rewarding to read. After just a few lines, one gets the sense of being in the presence of an original and incisive mind, a once-in-a-generation intellect. I am immensely grateful for the time I have been able to spend with Jung over the years. Many other readers have had similarly inspiring experiences reading Jung, which makes him one of the more talked-about and quoted psychologists of our age. As we delved deeper into the various texts, it became clear to us that many popular and academic treatments of Jung are not always informed by close readings of his work, but by the conceits of the present age and/or the agendas of the author. Jung even once said of himself, "Thank God I am Jung and not a Jungian" (Hannah, 1976, p. 78). Of course, there is nothing inherently wrong with agendas or conceits. We all have them. The problem is when we conflate "our stuff" with Jung's own words and thoughts. There are many who write about or teach Jung, but few genuine scholars of his work. A major goal in our ongoing collaboration was to be scholars rather than invoke the weight of Jung's name to bless projects and ideas he never advanced or approved of.

As brilliant as Jung is, he can also be maddeningly ambiguous, even intentionally obscure about the most central concepts within his analytical psychology. He sometimes contradicts himself between early and later work, and can even do so within the very same text. This is one of the reasons why selectively quoting Jung is such a problem. Jung also lapses into pages-long tangents or cites arcane examples from mythology or linguistics as "clear and convincing" evidence of a claim when they are tendentious supports at best. He is sometimes prone to impolitic or gratuitous statements about women or dark-skinned people which are difficult to defend. He puts commonly accepted terms to new use without first informing the reader, and he regularly violates basic rules of logic, grammar, and composition in a way one would not tolerate from a high school student. Many of his works seem like first drafts, with brilliant and generative ideas hastily sketched out, leaving the reader on the hook to conjure the examples and illustrations which he should have provided himself. One thing I often say to the group is that more than anything else, Jung needed a stronger editor. This volume attempts to perform some of these necessary editorial functions.

The Covid epidemic which began in the spring of 2020 required us to meet remotely for the first time. During the first pandemic semester, we decided to focus on the theme of Jungian *archetypes* by reading *Volume 9* (*Part 1*) of the *Collected Works*. The following semester we focused on the theme of *complexes* by reading selections from *Volume 8*. The readings from these two works struck immensely powerful chords in the group. Discussions were animated. The ideas influenced other projects we were working on in our careers and even inspired research which later became publications (see Dillon, 2021). It struck us that Jung's insights on the dynamic between complex and archetype were generally unappreciated and held great promise for the future of psychology.

When we discussed complexes and archetypes with our psychology colleagues outside of Jungian circles, their understanding of these terms was poor, which permitted them to blithely dismiss their larger implications. Of course, some of this disregard is due to our colleagues' prior philosophical commitments and orientations which make accepting Jung's ideas difficult or impossible, but a good portion of the blame is caused by the above-mentioned issues concerning the clarity, lack of examples, and overall poor persuasiveness of Jung's own writing. It was from experiences like these that the idea for the present volume was born. We set out to illustrate, clarify, and apply the highly generative concepts of complex and archetype with the hope the larger psychological community will more deeply appreciate and understand them. We do so largely by "adding flesh to the bones" of Jung's texts by providing examples and case applications which his original writings often lack. We also hope to show how these two great ideas are relevant to a society which is, in many important ways, different from Jung's own.

A brief word about our group and its expertise. Each author of the present volume is connected in some way to the University of West Georgia. The psychology program at West Georgia was founded in 1968 by several of Abraham Maslow's students who made the long journey south from Massachusetts to build one of the few programs in the United States exclusively dedicated to humanistic psychology. Over the years, the program expanded from its roots in the humanistic tradition to embrace transpersonal psychology, and more recently has adopted critical and psycho-social approaches. We award degrees at the bachelor's, master's, and doctoral levels. Save for the editor, each chapter of this volume is authored by a scholar or practitioner who brings this unique humanistic-transpersonal-social perspective to Jungian studies from an advanced degree in "Consciousness and Society," a unique method of training which emphasizes the examination of psychological life as it manifests in cultural and social phenomena. Each author brings this psycho-social perspective to the Jungian corpus. We hope our approach will illuminate hidden aspects of analytical psychology which will be valuable to those engaged more exclusively in Jungian Studies.

As noted in Chap. 2, complexes are "feeling toned" associations of perceptions, memories, thoughts, and desires which are activated by life events, relationships, or developmental stages. They behave like "animated foreign bodies" in the field of consciousness (see Jung, 1928/1969b, p. 11; Jung, 1934/1969a, p. 96). As Jung's work matured, he advanced the idea that most complexes are admixtures of both personal and archetypal material (Jacobi, 1959, pp. 22–23). Specifically, the complex comprises an outer *shell* and an inner *core*. The shell is largely composed of associations and amplifications from life experiences, significant relationships, and imaginal material from the culture's art, literature, philosophy, and religion. The core, or "nuclear element" of the complex, rests upon one or more archetypes, and is not derived from culture or experience (Jung, 1928/1969b).

We find complexes and archetypes not in the dark depths of the soul, but in the details of everyday life. Our book develops insights into these two central Jungian concepts by examining their embodiment in a wide range of contemporary social, cultural, and political phenomena. By exploring the dynamic interplay between complex and archetype, we bring these two foundational concepts to bear upon the emerging field of *psycho-social studies*, an approach which investigates the zone of intersection between the psychological and the socio-cultural. Building upon Lu and Yeoman's (2024) efforts to formulate a reliable and valid way of analyzing the psychological and archetypal significance of social phenomena, our project is one of the first in the United States to further the development of a uniquely Jungian approach to psycho-social studies.

The book is divided into two major parts: *complexes* and *case analyses*. Chapters 2, 3, and 4 (Part I) focus primarily on Jung's concept of *complexes* as the constellating region of intersection between the psyche and the social. Complexes manifest in our lives in numerous ways, including projections, dreams, parapraxes, and symptoms. Jung (1934/1969a) refers to complexes the *via regia* to the unconscious (p. 101) and even thought of calling his analytical psychology "complex psychology" since they were so central to his project. As one travels the royal road of the complex, one is inevitably led to the archetypes. Though they are shrouded by our personal experience, our trauma history, language, and our cultural history, the core of each complex contains an *archetype*, a numinous image with the power to animate or possess. Each chapter explores the deeper meaning and developmental implications of the complexes by examining the typical contexts in which they manifest: the therapeutic and personal growth context, modern science and society, and the discipline of psychology. We approach the archetype through the complex. We approach the complexes through everyday social and interpersonal life.

Chapter 2 shows what psychology misses when it ignores the dynamic interplay between psychic experience and social life, construing complexes as only external voices from society or internal products of the ego. Dillon explores two common obstacles to appreciating the role and power of complexes and illustrates how a proper understanding of the nature and function of the complexes can reveal the inner cause of our mental disturbances and open a productive avenue for growth and development.

Chapter 3 explores how the personification of complexes facilitates the advancement of self-knowledge. Steder argues that the intentional personification of complexes offers opportunities to encounter, engage, and disclose unknown aspects of personality resulting in a transformed personality through an expanded awareness of trigger situations and the attainment of a new attitude beyond the one-sidedness of the initial one. Steder concludes by providing an analytical description of dreams, literature, and psychopathology.

Chapter 4 surveys the small but important subset of Jungian literature seeking to reinterpret Jung's ideas regarding complexes and archetypes in light of the new science of *complexity*. It clarifies the connection between psychic complexes and complex systems, explores theoretical and clinical implications, and argues that a more transpersonal approach is needed to account for the difference between complexes and archetypes. The understanding emerging from Swogger's analysis calls for a revisiting of certain theoretical and clinical difficulties within Jung's thought.

Chapters 5, 6, 7, 8, 9 , 10, and 11(Part II) present case analyses which examine the way complexes and archetypes manifest in different domains of personal and social existence: romantic relationships, popular culture, video games, the clinical setting, parenting, pet-ownership, campus culture wars, and the vagaries and chores of everyday life. Each chapter reveals practical insights about how to productively engage the feeling-tones, dreams, and images present in the socially embodied complexes to unearth the guidance, depth, color, and energy which spring from the archetypes hidden within them.

Chapter 5 considers Kim Kardashian and Elon Musk as contemporary cultural embodiments of archetypes. Cochran shows that high-profile cultural figures spring from what he calls a *popular culture pantheon* which constellate as unconscious responses to the needs of the collective cultural consciousness at specific historical moments. These cultural figures also amplify cultural needs and desires, and shape individual understandings in the current era and beyond. Cochran demonstrates that the unconscious needs of a society are not separate from the individual but are expressed in the semiotic resources from which individuals come to know their world.

Chapter 6 explores the importance of play within Jung's analytical psychology. It presents video gaming as a modern creative medium within which self-reflection and individuation can occur during immersive gameplay. Using Campbell's (1949) hero's journey as a framing device, Grann focuses on *The Legend of Zelda* video game franchise and illustrates ways in which the game affords the player with opportunities to engage with various archetypes such as the Self, Orphan, Child, Persona, Wise Old Man/Woman, and Shadow. Grann concludes with some important theoretical reflections on the way archetypal material arises and facilitates self-discovery within video gaming and other contemporary virtual contexts.

Chapter 7 turns from the video screen to the realm of love and romance. Stover explores the relationship between those who seek the love of their life, whom she calls *Romantics*, and the process of individuation. She attempts to broaden Jung's view of "marriage as a psychological relationship" to include those who are committed to finding a partner but may not be actually married or partnered yet. Stover shows how commitment to the work of finding a partner can lead to psychological development through encounters with archetypes including the *Self*, *anima/animus*, and *syzygy*. Stover illustrates how these archetypes manifest in the common experiences Romantics face on their path to partnership and shows how engaging the path to such a love is individuation itself.

Chapter 8 stays with the focus on love and presents the historical context of Jung's notions of anima and animus. Swogger traces the origins of these notions in Jung's earliest articulations and argues that their gendered aspects are inessential according to Jung's most basic description of anima and animus as functions of relatedness between consciousness and the unconscious. Swogger's analysis shows that these archetypes might remain helpful principles with a range of psychological, clinical, and literary applications.

Chapter 9 explores the role that having (and not having) children plays in the process of individuation. It discusses the ways being a parent can facilitate individuation and explores the various archetypes and complexes activated by children which can be integrated more intentionally into the parent's personality. Stover and Dillon then consider modern trends indicating fewer people are choosing to have children and show that while parenting a real child can be an important part of individuation, it does not mean that having one's own child is the only way to accomplish this. The chapter provides some helpful tools to do this.

Chapter 10 turns from the realm of the family to the social embodiment of the sacred. Rich examines the diverse ways the archetype of the Self manifests in daily and social life through what he calls *sacred practices*. He explores four major ways the archetype of the Self manifests in sacred practices and urges us to see sacred practice as a *complex* in the sense that it helps us digest otherwise overwhelming archetypal material. Rich shows that if we can attend to the hidden material within whichever sacred practice we might adopt, we will be rewarded with spiritual growth and a greater sense of wholeness in life.

The final case in Chap. 11 offers a Jungian psycho-social analysis of the various "feeling tones" which have roiled campuses in the United States and across the world. Dillon argues that the emotional intensity surrounding these issues indicates not only complexes, but *one-sidedness*. This large-scale disavowal of psychic material creates conditions ripe for *possession*, wherein unconscious material behaves like an "animated foreign body." In this sense, Dillon shows that the modern academy is possessed by the repressed complexes which he calls the *angry gods* of the modern academy. Dillon assesses the negative consequences of this one-sidedness and presents various internal and external solutions for addressing this increasingly precarious situation.

Chapter 12 summarizes the key points from the various chapters of the book and addresses directions for the future. Through case analyses and theoretical chapters, we show that Jung's concept of the complex remains relevant as a model of the psyche, functioning as a generative basis for addressing critical issues pertaining to archetype theory and the continued development of Jungian psycho-social studies. We hope this book can contribute to the work to preserve and stretch Jung's work to address the needs of our time.

To conclude, I return to the various process points I made about our study group at the beginning of the chapter. After signing our book contract, we continued to meet twice a month for our reading group for the entire year leading up to the book's completion. But instead of reading Jung's texts, each meeting featured drafts of our own chapters. We read each chapter in advance of the meeting and workshopped the texts together during our time together. This work exhibited the same careful attention to text, curiosity, interpersonal respect, and ongoing effort to amplify and apply Jung's original ideas to new contexts that characterized all our previous meetings. This workshopping process not only improved the clarity and coherence of each chapter but helped us better join the separate chapters to one another and to the common theme of the volume. From my own experience writing an edited volume some 20 years ago, contributing chapters to several other edited volumes over the years, and reading many published edited works on my own, one of my main critiques of these kinds of books is that the chapters often stand completely alone, leading the volume to read not like a book, but like an assortment of different parts, a collective monologue rather than a focused discussion. This is mainly due to the way edited works are written. Authors rarely see the other chapters of the volume until the whole work is published. While each chapter of *Complex and Archetype* stands strong on its own, we worked together to compose the chapters to unfold with the same integrated voice of a single-authored work.

Competing Interests The author has no conflicts of interest to declare that are relevant to the content of this chapter.

References

Campbell, J. (1949). *The hero with a thousand faces*. Princeton University Press.

Dillon, J. (2021). Reassembling the real person: A Jungian and mythical-dramatistic approach to human development. *The Journal of Humanistic Psychology, 61*(5), 786–805.

Hannah, B. (1976). *Jung his life and work: A biographical memoir*. G. P. Putnam's Sons.

Jacobi, J. (1959). *Complex/archetype/symbol in the psychology of C. G. Jung* (R. Manheim, Trans.). Princeton University Press.

Jung, C. G. (1969a). A review of the complex theory (G. Adler, & R. F. C. Hull, Trans.). In G. Adler & R. F. C. Hull (Eds.), *The collected works of C. G. Jung: Vol. 8. Structure & dynamics of the psyche* (2nd ed., pp. 92–104). Princeton University Press. (Original work published 1934).

Jung, C. G. (1969b). On psychic energy (G. Adler, & R. F. C. Hull, Trans.). In G. Adler & R. F. C. Hull (Eds.), *The collected works of C.G. Jung: Volume 8. Structure & dynamics of the psyche* (2nd ed., pp. 3–66). Princeton University Press. (Original work published 1928).

Lu, K., & Yeoman, A. (2024). Jungian psycho-social studies: Akira, Greta Thunberg, and archetypal thematic analysis (ATA). *International Journal of Jungian Studies, 16*, 77–112.

PART I

The Nature and Importance of Complexes

CHAPTER 2

The Importance of the Complex in Modern Psychology: Toppling Two Dominant Models of the Psyche

James J. Dillon

The hot sun scorches Prometheus' arms, bound to a pillar of stone with inescapable fetters. As Hesiod tells it, Zeus sets a great winged eagle upon him, "…and it fed on his immortal liver, which grew the same amount each way at night as the great bird ate in the course of the day" (1988, p. 18). Prometheus wakes each morning to experience the same unendurable agonies of the previous day. The crime which justifies this dreadful punishment? Defying the will of Zeus, deceiving the gods through cleverness and trickery, ultimately stealing the gods' fire, and carelessly giving it to humankind. By Hesiod's account, Zeus takes fire away from human beings after Prometheus tries to trick him into eating a bone wrapped in attractive fat while giving humans the unattractive skin of an ox hiding nourishing meat. In other accounts, like those dramatized by Aeschylus (490 B.C.E./1975), Prometheus pities the vulnerable human creature, forced to live in darkness, soon to be annihilated by the angry Zeus. In either case, Prometheus simply cannot abide the state of affairs decreed by

J. J. Dillon (✉)
School of Social Sciences, University of West Georgia, Carrollton, GA, USA

J. J. Dillon (ed.), *Complex and Archetype*,
https://doi.org/10.1007/978-3-032-02609-5_2

the Father god and uses his fierce intellect to take matters into his own hands.

Prometheus is surely a hero to human beings (see Campbell, 1972). He finds himself in an unacceptable *initial situation* where the pantheon is ruled by raw power and might; he discerns a *liberating vision* of a world ruled by thought, planning, and reason; and then takes *bold action* to transform the world. But Prometheus is no hero to Zeus or the other gods. His actions are a radical disturbance of the sacred arrangement of roles which have been carefully assigned to each immortal being. He displays a reckless irreverence in his trickery of Zeus, and a glaring hubris in his gift to human creatures who may ultimately prove unworthy of it. In short, Prometheus is that member of the pantheon who always wants to be in control, though he is ill-suited to exercise power. He is that person in the group who always knows better than the others, is too clever by half, finds rules and precedent burdensome, and displays a stunningly naïve faith in intellect, planning, and future growth. Prometheus' story is ultimately a cautionary tale about restraining our irreverence and skepticism of divine decrees, demonstrating humility about the possibilities of knowledge and transformation, as well as balancing intellect and planning with nature and the other metaphysical forces which cannot be controlled.

The tendencies displayed by Prometheus are still very much with us in our modern culture, ever lurking in the background, structuring the way we see ourselves and our role in the cosmos. This chapter illustrates how these Promethean impulses have inspired two dominant ways of looking at the human soul in psychology. One view casts the psyche as consciousness, autonomy, and choice. The other sees the psyche as an unformed piece of clay which is passively shaped and molded by the life experiences which come its way. These two views together cause markedly negative developmental consequences by misunderstanding the powerful role of the unconscious, archetypes, and complexes in daily life. The chapter shows what psychology misses when it misconstrues the products of the unconscious as external voices from society or internal products of the conscious mind. In particular, it explores how focusing on complexes can lead to a more accurate picture of the psyche and remove the stubborn obstacles to growth which tend to bedevil us.

What Are Complexes?

Complexes are "feeling toned" associations of perceptions, memories, thoughts, and desires which are activated by life events, relationships, or developmental stages. They behave like "animated foreign bodies" in the field of consciousness (see Jung, 1928/1969d, p. 11; Jung, 1934/1969a, p. 96). Though Jung initially believed complexes resided mostly in the personal unconscious (Dieckmann, 2014, p. 69), as his work matured, he advanced the idea that most complexes are admixtures of both personal and archetypal material (Jacobi, 1959, pp. 22–23). Specifically, the complex comprises an outer *shell* and an inner *core*. The shell is largely composed of associations and amplifications from life experiences, significant relationships, and imaginal material from the culture's art, literature, philosophy, and religion. The core, or "nuclear element" of the complex, rests upon one or more archetypes, and is not derived from culture or experience (Jung, 1928/1969d). The dynamism and organizing power of the complex comes from the core; the activation of the complex is initiated through the shell.

The central feature of the complex is the *feeling tone*, a distinct emotional motif which behaves like a magnet, drawing things around it into itself (obsession), eventually splitting off from the ego and confronting it as an alien entity (possession). Though manifesting concretely in daily life as *feelings*, complexes appear in dreams and active imagination as *metaphorical images*, *symbols*, and *personified figures* (Jung, 1934/1969a, p. 97). Rather than being a pathological aberration, Jung has us view the psyche as primarily consisting of complexes. Dieckmann (2014) uses the image of the psyche as an *ecosystem of complexes.* He writes, "The complexes form the individual ecotypes that stand in more or less distinct relationship with one another" (p. 139). Though complexes often confront the clinician as pathological, they are not inherently morbid, but serve the developmental purpose of helping us approach the unconscious without being overtaken by it (Shalit, 2002).

While complexes help us digest otherwise overwhelming archetypal material, they become pathological when they are relegated too deeply to the unconscious, are (a) too one-sided, as when the negative or positive "pole" of the complex or archetype is emphasized to the exclusion of the other, or (b) when they are not brought into productive relationship with the ego and the other complexes which populate the psyche. To return to the image of the ecosystem, pathology is when one plant becomes invasive and starts to choke the life out of the other plants in the garden. This happens all too easily for most of us. Jung (1934/1969a) refers to complexes the *via regia* to the unconscious (p. 101). Properly understanding them is, therefore, key to human growth. What are the common obstacles to understanding?

Common Obstacles to Properly Understanding Complexes

I consider two common misunderstandings of complexes in this chapter. The first is a *tabula rasa* view of the psyche which mistakenly casts complexes as external voices, introjected relationships, or social practices (e.g., Bakhtin, 1973; Freud, 1923/1960; Hermans, et al., 1992; Vygotsky, 1978; Wertsch, 1991). The second common misunderstanding is what Jung calls the *ego complex* (Jung, 1920/1969h, p. 307). This view has us believe that consciousness, autonomy, and choice define the psyche. When confronted with unconscious material from the complexes, this perspective tells us it is simply a product of conscious imagination rather than a manifestation of psychic material from beyond the ego.

Psyche as Tabula Rasa

Though it has ancient roots (e.g., Lucretius, 99 B.C.E./1951), the *tabula rasa* view of the psyche is largely a modern account based upon the work of the British philosopher John Locke (1690/2000) and the psychologist John Watson (1970). The central idea is that children are born as a blank slate (*tabula rasa*) with no strong nature of their own. Locke (1690/2000) suggests that we consider the mind to be,

> …as we say, white paper, void of all characters, without any ideas … Whence has it all the materials of reason and knowledge? To this I answer, in one word, from Experience. In that all our knowledge is founded; and from that it ultimately derives itself. (p. 73)

Development is thus the story of how our particular life experiences write upon the blank page, forming us into what we eventually become. We are, from this perspective, "products of the environment." Given this assumption, any differences between adults are to be understood in terms of the influence of different social circumstances and life experiences, rather than inherent temperaments or abilities.

The *tabula rasa* view of the psyche is perhaps the most ascendant conception in psychology today, if not in our larger Western culture. Examples of these ideas are too legion to catalogue, so I mention just a few representatives here. Vygotsky (1978) writes, "Every function in the child's cultural development appears twice: first, on the social level, and later, on the individual level; first, between people (interpsychological) and then inside the child (intrapsychological)" (p. 57). Vygotsky urges us to see all interior mental processes as internalizations of external social relationships. He writes, "All the higher functions originate as actual relationships between individuals" (p. 57). Similarly, in his discussion of the formation of the superego, Freud (1923/1960) characterizes conscience as nothing more than the internalized voices of parents, teachers, law, morality, or religious figures. Or consider Butler's (2007) popular notion that gender does not reflect "nature," but is instead socially constructed through demands by others to perform social roles (p. 24).

Of course, there is much to like about the *tabula rasa* view. Assuming that all people are born "equal" in dignity and value is an essential ingredient to having a humane, democratic community. In addition, experience surely does shape and influence us in profound ways. And we should always look first to cultural and environmental circumstances to explain any differences between the people we observe. At the same time, using the *tabula rasa* view to understand *all* mental phenomena and explain all psychological differences involves a number of rather serious problems.

First, the strict *tabula rasa* view does not adequately reflect the complexity of the psyche or fully account for some deeper individual differences. Jung reserved some of his harshest criticisms for the *tabula rasa* view on the ground that it is simply an inaccurate model of the psyche. Jung (1936/1969c) writes,

> It is a mistake to suppose that the psyche of the newborn child is a *tabula rasa* in the sense that there is absolutely nothing in it. Insofar as the child is born with a differentiated brain that is predetermined by heredity and therefore individualized, it meets sensory stimuli coming from outside not with *any* aptitudes, but with *specific* ones ... These aptitudes can be shown to be inherited instincts and preformed patterns, the latter being the a priori and formal conditions of apperception that are based on instinct. (p. 66)

The *tabula rasa*'s inaccurate model of the psyche leads to specific misunderstandings of the psyche's many complexes. Jung notes that complexes have a definite inner pattern which transcends external circumstances. They are *imposed upon*, rather than *formed by* experience. He calls complexes, "objects of inner experience" which are "not to be met in the street and public places" (Jung, 1934/1969a, p. 100). He says it is no accident, for example, that each person develops a psyche with the same complex components of the *anima* or *animus*, *ego*, *persona*, *shadow*, etc., regardless of upbringing or circumstance.

Second, the *tabula rasa* view misunderstands the role of the environment. Specifically, external situations "constellate" complexes; they do not *construct* them. Jung (1934/1969a) writes, "...the outward situation releases a psychic process in which certain contents gather together and prepare for action" (p. 94). The *tabula rasa* conception correctly picks up on the fact that the environment and other people have a strong developmental role, but it grossly overstates their importance. Jung (1909/1989) writes,

> Just as the migratory and nest-building instincts of birds were never learnt or acquired individually, man brings with him at birth the ground-plan of his nature, and not only of his individual nature but situations that have existed since primeval times: youth and old age, birth and death, sons and daughters, fathers and mothers, mating, and so on. (p. 315)

We might say that our significant relationships and life experiences provide the *content*, but not the *form* of the complex.

Third, the *tabula rasa* view cannot account for the phenomenon of *resonance*. As I note above, external situations, relationships, and experience trigger, or "constellate" complexes. The *tabula rasa* view misunderstands this constellating role as a *constructive* one. If we are truly a white sheet of paper, experience can scribble upon us in any direction it will. But it appears that some words, people, and experiences impress themselves upon us more than others. Why from among the billions of possible external influences do we seize upon this or that one, and forsake the others? And why do people tend to have similar words, people, and experiences they resonate with? The reason is because these external factors resound with something more primary: our *nature*. Consider the example of choosing the right career (see Dillon, 2022). Out of all the "career words" presented to us by parents, teachers, and the wider social world—*astronaut*, *physical therapist*, *supply chain manager*, *television producer*—a resonant one will often glow a little brighter than the others and open up a shimmering path for us. For a person who has discerned such a resonant path, the words naming the path indeed come from other people, *but the glimmer of resonance does not.* This is because resonant words, people, and experiences reflect meanings that connect us to something deeper than what comes from parents, culture, or society.

Resonance also brings emotional power. Dillon (2022) considers some otherwise mundane words reported in the *New Testament* which are spoken to audiences by the early apostles. They purportedly "cut to the heart" of those who hear them (*Acts* 5:33). Or think of Socrates, who tells us of the agony he feels whenever his *daemon* disturbs him when he says or does something that is wrong. She jerks him back with a piercing, "No!" In such moments, Socrates is certain he must change course. The *tabula rasa* conception can only point to prior learning or cultural conditioning to explain these phenomena, which seems inadequate given these resonant experiences are often novel and surprising. It does not enable us to adequately explain why there would be so much feeling associated with *these* particular words, actions, people, and experiences compared with all the others.

At a larger level, the strict *tabula rasa* view cannot account for what Reno (2019) calls the *strong gods*, our deepest passions and loyalties, the things individuals and groups actually care about and fight over. The defining feature of the strong gods is the binding power of the feelings we have when we are around them. These gods call upon the deepest loves in our souls. He writes, "The strong gods are the objects of men's love and devotion, the sources of the passions and loyalties that unite societies" (p. xii). Some of these gods include: the nation, truth, transcendence (or God), children and their education, tradition, and authority. These are the things to which people devote their lives, around which they form cultures, and for which they will kill or die. The *tabula rasa* model presents a flattened world with no resonance or strong gods, a deracinated psyche which can be taught to love and value whatever others teach us to love and value.

The fourth problem with the *tabula rasa* conception is that it causes us to ignore our inner resources, to become overly dependent upon the environment and other people, to lack resilience, and even to develop a state of learned helplessness in the face of severe difficulty and suffering. Jung (1954/1969f) writes,

> The disastrous idea that everything comes to the human psyche from outside and that it is born a *tabula rasa* is responsible for the erroneous belief that under normal circumstances the individual is in perfect order … As a result of these prejudices, the individual feels totally dependent on his environment and loses all capacity for introspection. In this way his code of ethics is replaced by a knowledge of what is permitted or forbidden or ordered … He has not yet made the discovery that he might be capable of spontaneous ethical impulses, and of performing them—even when no one is looking. (p. 267)

Of course, looking to the environment to explain psychological phenomena is completely warranted in certain cases, but it becomes a bad habit when we rely on exogenous accounts as an axiomatic principle rather than as the particular situation warrants. Some psychological phenomena surely do have a social origin; but others do not. Vygotsky (1978) does not say *some* functions in the child's development appear first on the social plane and then on the psychological; he says *any* functions. As a result of an exclusive reliance on external accounts, we miss the opportunity to cultivate a proper understanding of phenomena which have an *endogenous* origin, and to take appropriate steps to nurture these inner realities which have their own purpose, power, and developmental course.

A final problem with the *tabula rasa* view concerns human growth. The ability to handle unconscious material follows a developmental course. From our initial state of weakness, we project psychic material which belongs to us onto others, particularly our parents and close caregivers. Jung (1928/1969d) notes, "Everything that works from the unconscious appears projected on others" and is enacted on the political and interpersonal stage (p. 53). He refers to this tendency to projection as a "tenacious prejudice" which can only be broken with considerable suffering, time, and effort. We can grow only when we develop sufficient ego strength to accept complex and archetypal material as our own rather than seeing it as coming to us from the familial or social world.

The disownership of unconscious material through projection creates conditions which are ripe for one-sidedness, pathology, and, ultimately, possession. As noted earlier, Jung (1934/1969a) claims that a complex in its extreme form behaves like an "animated foreign body" almost with its own consciousness (p. 96). So long as we are unaware of the psychic origin of these experiences, we run the risk of being possessed by them. Jung (1934/1969a) continues, "Everyone knows nowadays that people 'have complexes.' What is not so well known ... is that complexes can *have us*" (p. 96).

Consider an example. Jung (1909/1989) notes that there is a distinct difference between the *archetypal father* and our *actual father* out there in the world. He writes, "...behind the father stands the archetype of the father, and in this pre-existent archetype lies the secret of the father's power" (p. 320). The actual father is considerably less powerful than the child believes. In fact, a large store of the actual father's numinosity and power comes from the archetype rather than the person. Jung (1928/1969d) writes, "...the wicked father who forbade everything is far more inside than outside themselves" (p. 53). So long as the child projects this power upon the real person of the father (in the form of a complex), they do not recognize it as their own and thus experience it as "autonomous" or external to themselves. They run the risk of being "possessed" by the power of the father archetype. The initial steps in working with the strong feelings which derive from complexes (like the father complex here) involve discerning and owning the *internal* unconscious processes which have produced them. So long as we are in the grip of the *tabula rasa* model which tells us these "voices" are actual people we have met, we simply cannot do this.

Psyche as Consciousness: The Ego Complex

The second common obstacle to properly understanding complexes is the tendency to view the psyche and consciousness as synonymous. Jung (1951/1971a) refers to this view as the *ego complex.* It is ironic that a major obstacle in appreciating the power of the complexes is another complex. Jung typically uses the solitary word *ego* to connote the normal functioning of this part of the psyche. He uses the term *ego complex* to point to occasions when the ego behaves in a more exaggerated fashion. The ego complex sees the personal self as the singular god, rather than one member among a larger pantheon. It believes that consciousness, its defining feature, comprises the entirety of the psyche. It erroneously sees itself as the author of all psychic contents. When confronted with autonomous complex material from the unconscious, the ego complex will have us believe that we imagined it ourselves, that it would all not exist had we not intentionally brought it to life with our imagination. Jung (1934/1969a) says the ego complex,

> ...behaves like some one who hears a suspicious noise in the attic and thereupon dashes down into the cellar, in order to assure himself that no burglar has broken in and that the noise was mere imagination. In reality he has simply not dared to go up into the attic. (p. 99)

When confronting unconscious material which presents itself to us as symptoms, powerful and recurring emotional motifs, or the fantasy products of dreams and active imagination, the ego complex steps in and issues its singular refrain, "It is only my own thoughts!" (Jung, 1939/1969c, 132). Such hubris, Jung claims, serves the purpose of maintaining the supremacy of the ego complex, which must be protected at all costs from dissolution into the unconscious.

As with the *tabula rasa* view, the ego complex is pervasive in both academic and everyday settings. Consider popular admonitions suggesting what we can "create our own reality," as when Oprah Winfrey famously admonishes her viewers, "Remember, you are co-creating your life with the energy of your own intentions." Whenever I work with students in class doing active imagination and other inner dialogue activities, they routinely struggle during the exercise with an inner voice which tells them, "This is just my own imagination, right?" This voice impedes their ability to access additional unconscious material. Because of the ego complex, they find it difficult to imagine that psychic material can reach out to them, that they are not the authors of all that takes place in their souls. In academic circles, over the past 50 years, postmodern philosophies have severely critiqued the notion of objective reality. They have replaced it with the idea that knowledge is "constructed" and imposed through mechanisms of power and persuasion. While these same philosophies have claimed the ego is also a social construction, in practice many enter this ontological void and assert that the *autonomous ego* "establishes truth," for example, in the determination of one's gender, or deciding when life in the womb begins.

As with the *tabula rasa* view, there is much to like about the ego complex. Surely, we have power to make real and consequential choices in life. Developing a strong and independent ego is also an essential ingredient to individuation. And there is undoubtedly something special and unique about each and every person. But using the view provided by the ego complex to understand *all* mental phenomena involves a number of rather serious problems. First, the ego complex is *one-sided*. In its extreme form, it simply does not do justice to the full complexity of the psyche. Specifically, while it is true that the ego is the central complex of the psyche, integral, for psychological functioning and flourishing, it is by no means the *only* one. Jung (1920/1969h) notes that the psyche,

> ...is not an indivisible unity but a divisible and more or less divided whole. Although the separate parts are connected with one another, they are relatively independent, so much so that certain parts of the psyche never become associated with the ego at all or very rarely. I have called these psychic fragments "autonomous complexes," and base my theory of complexes on their existence. According to this theory the ego complex forms the centre characteristic of our psyche. But it is only one among several complexes. (p. 307)

Jung presents a model of the psyche comprising multiple complexes which "behave like independent beings" (1937/1969g, p. 121), and are like "fragmentary personalities" (1934/1969a, p. 97). These complexes are not authored or controlled by the ego. What the ego complex misses is the fact that the ego lives in the house (the psyche), but is not the whole house, much less its master.

Second, the ego complex's tendency to assume control over things it does not have and ignore the archetypal core of the psyche carries various negative developmental consequences. In particular, overcontrol by the ego can actually *cause* psychopathology. Jung (1958/1985) notes that, "A complex becomes pathological *only when we think we have not got it*" (p. 79, emphasis added). Shalit (2002) writes,

> Internally, it is the task of the complex to dismember the archetype, preventing it from overwhelming the developing child, enabling the archetypal core to have a valid but not devastating impact on the person. Complexes become autonomous due to the ego's defensive attitude, preventing the complex from entering the realm of the ego and conscious identity. Not the *content* of the complex but the *autonomous strength* it gathers in the shadow makes it pathological. (p. 58)

It is not the complexes, *but the state of the ego* which determines whether complexes are life-giving or pathological.

To explore exactly how this process of pathogenesis is determined by ego-positioning, it is important to distinguish between two types of pathological complexes: those of the *soul* and those of the *spirit*. With *soul complexes*, the ego loses a connection to the animating presence of another complex or archetype. We might refer to these simply as *neuroses*. Shalit

(2002) writes that people in the grip of such a complex, "seem to be without a *joie de vivre*, dull and spiritless, schizoid or asthenic" (p. 68). Jung (1920/1969h) notes that we experience soul complexes as *sickness* in that we feel the loss of something vital within ourselves (p. 312). With a soul complex, the ego sets up rigid defenses in the form of avoidance, phobias, obsessions, or compulsions so as to protect its rule. The benefit of soul complexes is that they enable the ego to perform executive functions and focus on what it finds important without unnecessary distraction (Jung, 1937/1969g, p. 121). The cost of soul complexes is a restriction of the psyche's full range of experiential life.

With *spirit complexes*, the power of the complex or archetype inundates and overpowers the ego as if from the outside. In extreme form, we might refer to these as *psychoses*. Jung (1920/1969h, p. 312) claims we experience spirit complexes as *possession*, a strange and uncanny presence not belonging to the ego. The complexes and archetypes which possess us may be deep and archaic, as when the ego is possessed by the chthonic Mother or terrible Father, or they may be closer to the surface of social life, as when the ego completely identifies with the persona. With spirit complexes, the ego is too weak; with soul complexes, the ego is too strong. Each instance of pathology directly depends upon the way the ego positions itself with respect to the unconscious and the other complexes. As Jacobi (1959) writes, "...it is solely the state of the conscious mind, the greater or lesser stability of the ego personality, that determines the role of the complex" (p. 27).

For individuation to take place, the ego must attain sufficient strength to be able to contend with the complex psychic forces beyond itself without being overwhelmed. But it also must not be so strong as to bar admission of complex psychic material into its sphere. Jung uses the metaphor of a *productive marriage* (*hieros gamos*) to explain this "just right" state between ego and unconscious. In this new relationship, there is an open dialogue between two human beings with equal rights, "each of whom gives the other credit for a valid argument and considers it worth-while to modify the conflicting standpoints by means of thorough comparison and discussion or else to distinguish them clearly from one another" (Jung, 1916/1971b, p. 297). For this marriage to form, the ego must not only develop into a stable entity, establishing what Jung calls a "conscious control point," but it must eventually be deposed from its need to control through the establishment of a "transpersonal control point" whose center is in the Self, just beyond the ego's grasp (Jung, 1928/1966b, p. 134).

We simply cannot establish a transpersonal control point if we are in the grips of the ego complex.

Doing the Work

This last section of the chapter explores "the work" we must do to grow, and how the two dominant models of the psyche impede it. Recall Jung's (1934/1969a) claim that the complex is the *via regia* to the unconscious (p. 101). From a Jungian perspective, the lion's share of growth work involves contending with the various complexes which arise in the course of daily life (Jung, 1939/1969b). But Dieckmann (2014) notes,

> ...the kind of complex a person has tends to be less important for the individual's psychic health than whether or not the individual is able to deal with the complex, to experience it consciously, and to employ its archetypal dominants and energies at the appropriate and sensible times and places. (p. 2243)

While specialized knowledge and skills related to particular complexes are useful, it is more important from a clinical perspective to develop a general ability to deal with *any complex*. What is involved with this global ability to deal with the complex? I summarize the major elements of this process in a list of "steps of the work."

The Steps of the Work

The steps of the work include (a) consciousness of strong feeling-tones and related behavioral disruptions of everyday life; (b) appreciating the psychic autonomy of the complex, that is, ceasing to treat this material as ego-authored (ego complex) or socially derived (*tabula rasa*); (c) coming to understand the specific kind of unconscious, complex-driven processes behind our emotional and behavioral disturbances; (d) divesting the complex of one-sidedness by excavating its repressed opposite pole; (e) experiencing and utilizing the archetypal power hidden within the complex; (f) integrating all the complexes of one's psyche under a single transpersonal directive organized by the archetype of the Self; (g) strengthening or establishing the *transcendent function*, a stable bridge spanning the gap between ego and unconscious, which enables productive use of unconscious material in the future.

As we explore these steps, it is important to embed them within proper images of development. There are at least three images Jung provides which are helpful here. In the first, Jung describes the process of growth as *adaptation to inner and outer reality*. The image is an ego working and stretching itself toward a state where it can appropriately interact with and accommodate whatever is "there" internally and externally. An ego which is unable (or unwilling) to deal with these realities is "less developed" than one which can. The second image of growth is the *regeneration of an ecosphere* described earlier in the chapter. The image here is an ego working as a steward to eliminate invasive plants (dominance by a singular complex) so as to allow the full diversity of the psyche's flora and fauna to thrive. This image casts psychological health as a state in which all the complexes of the psyche work together, are related to consciousness, and are ultimately subordinated to the workings of the archetype of the Self (the master gardener). The third image of growth is the *productive marriage* described in the paragraph above where we have free-flowing communication between two equal parties, ego and unconscious.

We can use these images of development to view the steps of the work in starker relief. The first step of the work involves the simple awareness that something is amiss in our souls. We do not need to know at this point what it is, or why it is happening. A simple awareness will do. We find ourselves in the grips of a persistent feeling-tone resounding in the background of our significant relationships or large portions of our day. Perhaps we (or others) are surprised, disturbed, or concerned by some aspect of our behavior. This moment is simply a turning to see that this issue is there. While I describe this awareness as "simple," getting to this place is no easy matter. It does not take much to deny or misinterpret the feeling-tones which plague us, or ignore distressing or self-destructive behavior. The "simple awareness" in this step involves immense trust, courage, sobriety, and honesty. Returning to our images of growth, this first step is the moment when the couple (ego and unconscious) admits there is a problem in the relationship, or when the gardener notices that something is choking the life of the other plants.

The second step of the work is perhaps the most consequential crossroad of the whole process. It has been the focus of almost this entire chapter. It is here we make a concerted effort to resist the pervasive tendency to view our haunting feeling tones and disruptive behaviors as the result of our relationships with culture or significant other people (*tabula rasa*), or to see them as a state of mind we have somehow authored (ego complex).

So long as we take the interpretive routes offered by the ego complex and *tabula rasa* models, we cannot really initiate the process of growth beyond step one at all.

As we resist the deep urges to project or assume control, we begin to explore in detail just what it is that has been gnawing at us, to *name the complex* (or complexes) at work in us. It is here where the gardener identifies the specific invasive species. If we identify the wrong problem, we cannot treat it properly. There are dozens of potential culprits which are quite beyond the scope of this chapter to explore. Perhaps we are in the grips of a *father complex* in which we exaggerate instincts related to intellect, spirit, authority, control, or self-assertion. Or perhaps we are in the grips of a *puer/puella complex* in which we fight the passage of time, refuse to grow up, and squarely face the difficulties of life. Perhaps it is a *mother complex*, *power complex*, *Salome complex*, etc. This detective work can be aided by the wisdom and skill of what Jung (1946/1966c) calls an *adept*: an experienced therapist or knowledgeable other willing to serve as guide or *psychopomp* through this arduous process (p. 221).

As mentioned earlier, a major function of the complex is to enable us to digest potentially overwhelming psychological reality into manageable bites. It does this by *splitting*, presenting just one side of a more paradoxical reality. Think here of the way a fairy tale breaks down the ambivalent nature of a multifaceted parent figure into two completely separate characters, one good and the other wicked. When we engage this step of the work, we divest the complex its one-sidedness by dealing with its repressed opposite pole. With human figures, for example, we work to see the mother or the father not as all good, or all bad, or all anything, but as a complex mixture of diverse and often contradictory human qualities. Dieckmann (2014) writes,

> Every good and successful analysis therefore has the task of mobilizing the opposite pole and allowing the human being within to be seen behind the projected complex in all of his or her ambivalence. (p. 274)

With this step, the role of the complex shifts from being a limiting and debilitating one to an expanding and strengthening one.

As we divest of one-sidedness, we begin to access, experience, and utilize the archetypal power hidden within the complex. The shell of the complex "opens downward" to the archetypal core, enabling us to engage the liberatory power and vivifying energy of the archetype behind the complexes (Dieckmann, 2014, p. 1278). Jacobi (1959) writes,

> The complex in its 'seminal function' even deserves a place of honor as the life-renewing and life-promoting source whose function it is to raise the contents of the unconscious to consciousness and mobilize the formative powers of consciousness. (p. 29)

The core of the complex, which had been hobbled by limiting fixations, expands and enriches psychic life. We experience the deep truth that healing energy comes from *nature*, not the ego or culture.

As we divest complexes of one-sidedness, psychic energy shifts from the "conscious control point" of the ego to the "transpersonal control point" of the unconscious. We come to appreciate that this work of individuation is not a conscious process, but is directed by a natural, unconscious master plan. We not only begin to experience archetypal power within the complex as described in the step above, but we move toward integrating all the complexes of the psyche under a single transpersonal directive organized by the *archetype of the* Self. Dillon (2021) presents a larger discussion of the particular stages of this universal process of individuation. With the previous step, we take advantage of the compensatory energy emanating from the repressed opposite pole of a single complex; with this new step, we avail ourselves of the compensatory power of the other complexes of the psyche (see Jung, 1954/1969f, p. 261). Dieckmann (2014) writes,

> In the healthy psyche, an entire system of different complexes, each with its unique quality, are related to one another. Through a partial identification, the healthy ego can make use of them when necessitated by various life situations to master the task at hand. (p. 412)

A diversity of complexes flourishes in the garden of the psyche rather than being dominated by the growth of a single, one-sided plant.

These latter steps of the work are facilitated by the strengthening or construction of what Jung (1916/1971b) calls the *transcendent function*, a new structure of the ego whose function is to join together two separate and often opposed psychological systems: the discursive logical system of the ego and the imagistic metaphorical system of the unconscious. As the transcendent function brings these opposing systems together, it enables us to consciously process unconscious psychic material at a *symbolic* rather than a literal or behavioral level. A central tenet of analytical psychology is that we "see through" feelings, symptoms, and compulsive behaviors to the unconscious manifesting itself in the form of personified images, figures, and animated symbols. As Hillman (1975) notes, when we "introspect," we are not thinking about a something, but *talking with a someone*. To fully understand this unconscious material, we must have Jung's "dialectical discussion" with it. The transcendent function enables this inner dialogue, which is staged in active imagination, intensive journaling, role play, meditation, or prayer. As we do this, complexes begin to lose their compulsive character,

> They slough off their mythological envelope, and by entering into the adaptive process going forward in consciousness, they personalize and rationalize themselves [so that] a dialectical discussion becomes possible. (Jung, 1946/1969e, p. 187)

With the establishment of the transcendent function, a more open relationship is established between ego and unconscious, which leads to our ability to productively engage feeling-tones, dreams, fantasy, images, and art for guidance, depth, color, and energy in daily living (see Dillon, 2021, p. 793). We are now able to assist the Self in its patient work to achieve wholeness in us.

Confronting the One-Sidedness of Distorted Foundational Myths

The model of the psyche offered by analytical psychology incorporates the truths within the *tabula rasa* model and the ego complex, but it does not make them the only factors of psychic life. When environmental malleability or ego control become the defining psychological factor, it causes a serious *one-sidedness* in our consciousness which can impede our efforts to grow. Perhaps most seriously, when we are under the sway of the *tabula rasa* or ego complex, we come to identify with the *heroes of distorted foundational myths*. Along with Jung (1955), scholars from various disciplines such as Berman (1981), Campbell (1972), Cassirer (1953), Gebser (1986), Langer (1942), Neumann (1995/1949), and Whitmont (1969) have argued that the depths of the human psyche assume a mythical-symbolic form. While we consciously live our lives at an abstract level founded upon rational and scientific concepts, a simple scratch of the surface—a day or night dream, stressful event, unfocused attention—reveals the vivid mythical substrate lurking within. Similarly, though our pathology and suffering may express itself at a surface level as cognitions, feelings, sexual urges, or power impulses, at bottom, symptoms manifest as symbols and "mythologems" (Jung, 1945/1966a, p. 92). The psychological difficulties caused by the *tabula rasa* model and the ego complex ultimately rest upon a distorted mythical base structure centered upon the figure of Prometheus.

In the myth which animates the *tabula rasa* model, we unconsciously identify with the hero Prometheus, and *only* Prometheus. We thereby adopt a reflexively oppositional stance toward nature and what is believed to be "fixed." We put too much stock in the idea of progress and unlimited possibility. We overemphasize the transformative power of knowledge, learning, cultural influence, and the ability of technology to solve problems. Everything is believed to be malleable; each day is new. In Chap. 9, we discuss the *Prometheus complex*, which is borne of the archetype of the child. It concerns a pitched mania for progress in parenting, education, and politics. Under the spell of the Prometheus complex, we look to the child as a means of continuing the steady march of history away from the dark past toward a future enlightenment. We use our children and the educational system to build a world purportedly better than the one we and our ancestors grew up in. We frantically shape and educate the child toward this desired ideal through a process Jung (1940/1969i) calls *furor paedogogicus* (p. 175). What this complex ignores is that the child is not just "the future," but a reminder to the adult of the still existing state of nature and the past. Jung says the furor induced by this complex, is "…a god-sent method of by-passing the central problem … namely *the education of the educator*" (p. 175, emphasis added). Within this distorted myth, there is no nature, tradition, or inner wisdom/inheritance to draw upon. There are no limits to respect as we manically shape ourselves and others into whatever form we desire through knowledge, culture, and learning.

These are some of the features and negative consequences of the distorted myth within the *tabula rasa* model of the psyche. The ego complex rests upon the base Prometheus myth as well. Shalit (2002) calls Prometheus the "archetypal image" of the ego complex (p. 47). In the distorted myth which animates the ego complex, we similarly identify with the hero Prometheus, but we focus here on his relationship to the other gods. We cast Prometheus as the ego and the rest of the pantheon as the unconscious. Prometheus simply dispenses with the role and power of the other gods, and takes them all upon himself. He knows better than all the others, and will acknowledge no authority greater than his own. Within this distorted myth, the ego simply assimilates the other parts of the psyche into itself. But arrogating such control to oneself requires a depleting hyper-vigilance. We take on unfulfillable tasks and exhaust ourselves in trying to master them. But such arrogation brings no real reward. As Dieckmann (2014) notes, when we succeed in fulfilling these Herculean tasks, we are never satisfied, but sink into a depression or direct perfectionistic aggression against ourselves (p. 423).

This chapter contends that when we misconstrue the complexes, our model of the psyche is inaccurate, and our view of growth distorted. This is not only an academic matter, but something which carries real developmental consequences. To the extent we come under the sway of the *tabula rasa* model, we cannot take advantage of the resources, direction, and inner purpose seeking to realize themselves through our nature. To the extent we come under the sway of the ego complex, we overvalue control, assume things are authored by the ego which are not, and lose precious contact with significant portions of our inner life. We can escape each trap through a fuller appreciation of the entire psychic ecosystem, an inner landscape which contains not just a single complex, myth, and hero, but *dozens*. The hero is not knowledge, learning, or the ego, but as Shalit (2002) notes, our "...capacity to turn toward and connect with the Self, to venture into the darkness of the shadow and bring forth instinctual and archetypal energies from the depths" (pp. 46–7). Human existence is too complex and multifaceted for just a single complex and myth. The diverse events of life which confront us, particularly those involving nature and limits, demand that we make productive use of the full range of the complexes in the psyche, not just one. The *tabula rasa* and ego complex impede our ability to do this. Our commitment to human growth must, therefore, lead to the toppling of the ego complex and the *tabula rasa* as unitary models of the psyche. Given their entrenchment, this will be difficult work, but the cost of quiescence could be our very souls.

Competing Interests The author has no conflicts of interest to declare that are relevant to the content of this chapter.

References

Aeschylus. (1975). *Prometheus bound* (J. Scully & C. J. Herington, Trans.). Oxford University Press. (Original work published 490 B.C.E.).

Bakhtin, M. M. (1973). *Problems of Dostoevsky's poetics*. Ardis.

Berman, M. (1981). *The reenchantment of the world*. Cornell University Press.

Butler, J. (2007). *Gender trouble: Feminism and the subversion of identity*. Routledge.

Campbell, J. (1972). *The hero with a thousand faces*. Princeton University Press.

Cassirer, E. (1953). *Language and myth*. Dover Books.

Dieckmann, H. (2014). *Complexes: Diagnosis and therapy in Analytical Psychology*. Chiron Publications. https://www.amazon.com/Complexes-Diagnosis-Therapy-Analytical-Psychology-ebook/dp/B00OYAGD2G/ref=sr_1_1?crid=CJPERN3AF8H2&keywords=complexes%3A+diagnosis&qid=1690461953&s=digital-text&sprefix=complexes+diagnosis%2Cdigital-text%2C89&sr=1-1

Dillon, J. J. (2021). Reassembling the real person: A Jungian and mythical – Dramatistic approach to human development. *Journal of Humanistic Psychology, 61*(5), 786–805.

Dillon, J. J. (2022). *The joy of duty: Human happiness and ethical obligation*. Ethics International Press.

Freud, S. (1960). *The ego and the id* (J. Strachey, Trans.). W.W. Norton. (Original work published 1923).

Gebser, J. (1986). *Ever present origin, part one: Foundations of the aperspectival world*. Ohio University Press.

Hermans, H. J. M., Kempen, H. J. G., & Van Loon, R. J. P. (1992). The dialogical self: Beyond individualism and rationalism. *American Psychologist, 47*, 23–33.

Hesiod. (1988). *Theogony and works and days* (M. L. West, Trans.). Oxford University Press.

Hillman, J. (1975). *Re-visioning psychology*. Harper.

Jacobi, J. (1959). *Complex/archetype/symbol in the psychology of C. G. Jung* (R. Manheim, Trans.). Princeton University Press.

Jung, C. G. (1955). *Modern man in search of a soul*. Mariner.

Jung, C. G. (1966a). Medicine and psychotherapy (R.F.C. Hull, Trans.). In H. Read, M. Fordham, G. Adler, & W. McGuire (Eds.), *The collected works of C. G. Jung: Vol. 16. The practice of psychotherapy* (2nd ed., pp. 84–93). Princeton University Press. (Original work published 1945).

Jung, C. G. (1966b). The aims of psychotherapy (R.F.C Hull, Trans.). In H. Read, M. Fordham, G. Adler, & W. McGuire (Eds.), *The collected Works of C.G. Jung: Vol. 16. The practice of psychotherapy* (2nd ed., pp. 36–52). Princeton University Press. (Original work published 1928).

Jung, C. G. (1966c). The psychology of the transference (R.F.C. Hull, Trans.). In H. Read, M. Fordham, G. Adler, & W. McGuire (Eds.), *The collected works of*

C. G. Jung: Vol. 16. The practice of psychotherapy (2nd ed., pp. 163–323). Princeton University Press. (Original work published 1946).

Jung, C. G. (1969a). A review of the complex theory (G. Adler, & R.F.C. Hull, Trans.). In G. Adler & R. F. C. Hull (Eds.), *The collected works of C. G. Jung: Vol. 8. Structure & dynamics of the psyche* (2nd ed., pp. 92–104). Princeton University Press. (Original work published 1934).

Jung, C. G. (1969b). Concerning rebirth (R.F.C. Hull, Trans.). In H. Read, M. Fordham, & G. Adler (Eds.), *The collected works of C.G. Jung: Vol. 9 (part 1). Archetypes and the collective unconscious* (2nd ed., pp. 112–147). Princeton University Press. (Original work published 1939).

Jung, C. G. (1969c). Concerning the archetypes, with special reference to the anima concept. (R.F.C. Hull, Trans.). In H. Read, M. Fordham, & G. Adler (Eds.), *The collected works of C.G. Jung: Vol. 9 (part 1). Archetypes and the collective unconscious* (2nd ed., pp. 54–72). Princeton University Press. (Original work published 1936).

Jung, C. G. (1969d). On psychic energy (G. Adler, & R.F.C. Hull, Trans.). In G. Adler & R. F. C. Hull (Eds.), *The collected works of C.G. Jung: Vol. 8. Structure & dynamics of the psyche* (2nd ed., pp. 3–66). Princeton University Press. (Original work published 1928).

Jung, C. G. (1969e). On the nature of the psyche (G. Adler, & R.F.C. Hull, Trans.). In G. Adler & R. F. C. Hull (Eds.), *The collected works of C.G. Jung: Vol. 8. Structure & dynamics of the psyche* (2nd ed., pp. 159–234). Princeton University Press. (Original work published 1946).

Jung, C. G. (1969f). On the psychology of the trickster-figure (R.F.C. Hull, Trans.). In H. Read, M. Fordham, & G. Adler (Eds.), *The collected works of C.G. Jung: Vol. 9 (part 1). The archetypes and the collective unconscious* (2nd ed., pp. 255–272). Princeton University Press. (Original work published 1954).

Jung, C. G. (1969g). Psychological factors determining human behaviour (G. Adler, & R.F.C. Hull, Trans.). In G. Adler & R. F. C. Hull (Eds.), *The collected works of C.G. Jung: Vol. 8. Structure & dynamics of the psyche* (2nd ed., pp. 114–125). Princeton University Press. (Original work published 1937).

Jung, C. G. (1969h). The psychological foundations of belief in spirits (G. Adler, & R.F.C. Hull, Trans.). In G. Adler & R. F. C. Hull (Eds.), *The collected works of C.G. Jung: Vol. 8. Structure & dynamics of the psyche* (2nd ed., pp. 301–318). Princeton University Press. (Original work published 1920).

Jung, C. G. (1969i). The psychology of the child archetype (R.F.C Hull, Trans.). In H. Read, M. Fordham, G. Adler, & W. McGuire (Eds.), *The collected Works of C.G. Jung: Vol. 9 (part 1). The archetypes and the collective unconscious* (2nd ed., pp. 151–203). Princeton University Press. (Original work published 1940).

Jung, C. G. (1971a). Aion: Phenomenology of the self. In J. Campbell (Ed.), *The portable Jung* (pp. 139–162). Penguin. (Original work published 1951).

Jung, C. G. (1971b). The transcendent function. In J. Campbell (Ed.), *The portable Jung* (pp. 273–300). Penguin. (Original work published 1916).

Jung, C. G. (1985). Psychotherapy and a philosophy of life (G. Adler, & R.F.C. Hull, Trans.). In G. Adler & R. F. C. Hull (Eds.), *The collected works of C.G. Jung: Vol. 16. Practice of psychotherapy* (2nd ed., pp. 76–83). Princeton University Press. (Original work published 1958).

Jung, C. G. (1989). The significance of the father in the destiny of the individual (G. Adler, & R.F.C Hull, Trans.). In G. Adler & R. F. C. Hull (Eds.), *The collected works of C.G. Jung: Volume 4. Freud and psychoanalysis* (pp. 302–323). Princeton University Press. (Original work published 1909).

Langer, S. (1942). *Philosophy in a new key: A study in the symbolism of reason, rite, and art.* Harvard University Press.

Locke, J. (2000). *An essay concerning human understanding.* Batoche Books. (Original work published 1690).

Lucretius. (1951). *The nature of the universe* (R. E. Latham, Trans.). Penguin Classics. (Original work published 99 B.C.E.).

Neumann, E. (1995). *The origins and history of consciousness.* Princeton University Press. (Original work published 1949).

Reno, R. (2019). *Return of the strong gods: Nationalism, populism, and the future of the west.* Regnery Gateway.

Shalit, E. (2002). *The complex: Path of transformation from archetype to ego.* Inner City Books.

Vygotsky, L. S. (1978). *Mind in society.* Harvard University Press.

Watson, J. B. (1970). *Behaviorism.* W.W. Norton.

Wertsch, J. V. (1991). *Voices of the mind: A sociocultural approach to mediated action.* Harvard University Press.

Whitmont, E. C. (1969). *The symbolic quest.* Princeton University Press.

CHAPTER 3

The Role of Complex Personification in Facilitating Self-Knowledge

Michael V. Steder

Who am I, what is my place in the world, and what are my goals? Such questions of identity, belonging, and purpose are at the heart of our committed interest to ourselves and others and at the heart of our issues with stagnation, isolation, and confusion. Exploring these questions, and the commitments and issues they invoke, constitutes a pursuit of self-knowledge which, according to Jung (1912/1972), involves communication between unconscious complexes and the conscious ego. The result of this process is an expanded perspective on identity and belonging, and a deepened investment in one's projects. This chapter explores how the personification of complexes facilitates the advancement of self-knowledge.

Jung's concept of complexes is a central principle of his theory of psyche. The autonomous formation and activity of complexes represent the energetic contents and impressions constituting an individual's personal unconscious, the hidden domain of the psyche. As such, complexes demarcate unknown and unrecognized characteristics of identity and experience, revealing gaps or blind-spots in the attainment of self-knowledge. While the presence and influence of complexes typically disrupt the process of self-knowledge, the personification of complexes offers

M. V. Steder (✉)
University of West Georgia, School of Social Sciences, Carrollton, GA, USA

J. J. Dillon (ed.), *Complex and Archetype*,
https://doi.org/10.1007/978-3-032-02609-5_3

opportunities to encounter, engage, and disclose unknown aspects of personality by constellating unconscious characteristics of identity and experience. I explore how complex personification can facilitate self-knowledge in four sections of the chapter.

The first section describes the psychological dimensions of complexes as Jung sees them. These dimensions have two interrelated aspects: *unconscious contents* and *personification*. The chapter unpacks each of these aspects, yielding a portrait of complexes as energetic constellations of unconscious tension dissociated from consciousness with the propensity for autonomous activity to give imaginative shape to feeling-toned-fixed-ideas. The next section addresses the importance of self-knowledge in analytic psychology. Self-knowledge hinges on the notion of a hidden self, separated from conscious awareness. This idea suggests that self-knowledge deals with issues of plurality vs. unity, ego one-sidedness, and lost potentiality. The hidden self, and the one-sidedness it produces, results in a disconnected ego of habitual attitudes and actions that is susceptible to dissociation and complex activity. Self-knowledge is important because it is a call to rediscover Self through the transformation of ego one-sidedness by way of the influence, direction, and integration of complex activity. The final section shows how complex personification facilitates self-knowledge in three stages: *impression*, *naming*, and *integration*. *Impression* refers to the initial, autonomous, eruption of complex activity in trigger-situations and symptom expression. This first contact is followed by the constellating process of *naming* which gives shape to the complex and allows the ego to recognize the complex as an "other." *Integration* is a discursive exchange between the values, ideals, and actions of the ego and those of the personified complex. This exchange results in a transformed personality through an expanded awareness of the trigger-situation and attainment of a new attitude beyond the one-sided attitude previously held by the ego.

Psychological Dimensions of Complexes

As Dillon notes in Chap. 2, "complexes are feeling toned associations of perceptions, memories, thoughts, and desires which are activated by life events, relationships, or developmental stages" (see Jung, 1934/1969b, p. 11). Jung (1934/1969a) writes that a complex,

> [I]s the *image* of a certain psychic situation which is strongly accentuated emotionally and is, moreover, incompatible with the habitual attitude of

> consciousness. This image has a powerful inner coherence, it has its own wholeness and, in addition, a relatively high degree of autonomy ... and therefore behaves like an animated foreign body in the sphere of consciousness. (p. 96)

Once activated, complexes exert their influence in a variety of ways such as compulsive acts of competitiveness, debilitating moments of sadness, and obsessive longing. To understand the relationship between complexes and self-knowledge, the psychological dimensions of complexes uncovered by Jung need to be brought into focus.

The *unconscious contents* of a complex are represented by a group of perceptions, memories, thoughts, and desires resulting from a dual process of dissociation and association (Jung, 1912/1972, 1973/1981, 1902/2014). Dissociation directs perceptions, memories, thoughts, and desires of disturbing and unreconciled life events, relationships, and developmental stages away from conscious awareness and understanding (Jung, 1912/1972, 1902/2014). In conjunction with this process, the content is directed to the unconscious where the process of association gathers the content around a shared affect such as anger, aggravation, sadness, revulsion, inferiority, bliss, pride, amusement, affection, or confidence, and connected to an archetypal core such as the *persona*, *shadow*, or *anima* (Jung, 1934/1969b, 1916/1969f, 1912/1972). The constellating affect of a complex comprises its *feeling-tone*: the energetic value or nuclear element of its expression or influence. Jung (1928/1969c) writes,

> The nuclear element is characterized by its feeling-tone, the emphasis resulting from the intensity of affect ... It produces a specific constellation of psychic contents, thus giving rise to the complex, which is a constellation of psychic contents dynamically conditioned by the energetic value. (pp. 11–12)

The energetic value of a complex's feeling-tone determines its intensity to gather unconscious content and influence consciousness. The degree of intensity derives from *tension* generated in the polarity between consciousness and the unconscious.

Tension between consciousness and the unconscious increases the farther the contents and feeling-tones of a complex are removed from the awareness, consideration, and acknowledgment of the ego. For Jung (1934/1969b, 1951/1971), the ego represents the center of consciousness because it is most readily identified with a person's recognized and understood bodily sensations, thoughts, and actions. As the center of consciousness, the ego's primary function is to solidify a consistent sense of identity and efficiently recognize and accomplish definitive tasks through the process of *directed judgment*. As Jung (1916/1969f) states, "[t]he definitiveness and directedness of the conscious mind are extremely important ... Without them science, technology, and civilization would be impossible, for they all presuppose the reliable continuity and directedness of the conscious process" (pp. 69–70). However, the ego's directed judgment leads to psychological tension between consciousness and the unconscious because, "....the quality of directedness makes for the inhibition or exclusion of all those psychic elements which appear to be, or really are, incompatible with it" (Jung, 1916/1969f, p. 70). This produces a buildup of inhibited and excluded psychic elements in the unconscious. The greater the number of excluded contents, or the greater their incompatibility with the ego, the greater the psychic tension. As psychic tension increases, so does the energetic intensity gathered and exerted by the complex. As a result, "[t]he further[sic] we are able to remove ourselves from the unconscious through directed functioning, the more readily a powerful counter-position can build up in the unconscious, and when this breaks out it may have disagreeable consequences" (Jung, 1916/1969f, p. 71).

The intensity of energy gathered and exerted by a complex determines the degree of its autonomous influence on the thoughts, behaviors, and emotions of the ego. The greater the intensity, the more readily a complex will influence the ego and the more impactful or disruptive this influence will be. Thus, the more separated a complex is from the ego, the more it will act as an animated foreign body intruding on the ego's actions and experiences. At the low intensity end, a complex exerts its influence on the ego as spontaneous thoughts, behaviors, or emotions that occur outside the ego's control (Jung, 1973/1981, 1902/2014). At the high intensity end, a complex has the propensity to act as an independent center of consciousness, what Jung refers to as a "splinter psyche" (Jung, 1934/1969a). Such complexes act as uncontrollable intrusions which seem to have minds of their own as displayed by the hallucinations and fantasies in schizophrenia and alternate personalities in dissociative identity disorder.

Feeling tone and tension are the dynamic factors related to the other significant psychological dimension of complexes: *personification*. As Jung (1927/1969e) writes, "...every autonomous or even relatively autonomous complex has the peculiarity of appearing as a personality, i.e., of being personified" (p. 196). Personification is an autonomous, unconscious process that figures the abstract dynamic factors of a complex in a relational context of *otherization*, *formation*, and *communication* with the ego. This is significant because "[p]ersonifying or imagining things becomes crucial for moving from an abstract, objectified psychology to one that encourages animistic engagement with the world" (Hillman, 2013, p. 69).

I define *otherization* as a psychological process of experiencing and regarding an idea or feeling as separate or different from an individual's personality, identity, or sense of self. As noted above, a complex consists of a conglomerate of psychological content separated from conscious awareness and held together by the energy of its feeling tone. However, the separate quality of a complex is typically unrecognized, misattributed, or rejected by the ego. If a person is suddenly overwhelmed with a feeling of depression, and the thoughts and memories accompanied by that feeling, they often say "*I am* depressed," or "Another person or situation is *making me* depressed," or "*My* depression is caused by *my* brain's chemical imbalance." In each case, the separate quality of the depression complex is missing, resulting in the person identifying with depression as their state of consciousness. In the first example, the separate quality of the complex is unrecognized since the person directly identifies the depression as their own. Misattribution of the separate quality of the complex occurs in the second example because depression is recognized as an effect of the environment taken on by the ego. Rejection of the complex's separate quality occurs in the third example since depression is reduced to the ego's brain-chemical processes.

When a complex is personified, its separate quality is constellated as a distinct figure of psychological content and emotion *other* than the ego. Through personification, a person's sudden feeling and impressions of depression remain with the complex while the complex takes on a form and position which the ego can relate to as other. This creates some distance between the individual experiencing depression and the feelings and ideas associated with depression which can relieve their suffering and hopelessness. As such, therapists such as Ira Progoff, a holistic depth psychologist, employ specific techniques to promote personification. Progoff (1975) developed the intensive journal method, influenced by Jung's method of active imagination, to promote personification for the purpose of developing an individual's "...own capacities for growth and psychological well being" (p. 128). The journal, Progoff (1975) writes, "can be considered a companion, a portable alter ego, and an intimate friend who will respond and discuss with a person in dialogue" (p. 128). By writing an intensive journal, an individual is able to engage their complex as a distinct other through dialogue. Dimaggio and Stiles (2007) discuss how personification is useful in eliciting and engaging the multiple internal parts clients and therapists express during psychotherapy by focusing closely on the voice, attitude, and behavioral changes that accompany shifts in subject position and facets of personality. Dimaggio and Stiles (2007) promote personification by encouraging the client and therapist to notice nuanced changes in their voice, attitudes, and behaviors and act them out through role-playing or the two chair technique, taking the time to reflect on each subject position or facet of personality as a unique, independent person. In the field of physical illness treatment, Shahar and Lerman (2013) discuss how giving human characteristics to physical illness helps improve the resilience and emotional distress of individuals dealing with chronic illness. They argue that as long as it is not persecutory, "...personification is potentially adaptive because of its *transformative* nature: it changes an event or situation from an external obstacle to an internal sense of purpose or meaning" (p. 50). Relatedly, Shahar and Lerman (2013) suggest utilizing multiple modalities of personification such as a) cognitive behavioral approaches which promote personifying feelings or encouragement and engagement, b) family systems models which personify aspects of an illness as a helpful or educational figure, and c) psychodynamic approaches which focus on personifying malevolent representations of an individual's inner world related to the illness to give shape and characteristics to hidden or abstract qualities. As these various techniques of personification show, personification allows a person to recognize groups of feelings and thoughts which populate their psyche besides the ego. By establishing them as "other," a distance is created that makes room for analysis, personal development, and healing.

Personification not only establishes a complex as a node of thoughts and feelings independent of the ego, but it also provides the complex form and character for the ego to confront. With *formation*, feeling-toned associations of ideas take shape as figures with character traits that can be related to and explored. Otherization distinguishes a complex from the ego, but without a form the complex remains in darkness, making it difficult for a person to identify and understand its influences. As a constellation of associations of thoughts and feelings, a complex has a wide array of spontaneous, subtle, and confusing influences across a multitude of situations that are difficult to organize into a central theme. Even though a single complex of depression is exerting its influence, a person may experience depression as a listless sadness in one instance, as a compelling creativity in another. They may be motivated to act anti-socially is one situation and find solidarity with others in another. Without a definitive form, it is difficult for a person to recognize and understand how such different experiences and actions can be influenced by the very same complex. Through personification, however, a complex is brought into the light as a figure for the ego to behold with expressive characteristics consistent with its vast influence.

While personification requires the autonomous quality of a complex, personification does not occur automatically, except in pathological conditions such as dissociative identity disorder or schizophrenia. This is because of the generally dismissive attitude of our modern, highly developed rational ego operating at the expense of the dynamic life of the unconscious. For Jung (1920/1969d), before the evolution of the ego, humans lived in two worlds, the physical and the spiritual world. The spiritual world is closer to the unconscious and is experienced as spirits, deities, and demons in various images. The physical world is closer to consciousness and is both logical and discursive. Once the ego develops as the primary locus of experience, the spiritual is dismissed as unreal and inconsequential. This attitude is reflected in the way modern consciousness ignores or undervalues the importance of dreams. For pre-modern humans, the dream world, which is populated by figures and images of the spiritual realm, is seen as being just as significant as the waking world. It conveys important information for an individual's and community's well-being. For the modern ego, however, dreams are viewed as irrational non-sense with little to no importance, while the process of rational thinking and judgment are believed to be the only important aspects of reality.

For Jung (1964, 1934/1969b), the autonomous personifying activity of complexes is most readily experienced in dreams and are the psychological foundation of early, pre-modern belief in spirits. Once ego-consciousness develops as the primary psychological reality, the animating expression of autonomous complexes are explicitly dismissed, resulting in a subversion of the personifying capacity of complexes. Complexes still function autonomously but their expressions are subtle and abstract in the waking state in accordance with the directional focus of consciousness. Their personifying capacity is still available to modern consciousness in the form of dream images which can erupt into consciousness when a high intensity of tension between consciousness and the unconscious occurs or when techniques are utilized to reduce the abbreviating and dampening influence of the rational ego.

Even with the difficulties of the infringement of ego directedness on a complex's propensity to personify, we are still familiar with the formative and expressive personification from ancient myths in figures such as Zeus, Odin, and Shiva. Each figure is a personification of nature or of the hopes, fears, values, and vices of human culture. The image and characteristics of each figure symbolize a totality of associations around a central theme that would take many paragraphs of description and justification to reveal in words. As Jung (1912/1972) writes,

> The symbol is not a sign that disguises something generally known. Its meaning resides in the fact that it is an attempt to elucidate, by a more or less apt analogy, something that is still entirely unknown or in the process of formation. (p. 291)

Relatedly, when a complex is personified, the many associations and influences of the complex are given a shape and character for the ego to recognize and explore without getting stuck attempting to list an exhaustive inventory of every moment of influence and every relevant association. In the case of a depression-complex, for example, personification reveals the complex as an independent figure with definitive features and characteristics indicative of the influences and impressions it exerts on a person's ego. The figure could be a belittling individual in the person's life, a pop culture figure representative of despair or failure, or a real or fictional successful character that reminds the person of his or her inadequacies. The list of possible figures is inexhaustible. The formation aspect of personifying a complex is specific to an individual's particular complex and their unique history. The importance of personification formation is not the figure itself, but in its influence and the message it is attempting to convey.

While otherization separates a complex from the ego and formation gives it shape and character, *communication* is the interactive aspect of personification. I define communication as the relational field that arises in a personified complex's interaction with an individual's ego. Before personification, the influence of a complex is hidden from the ego's awareness because its feeling-tone and fixed ideas are not recognized as distinct from the ego's conscious thoughts and feelings. Once a complex is personified, it is revealed as an independent figure of the individual's psyche with thoughts and feelings apart from the ego. A space is now established for communication to take place. Within this space the person has the opportunity to familiarize himself or herself with the nuances of the complex's influence in the same way he or she would become familiar with another person. Jung (1934/1969b) refers to this process as *active imagination*, which he defines as "...a sequence of fantasies produced by deliberate concentration" (p. 49). Jung uses the phrase "deliberate concentration" to distinguish his method from Freud's free association, and to highlight his focused precision on remaining with and amplifying the emotional state or feeling-tone of the encountered complex. Jung (1934/1969b) writes, "Fantasy must be allowed the freest of possible play, yet not in such a manner that it leaves the orbit of it object, namely the affect, by setting off a kind of 'chain reaction' association process" (p. 82).

Active imagination evokes spontaneous fantasies of a complex by reducing an individual's conscious judgment and concerns, remaining focused on the feeling-tone of the complex, and elaborating on the images that are formed to enrich and clarify the complex's associations and feeling-tone (Jung, 1934/1969a, 1954/1985). Following Jung's groundwork, many therapists have taken up active imagination as a method to access the unconscious and help patients become familiar with unknown and denied aspects of their personality. Through communication, the ego is not just passively influenced by the thoughts and feelings exerted by the complex, but becomes involved as an active participant with another active participant each attempting to understand the other. While written and spoken dialogue are the most common types of communication, other media such as drawing, sculpting, and physical action are also possible. Regardless of the communication employed, it is the message that matters. Before being personified, a complex is like an ignored or neglected child acting out for attention and recognition because his or her thoughts, feelings, concerns, and wants are not acknowledged. As a result of personification, the complex is given a voice and is able to bring the importance of its feeling-tone and association of unconscious content to an individual's awareness. In the ensuing communication between the complex and the individual's ego, the thoughts, feelings, concerns, and wants rejected or ignored by the ego are able to be developed, explored, and debated, allowing the person to recognize and consider unrealized aspects of their identity, leading to the expansion of self-knowledge.

The Importance of Self-Knowledge

In order for complex personification to facilitate self-knowledge, there must be an unknown self that needs to be found or developed, a self that is different from an individual's consciously recognized personality and identity. The psychological notion that people have an unknown self was first introduced and developed by Freud (1961) and the psychoanalytic tradition (Ellenberger 1970). According to Freud, the consciously recognized personality and identity of a person is only a small part of the individual's total psyche and personality. Freud (1961) defines the ego as the consciously recognized part of the psyche. He defines the total psyche not as the Self as Jung does, but as a three-part structure of id, ego, and superego (Ellenberger, 1970). While the ego is regarded as the conscious part of the psyche, Freud (1961) stresses that the id and superego are hidden from conscious awareness as unconscious structures. These unconscious structures influence a person's thoughts, feelings, motives, values, and fantasies outside of their awareness and require psychoanalytical therapy to be consciously revealed and known. As such, an individual's assumed unity of their ego personality is a false assumption covering up the fact that the total personality is a plurality of id, ego, and superego.

As a student of Freud, Jung (1934/1969a, 1912/1972) begins with the premise that the total personality is both conscious and unconscious and stresses the idea that most of an individual's personality is hidden. However, in establishing his own theories and building his own psychological tradition, Jung (1934/1969b, 1951/1971, 1912/1972) expands on Freud's three structure personality system with his notions of Self and complexes. While Freud avoids discussing the Self in favor of the id, ego, superego relationships, Jung spends a great deal of time and effort developing the notion of a hidden Self. He refers to the Self as the unifying archetype of psychical wholeness characterizing the totality of the conscious and unconscious parts of an individual's psyche. For Jung, the Self is hidden from conscious awareness because its unconscious parts need to be uncovered and made conscious, a process Jung refers to as *individuation*. Thus, the hidden Self is potential wholeness. An individual's ultimate developmental goal is to actualize this wholeness through the process of individuation, a process which uncovers the hidden Self.

Jung's notion of a hidden Self expresses a dichotomy between psychological unity and plurality. According to Jung, the ego is what we commonly refer to when we say "I," "me," or "mine." The ego is the center point of consciousness and our immediate awareness of our identity and personality: our explicit gender, place in our family, social position, occupation, accepted or willed attitude, explicit or recognized traits, values, and wants (Jung 1934/1969b, 1951/1971). As such, the person regards their ego as the apparent singular unity of their personality and fortifies that singularity by maintaining a close affiliation to its recognized qualities and regards anything apart from those qualities as not belonging to their personality and thus not to be identified with (Jung, 1951/1971, 1912/1972, 1921/1976). In contrast, the Self is not a singular unity but a unified plurality, a unifying archetype which holds all conscious aspects and unconscious aspects of an individual's personality together (Jung, 1964, 1934/1969b, 1951/1971). As Jung (1951/1971) states, the Self is the total personality because it represents the whole psyche, not just an individual's conscious aspects or unconscious aspects. However, unlike the ego, the plural unity of the total personality is hidden due to the unconscious aspects Jung refers to as archetypes and complexes.

> ...the self is a quantity that is supraordinate to the conscious ego. It embraces not only the conscious but also the unconscious psyche ... it transcends our powers of imagination to form a clear picture of what we are as a self... since however much we may make conscious there will always exist an indeterminate and indeterminable amount of unconscious material which belongs to the totality of the self. (Jung, 1912/1972, p. 177)

Since the Self is hidden from a person's conscious awareness, the ego believes itself to be the total personality. This results in a condition that Jung refers to as *one-sidedness*, a psychological state that occurs because of the ego's "me/not me" distinction (1934/1969a, 1912/1972, 1921/1976). According to Jung (1934/1969b), two of the primary functions of the ego are judgment and categorization. The ego judges sensory information that reaches conscious awareness in order to classify it into various categories such as good or bad, painful or pleasurable, active or passive. This categorization is central to a person's ability to make sense of the world, focus their attention, and efficiently pursue their goals. With regard to personality, the ego's judgment categorizes an individual's "me" from the "not me" along the lines of gender, type of thinking, type of feeling, type of sensation, social status or group, occupation, attitude, and behavioral traits (1969a/1934, 1964). For example, through this judgment, a person's ego-personality is formed and identified as "me" with statements such as "I'm male," "I'm reserved," "I'm sensitive," "I'm rebellious," "I'm joyful," and "I'm imaginative." This identity becomes reified in contrast with the "not me" through reverse statements such as "I'm not female," "I'm not outgoing," and "I'm not gloomy." However, as Jung states, the formation of the ego-personality comes at the cost of a one-sided identity or sense of self since many of the characteristics categorized as "not me" are actually rejected, unrecognized, or potential aspects of an individual's personality (1969a/1934, 1971/1951). As a result of this one-sidedness, these rejected, unrecognized, and potential aspects are relegated to the unconscious, leaving the person to mistakenly identify the ego-personality as their total personality.

With the establishment of a one-sided ego-personality, a developmental stagnation takes place that leads to lost potentiality because potential adaptive qualities and aspects of personality are not given the opportunity to be explored or realized (Jung, 1934/1969b, 1951/1971, 1912/1972). As a singular unity, the ego-personality is fortified against anything that could threaten its solidity or singularity which an individual establishes with statements of negation such as "I could never go to a party with so many people," or "I will never follow the status quo," or "there is nothing feminine about me." These statements indicate lost potentiality because they limit the plethora of characteristics and behaviors a person can explore and identify with, resulting in an inability to try new things, form new relationships, and adapt to new or novel personal and social conditions. While this developmental stagnation takes place with the ego-personality, the unconscious compensates with an eruption of activity that is both disturbing and illuminating (Jung, 1934/1969a, 1934/1969b).

As Jung states, the greater the one-sidedness and the more the ego is disconnected from the unconscious, the more energetic the unconscious becomes via the formation and activity of complexes. With increased one-sidedness and lost potentiality of personality development, the activity of complexes increasingly exert disturbing and directing influences on an individual's thoughts, feelings, attitudes, and behaviors (Jung, 1934/1969a, 1912/1972). The person experiences the impressions of a complex as strange, uncharacteristic infringements that destabilize their sense of identity. Since these impressions stem from the unconscious, the person has difficulty identifying their source. The source of these impressions is often identified with other people via projection by statements such as "I'm never so outgoing but I lose control of myself when I'm around that person." Or the source of the impression is internally ambiguous indicated by statements like "I know this movie is funny, but something must be wrong with me today because I just feel sad." In either case, the activity of the unconscious is a jarring influence on an individual's sense of personal stability which disrupts their habitual thoughts, feelings, and behaviors in such a way that they form pathological tendencies like obsession and depression. However, the disruptive activity of the unconscious has an illuminating potential because it directs a person's attention away from the habitual one-sidedness of the ego toward the unrecognized, dismissed, or rejected aspects of their personality. As such, the activity of the unconscious is a call to Self-knowledge, a call to reveal the hidden Self by way of uncovering complexes.

Facilitating Self-Knowledge Through Complex Personification

In the first section, I described the psychological dimensions of complexes as unconscious contents and personification. I then unpacked how self-knowledge is grounded in Jung's notion of the hidden Self. The question I take up in this section deals with just how complex personification facilitates self-knowledge. The facilitation of self-knowledge through complex personification occurs in three stages: impression, naming, and integration. These stages are primarily based on Jung's (1969) essays, *The Transcendent Function* and *The Structure and Dynamics of the Psyche*. I use a depression-complex as an example to describe each stage.

Stage 1: Impression

I refer to the first stage as *impression* because the initial activity of the unconscious is experienced as an ambiguous and spontaneous feeling, idea, or behavior that "impresses itself" upon an individual's conscious awareness. At this stage, the source of the impression is not identified as a complex, but is experienced as an intrusion or disruption of the person's commonly recognized personality and identity. The impression is a complex's first contact with an individual's ego and is often expressed as a symptom of a pathology. In the case of a depression-complex, the impression could be a feeling of sadness, a suicidal or self-destructive thought, or an inability to begin or complete a project. In whatever way the impression manifests, it occurs apart from, or in opposition to, a person's will or intent. While the impression is spontaneous, its spontaneity is not arbitrary, but is triggered or activated by a specific internal or external context or situation (Jung, 1912/1972). The feeling of sadness may occur when an individual goes to a party with friends. A suicidal thought may occur when an individual is remembering a time at school when they were 12. The inability to start or complete a project may occur when an individual is feeling a sense of accomplishment. The recognition of the relationship between the impression and the trigger situation is important because the activity of the complex is conveying a message about the situation or trigger that is unacknowledged by the one-sided ego-personality (Jung, 1934/1969b). The first contact of a complex is often regarded as an intrusion with statements like, "I know I should be enjoying this party, but this sadness is overwhelming me," or "I really want to finish painting this room, but it just feels so pointless." Regardless of the way the impression of the complex is manifested, the particular situation in which it occurs, or the degree to which it possesses an individual's thoughts, feelings, or behaviors, this stage is the complex's introduction to the ego and an invitation to get to know what it has to offer.

Stage 2: Naming

While the first stage is the complex's invitation to the ego to recognize its existence, the second stage concerns the otherization and formation of the complex described in the previous section. As Jung (1934/1969a) notes, while the symptom expression and activity of a complex directs the ego's attention to the domain of the unconscious, the existence of the complex must be regarded as "other" from the ego in order for the complex to convey its message. To be regarded as "other," the complex must have a form set apart from the ego. In other words, the complex must be *constellated* and *named*. The constellation and naming of a complex are directly related to the impression of its intrusion, disruption, and the situation or trigger in which it occurs. As Jung (1934/1969a) states,

> [t]his term [constellation] simply expresses the fact that the outward situation releases a psychic process in which certain contents gather together and prepare for action. When we say that a person is "constellated" we mean that he has taken up a position from which he can be expected to react in a quite definite way. (p. 94)

For Jung (1934/1969b), this step requires the ego to adopt a receptive position and allow the complex room to take shape and articulate itself without judgment via active imagination. Through active imagination, the complex takes shape by allowing the emotional and ideational association of its impression to expand into an enriched image and detailed articulation of its characteristics. He writes, "....[T]he elaboration of the mood is, as it were, a picture of the contents and tendencies of the unconscious that were massed together in the depression" (Jung, 1916/1969f, p. 82). If the impression of the complex is sadness, active imagination gives a space to that sadness and allows it to deepen and fill itself out. As sadness, its central characteristic may be melancholy, listlessness, lack of energy, and heaviness. Through active imagination, these qualities may bring forth an image that may refer to the individual's personal life such as an apathetic family member, or may appear as a cultural figure such as a character from a book or film. In either case, through naming, the initial and general feeling of sadness is refined and more directly aligned with the trigger situation in such a way that the feeling-toned, unconscious content of the complex is described in the fullest visual, linguistic, auditory, tactile, and olfactory detail possible, to the point where the complex in not only cast as an "other," but is named, demarcated, and given a definitive perspective on the trigger situation. Once the complex is formed and named as a definitive figure and perspective, the third stage is set.

Stage 3: Integration

The third stage of the self-knowledge process equates with what Jung (1916/1969f) refers to as the establishment of the transcendent function: a symbolic mediation between the attitude and contents of the unconscious and the position and assertions of the ego which can result in the transformation of the ego's identity, attitude, and behavior. After the personification of the complex establishes its perspective and articulates its ideas and attitude to the fullest degree possible, the person is able to enter into an open dialogue with it. This discourse is not a one-sided ego judgement or dismissal of the complex, nor is it a wholesale acceptance of the stance or attitude offered by the personified complex. Rather, it is a true discussion between the ego-personality and the complex in which both parties are heard, debated, and considered (Jung, 1916/1969f).

It is important to note in this context that the person is quite familiar with the ideas, feelings, and ideals of the ego-personality and identifies with them, but the impression of fixed ideas and feeling tones presented by the complex are new to the individual and present a fresh perspective on the trigger situation. Returning to the example of the depression-complex, the personified apathetic family member may offer a perspective on melancholy that informs the person that although their ego-personality asserts a care-free attitude of enjoyment consonant with a party life-style, that one-sided attitude has dismissed desire to establish more serious relationships and hides an anxiety to strive for a higher purpose. In weighing the assertions of the personified complex with the ego-personality, the individual reveals aspects of the unconscious that can expand their personality beyond the one-sidedness of the ego-personality, increasing the range of the available thoughts, feelings, ideals, and behaviors available to their identity and increase their adaptability to current and new opportunities.

In conclusion, I have offered a preliminary sketch of how complex personification can facilitate self-knowledge to reveal unconscious aspects and expand a person's identity beyond the narrow limits of a one-sided ego-personality. I began by describing the psychological dimensions of complexes which are unconscious contents dissociated from consciousness with energetic tension. These dissociated contents gather together as feeling-toned associations of ideas with the propensity to autonomously influence an individual's conscious thoughts, feelings, and behaviors. As autonomous factors of the unconscious, complexes can become personified as figures with characteristics that can be communicated with as "others." Next, I unpacked the importance of self-knowledge with regard to Jung's notion of the hidden self and contrasted it with the ego-personality. Finaly, I described how complex personification facilitates self-knowledge in three stages I refer to as: impression, naming, and integration. By examining these hidden processes, the chapter highlights the therapeutic potential of engaging with personified complexes and underscores the importance of self-knowledge in psychological health and personal development.

Competing Interests The author has no conflicts of interest to declare that are relevant to the content of this chapter.

References

Dimaggio, G., & Stiles, W. B. (2007). Psychotherapy in light of internal multiplicity. *Journal of Clinical Psychology, 63*(2), 119–127. https://doi.org/10.1002/jclp.20335

Ellenberger, H. F. (1970). *The discovery of the unconscious: The history and evolution of dynamic psychiatry*. Basic Books.

Freud, S. (1961). *New introductory lectures on psychoanalysis* (J. Strachey, Trans.). W.W. Norton.

Hillman, J. (2013). *Archetypal psychology*. Spring Publications, Inc.

Jung, C. G. (1964). *The collected works of C. G. Jung: Vol. 10. Civilization in transition* (G. Adler, & R. F.C. Hull, Trans.). Princeton University Press.

Jung, C. G. (1969a). A review of the complex theory (G. Adler, & R.F.C. Hull, Trans.). In G. Adler & R. F. C. Hull (Eds.), *The collected works of C. G. Jung: Vol. 8. Structure and dynamics of the psyche* (2nd ed., pp. 92–104). Princeton University Press. (Original work published 1934).

Jung, C. G. (1969b). Archetypes of the collective unconscious (R. F. C Hull, Trans.). In H. Read et al. (Eds.), *The collected Works of C.G. Jung: Vol. 9 (part 1). The archetypes and the collective unconscious* (2nd ed., pp. 3–72). Princeton University Press. (Original work published 1934).

Jung, C. G. (1969c). On psychic energy (G. Adler, & R.F.C. Hull, Trans.). In G. Adler & R. F. C. Hull (Eds.), *The collected works of C.G. Jung: Vol. 8. Structure & dynamics of the psyche* (2nd ed., pp. 3–66). Princeton University Press. (Original work published 1928).

Jung, C. G. (1969d). The psychological foundations of belief in spirits (G. Adler, & R.F.C. Hull, Trans.). In G. Adler & R. F. C. Hull (Eds.), *The collected works of C.G. Jung: Vol. 8. Structure & dynamics of the psyche* (2nd ed., pp. 301–318). Princeton University Press. (Original work published 1920).

Jung, C. G. (1969e). The structure of the psyche (G. Adler, & R.F.C. Hull, Trans.). In G. Adler & R. F. C. Hull (Eds.), *The collected works of C.G. Jung: Vol. 8. Structure & dynamics of the psyche* (2nd ed., pp. 139–158). Princeton University Press. (Original work published 1927).

Jung, C. G. (1969f). The transcendent function (G. Adler, & R.F.C. Hull, Trans.). In G. Adler & R. F. C. Hull (Eds.), *The collected works of C.G. Jung: Vol. 8. Structure & dynamics of the psyche* (2nd ed., pp. 67–91). Princeton University Press. (Original work published 1916).

Jung, C. G. (1971). Aion: Phenomenology of the self. In J. Campbell (Ed.), *The portable Jung* (pp. 139–162). Penguin. (Original work published 1951).

Jung, C. G. (1972). *The collected works of C. G. Jung: Vol. 7. Two essays in analytical Psychology* (G. Adler, & R. F.C. Hull, Trans.). Princeton University Press. (Original work published 1912).

Jung, C. G. (1976). *The collected Works of C. G. Jung: Vol. 6. Psychological types* (G. Adler and R. F.C. Hull, Trans.). Princeton University Press. (Original work published 1921).

Jung, C. G. (1981). *The collected works of C. G. Jung: Vol. 2. Experimental researches* (G. Adler and R. F. C. Hull, Trans.). Princeton University Press. (Originally published 1973).

Jung, C. G. (1985). *The collected works of C. G. Jung: Vol. 6. Practice of psychotherapy* (G. Adler & R. F. C. Hull, Trans.). Princeton University Press. (Original work published 1954).

Jung, C. G. (2014). *The collected works of C.G. Jung: Vol. 1. Psychiatric studies* (R. F. C. Hull, Trans.). Princeton University Press. (Original work published 1902).

Progoff, I. (1975). *At a journal workshop: Writing to access the power of the unconscious and evoke creative ability*. Dialogue House Library.

Shahar, G., & Lerman, S. F. (2013). The personification of chronic physical illness: Its role in adjustment and implications for Psychotherapy Integration. *Journal of Psychotherapy Integration, 23*(1), 49–58. https://doi.org/10.1037/a0030272

CHAPTER 4

Jung's Structure of the Psyche in Modern Perspective

Benjamin J. Swogger

In the decades since Jung's death, complexes and archetypes have met with different fates as regards their scientific understanding, a result perhaps reflective of their differing origins. On the one hand, the experimental paradigm of the word-association procedure—out of which arose the notion of the *autonomous complex*—ensured Jung's contemporaneous scientific reputation. Even today, in the history of psychology, Jung is remembered primarily for his empirical research on the association method and the description of psychological types to which it gave birth (see, e.g., Green, 1997). On the other hand, the concept of archetypes emerged from the mythological context surrounding Jung's *Red Book* experiences (Jung, 2009), which, far from representing a scientific endeavor, are best situated, Shamdasani (2021) estimates, as part of the Western visionary tradition. Nevertheless, however different the conditions from which these concepts evolved, it is clear that for Jung they were intimately linked.

B. J. Swogger (✉)
University of West Georgia , School of Social Sciences, Carrollton, GA, USA
e-mail: bs00067@my.westga.edu

J. J. Dillon (ed.), *Complex and Archetype*,
https://doi.org/10.1007/978-3-032-02609-5_4

In his 1931 essay "Analytical Psychology and *Weltanschauung*" (Jung, 1931/1969a), Jung posited that "over and above" the psychic complex is the autonomous "dominant" of the unconscious.[1] Dominants are felt to be "strange and incomprehensible," for which reason the human mind disposes to "personifying them as spirits, demons, and gods" (p. 369). Dominants "express themselves…in religion" (p. 370) and mythology, always with the affective intensity of "compelling necessities" (p. 372). It is the dominant, or archetypal, dimension of a complex which infuses it with its dynamism:

> Naturally the image of the individual mother is impressive, but its peculiar impressiveness is due to the fact that it is blended with an unconscious aptitude or inborn image which is the result of the symbiotic relationship of mother and child that has existed from eternity. (p. 372)

Here, "symbiotic" is an apt description not only for the relationship between mother and child but also for that between complex and archetype. Any scientific rendering of these fundamental and interwoven concepts should, therefore, be capable of doing justice to both.

To that end, this chapter investigates one prominent effort to bring Jung's ideas into alignment with recent scientific advancements, namely, the reinterpretation of complexes and archetypes in terms of the new science of *complexity*. Featuring the phenomena of *self-organization* and *emergence*, the chapter shows that while complexity science is eminently suited to describing autonomous complexes as Jung conceived of them, it fails to account for the theory of archetypes which would otherwise necessitate radical revisioning. By highlighting this discrepancy, the chapter advocates for the Pauli-Jung conjecture (Atmanspacher & Fuchs, 2014) as a way out of this dilemma and concludes with a look at future directions. The understanding emerging from such an analysis carries with it the potential for revisiting certain theoretical and clinical difficulties within Jung's thought as well as opening new vistas for carrying his work further into the twenty-first century.

[1] *Dominant* was a term first used by Jung in 1917 (Jung, 1917/1920) to refer to universal, invariant forms. It was chronologically intermediate to his use of *primordial image* in 1911 (Jung, 1911–1912/1991) and *archetype* in 1919 (Jung, 1948/1969b). For differing interpretations as to Jung's source for the term dominant, see Noll (1997) and Shamdasani (2003, p. 309).

Autonomous Complexes as Self-Organizing Psychic Structures

In her introduction to Jung's Zofingia lectures, Marie-Louise von Franz (1983) interprets Jung's sympathy for vitalism as a step in the direction toward the modern possibility of "'self-organization' by a spiritual agency" (p. xvii). While the allusion to a spiritual agency represents something *other* than self-organization as understood today in the study of complex systems (Yates, 1987), it is worth considering whether the spirit of these ideas might be interpreted as prefiguring the type of spontaneous pattern formation that *would* be considered self-organization.

In the first of these addresses, "The Border Zones of Exact Science," Jung attacked the dominant materialist paradigm of the time in his evaluation of the origin of life. Living matter, he contended, would have had to exist from the very beginning or else have encountered some vital force, since "organic beings never develop out of inorganic matter, but only through contact with life. If ever a law was absolute, then it is this, that *omne vivum ex vivo* [all life from life]" (Jung, 1983, p. 16). Given the implausibility that a living cell from which all life emerged existed at the outset of the creation of the universe, one must therefore explain how the first cell came to be in the first place. Following the dictum that all life comes from life, Jung accordingly postulated that the primordial life force is necessarily immaterial, since, by definition, no *other* living entity could have existed prior to the *first* living entity.

But while Jung was correct in assuming that an energy influx is necessary for the creation of dynamic structure, it is not so apparent that the involved matter or energy need be vital. In an experiment by Kondepudi, Kay, and Dixon (2015), for instance, metal beads were shown to spontaneously form branching, protein-like shapes when exposed to electricity in a petri dish of oil surrounded by a grounding ring (Fig. 4.1). Initially arranged haphazardly in the oil (an insulating substance), the beads responded to the electricity by "snapping" into place as a sort of conduit for the electricity to reach the ground. This suggests that energy throughput leads to remarkable structural self-organization including organism-like energy-seeking behavior and even, the authors report, self-healing.

Yet despite this apparent vitality, these results can be explained using the known laws of physics. The second law of thermodynamics dictates that a given system strives for maximal entropy, which in this case is achieved when the electricity is dissipated via the metal beads to the

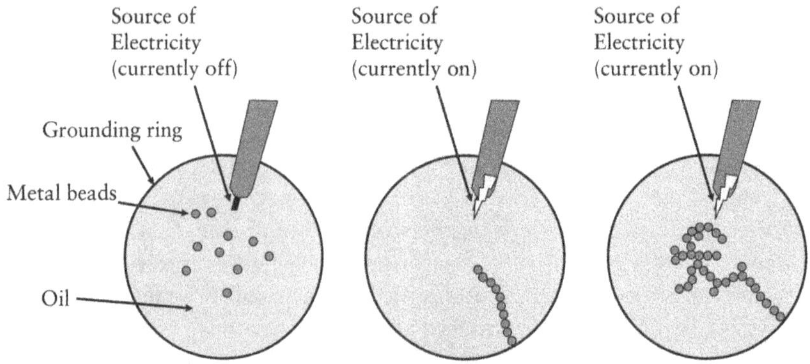

Fig. 4.1 Spontaneous self-organization of inanimate matter. (Note: Reprinted with permission from Blau and Wagman (2023, p. 278). Copyright 2023 by Julia J. C. Blau and Jeffrey B. Wagman)

grounding ring. So while the total system dramatically *increases* in entropy (in accordance with the law), the beads themselves appear to move from a state of *higher* entropy to *lower* entropy (from *disorder* to *order*, hence the popular characterization of this process as "order out of chaos"). Though Jung makes much of the first law of thermodynamics (the conservation of energy) in the Zofingia lectures and elsewhere, the second law as it relates to systems far from thermodynamic equilibrium, like the one in this example, had not yet been worked out *in toto*. Jung was, therefore, ahead of his time with respect to his intuition that, given sufficient energy, simple elements could be organized into complex aggregates. After his early foray into physical science, he turned his attention toward the psyche.

In his medical dissertation "On the Psychology and Pathology of So-called Occult Phenomena," Jung (1902/1970a) explained somnambulistic hallucinations as a result of "a certain autonomy of the psychic elements" (p. 46). Following Pierre Janet's assessment in *L'Automatisme* that a split-off personality consisted of disaggregated psychic phenomena organized by suggestion, Jung similarly interpreted the "channeled" personalities of his medium as a constellation of associated psychic content charged by unconscious sexual anticipation. This peculiar self-organization of the psyche would go on to represent the principal feature of his signature concept: the *autonomous complex*.

Although Jung stopped short of referring to complexes as autonomous in his seminal word-association studies (Jung & Riklin, 1904/1973), he clearly described them as such on account of their structural independence from the ego and the instigating role of affectivity in constellating them.[2] Several years later, referring to the spontaneous organizing effect of sufficient emotional charge, he stated:

> For this property of the complex, I have introduced the term *autonomy*. I conceive the complex to be a collection of imaginings, which, in consequence of this autonomy, is relatively independent of the central control of the consciousness, and at any moment liable to bend or cross the intentions of the individual. (Jung, 1913/1973, p. 601)

With the notion of autonomous complexes, Jung came remarkably close to contemporary understandings of self-organization: instead of metal beads and electricity (Fig. 4.1), Jung posited a "collection of imaginings" and *libido* or *psychic energy* (Jung, 1928/1969c). These obvious resonances, however, are observable only in retrospect, as Jung intuited ideas that only became explicitly developed much later. But while Jung lacked recourse to terminology that might more precisely describe such phenomena as the psychic dynamics characterizing constellation of a complex, modern complexity science furnishes vocabularies that are well equipped to describe such dynamics. In what follows, complex constellation is expressed in the language of complexity in order to highlight not only the impressive agreement of these approaches with Jung's ideas but also their utility for capturing a broad spectrum of theoretical and clinical considerations.

Complexity: The Language of Complexes

Jung's written record on complex constellation coincides remarkably well with contemporary complexity perspectives. Consider the following selection:

> The superstition held by all races that hysterical and insane persons are 'possessed' by demons is right in conception. These patients have, in fact, autonomous complexes, which at times completely destroy the self-control. There

[2] For a fuller account of the importance of affectivity for Jung's word-association experiments, see Swogger and Dillon (2023).

> superstition is therefore justified, inasmuch as it denotes 'possession,' because the complexes behave quite independently of the ego, and force upon it a quasi-foreign will. (Jung, 1913/1973, p. 602)

Here, Jung unwittingly referred to two cardinal features of self-organizing forms: *phase transitions* and the principle of *circular causality*. Phase transitions denote the critical points whereby local interactions (such as the typical associative activity of mental contents before constellation as a complex) become global patterns (the constellation of the complex from mental contents). In typical conscious states, the interactions between potential complex-forming mental contents are insufficiently strong to overtake the constellating power of the ego-complex and are therefore subordinate to it. But the change in affect resulting from some outside stimulus (e.g., the stimulus word in Jung's word-association procedure) provides the energy necessary for the self-organization of certain mental contents into a complex, akin to the spontaneous ordering of metal beads when electricity is sent coursing through oil in a petri dish (Fig. 4.1). The autonomous complex then competes with the ego-complex for dominance of the system, and if sufficiently strong, the autonomous complex usurps the ego which then becomes but one constituent part of the global psychic pattern dominated by the autonomous complex. In such a case, the affective or emotional state acts as the *control parameter* leading the system into another of its possible states characterized by the *order parameter*. The order parameter, as the characterization of the dominant pattern, can be thought of as a description of the psychic state (e.g., possession by the mother/father complex or parent/child complex). A change in the order parameter, such as that from ego-consciousness to a state of possession, is brought about by a change in the control parameter, which, in this case, means a change in emotional state. The order parameter then *constrains* the activity of its constituent parts which now include the ego. In other words, the autonomous complex *subordinates* the ego-complex, and the individual is in a state of *possession by a complex*. This process of constraint by the order parameter over the very parts of the system that give rise to the order parameter leads to a situation in which each *causes* the other: the order parameter governs the behavior of the parts, and the parts, by making up the order parameter, lead to its emergence. This is the principle of circular causality. Functionally, the system locks into a specific pattern until perturbed again from the outside or altered by internal fluctuations.

Circular causality, order parameters, and control parameters are terms which derive from the mathematical language of dynamical systems and are associated with German physicist Hermann Haken's system of *Synergetics*. As an approach to the study of structural self-organization, Synergetics has found application across a wide variety of domains including psychology broadly (Kelso, 1995), psychotherapy (Tschacher & Haken, 2019), even Freudian theory (Frank, 2019, p. 276). In Jungian circles, this work has been taken up by Nancy Krieger, whose book *Bridges to Consciousness: Complexes and Complexity* is the most sustained effort at applying the study of complex systems, in the form of Haken's Synergetics, to Jung's thought. Krieger (2014) suggests that complexes can be conceived as "attractor state[s] within the psychic landscape" (p. 1), referring to the modeling procedure whereby quantitative variables of a given system, including the control parameter and order parameter, feed into a set of equations that can be mapped as the system's *phase space* or *attractor landscape*. The simplest kind of attractor, a *point attractor*, essentially measures the stability of a given pattern of the system, as is intuitively grasped by its graphic representation (Fig. 4.2). The depth of the attractor corresponds to its stability, and one can imagine that in healthy individuals most complexes are represented by attractors that are shallower (less stable) than the ego-complex. Were this not so, the ego would be under constant threat of possession by the various autonomous complexes. Ostensibly, many complexes merely disrupt the functioning of the ego-complex without completely taking it over, as in the interferences demonstrated in Jung's word-association tests and, more practically, as indicated by ordinary experience. Only those complexes with extremely high valence possess enough stability for the psychic system to be shifted into an entirely new pattern as in the transition from (b) to (c) in Fig. 4.2.

The phase space is a fluid, dynamic landscape, evolving over time, with attractors forming, combining, and flattening, but it is important to note that in physical systems, variables are measured *quantitatively* and graphs such as these model the *actual* dynamics of the system. Since both the control parameter and order parameter in this example are *qualitative*, the phase space is only an illustration and not, of course, an actual depiction of psychic dynamics. Nevertheless, thinking in terms of attractor landscapes remains a helpful metaphor and can help makes sense of the work done in analysis.

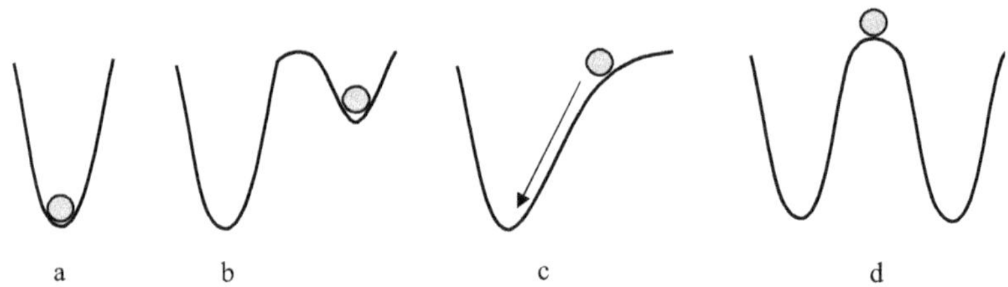

Fig. 4.2 A hypothetical phase space. (Note: (**a**) A point attractor representing a stable state of the system. (**b**) The system is stable in the ego-complex pattern (right attractor), but an autonomous complex represents a potentially more stable pattern (left attractor). (**c**) The landscape from (**b**) has shifted such that the ego-complex pattern loses its stability, and the autonomous complex attractor stabilizes the system into its pattern (i.e., possession). (**d**) At certain critical points where two or more stable states exist, a perturbation (e.g., one-sided viewpoint) is required to break the symmetry)

A Clinical Example

In his book *Complexes: Diagnosis and Therapy in Analytical Psychology*, Dieckmann (1999) describes his experience working with a young female patient who grew up idolizing her father and who, at seventeen, married a man her father's age. After she gave birth to a child, her marriage quickly deteriorated upon learning of her husband's professional dishonesty and sexual perversity. Following her divorce, the patient supported herself through a series of ill-advised affairs with older, married men, though at the cost of her psychic health as her worsening neurosis finally forced her into therapy. Based on the patient's anamnesis and clinical presentation, Dieckmann identified four operative complexes: (a) a positive father complex based on the revered figure of the patient's father, a successful professor with whom the patient was particularly close; (b) a negative father complex consisting of all the aggressive and sexual shadow aspects that the patient did *not* meet with in her father and so were projected onto her husband, though not without good reason; (c) a peculiar mother complex in accordance with the patient's cool, distant relationship with her mother which resulted in the patient perceiving her mother *through the eyes of the father* in the form of a trophy wife, empty of herself, serving only to add glint to the father's success; and (d) a child complex in the form of a certain infantilism resulting from the patient's closeness with her father which kept her in a state of perpetual dependency.

Equally important as these four constellated complexes are the manifold aspects of the father and mother complexes that were *not* cathected by the patient. These include: (e) the father as wise mentor and facilitator of individuation, since the patient's relationship with her father was one of subordination rather than apprenticeship and learning; (f) the father as positive hero, since the patient's unallayed admiration for her father was based on his conventional, if unimaginative, academic success and not on any real or perceived aptitude for ingenuity, courageousness, and inspired action; (g) the father as negative hero, since neither was he a failure, an idle dreamer, nor feeble; (h) the mother in her positive manifestations as caregiver, warmth bringer and protectress, since the patient's relationship with her mother was entirely devoid of these elements; and (i) the mother in her negative manifestations as ensnarer and devourer, since the patient's relationship with her mother was far too ambivalent for these either.

In the language of complexity, the patient's constellated complexes can be represented by attractors in her psychic landscape which happen to be more or less in contact with her ego-complex since she is able to report conscious experiences of the four primary complexes (a-d) in the form of fondness for her father, animosity toward her husband, distance from her mother, and childlike dependence. Proximity to the ego-complex ostensibly keeps these attractors shallower, more adaptable, and less likely to dominate the system as a whole; but the other, uncathected aspects of these complexes (e–i) represent energetic potentials that can be depicted as very deep attractors which, owing to the depth of their unconsciousness, possess the capacity, if constellated, to forcefully overtake the ego-complex or else become violently projected. Though he does not state it in these terms, it is precisely for this reason that Dieckmann views the work of therapy as one of *diffusing* the patient's psychic energy among as many attractors of the major complexes as possible rather than leaving it concentrated at only a few points. In doing so, he facilitates the process of bringing powerful, potentially eruptive unconscious complexes in touch with consciousness and so significantly expands the possible *conscious responsivity* of the patient while significantly lessening the potentially destructive impact of *unconscious reactivity*. Dieckmann (1999) states:

> Ideally, a moderately healthy person would expect all the core elements of the [major] complex[es] to be cathected to a greater or lesser degree. In this sense...a therapeutic concept...could aim at activating more complex core elements and associating them with the ego-complex. Then the ego-complex

> could draw on their various possibilities in relevant situations, which only then makes the plasticity of life into a living totality. (p. 56)

In this respect, the patient's psyche becomes more flexible and resourceful—in a word, *dynamic*—and indeed, Dieckmann comes remarkably close to dynamic systems approaches to cognition and action like that of Thelen and Smith (1994) who define a healthy dynamic system as "one that is always on the move and that lives on the edge of multiple attractors," adding that "such a system could move in and out of *almost* stable states of dramatically different kinds with small amounts of energy—with small forces" (p. 244). This contrasts with the type of rigid, unaccommodating landscape characterized by "very deep and narrow attractors." They elaborate:

> An attractor that is too deep means that the system would stay stuck in that state unless perturbed greatly. A system that did one thing would not be intelligent... Rather, an intelligent system is one that lives on the edge of many close attractors—dipping in along the side of an attractor and out again, perhaps never falling all the way to the bottom. (pp. 244–245)

Dieckmann goes on to show how the process of analysis, by attending to images and amplifying symbols, is particularly conducive to facilitating the traversal of new pathways in the patient's psyche and breaking away from worn ones. He depicts graphically the results of his work with a particularly challenging "borderline" patient who successfully redistributed concentrated libido among various attractors of the father and mother complexes as part of her individuation process involving the establishment of a more balanced psychic landscape. Dieckmann clarifies, however, that to effect such a rebalancing is not to advocate for a homogenization of the psyche among patients but to help patients open to the fullness and richness of psychic possibility as it exists for them. "Diversity [of psychic complexes]," he states, "imparts to the individual a unique destiny and personality" (Dieckmann, 1999, p. 57).

As is apparent, one can do incredibly valuable clinical work with complexes in the fashion described here, but it would not be quintessentially Jungian if the *archetypal* aspects of these complexes were not recognized, as Stover and Dillon each do for the parental complexes in this volume, and Dieckman does by relating them to such archetypal figures as the Apollonian god, the senex, and puella. For Jung, the mythological nature of the autonomous complex seemed to lend itself to something greater than even the remarkable effects it produced in the word-association tests and the validation it seemed to give to Freud's ideas regarding repression. In fact, as early as his 1907 book *The Psychology of Dementia Praecox*, Jung (1907/1960b) recognized that "it may be that the concept of the feeling-toned complex goes a little beyond the scope of Freud's views" (p. 38). In the same book, Jung mentioned Daniel Paul Schreber a number of times and, after introducing Schreber's book *Memoirs of My Nervous Illness* to Freud, which led to Freud's well-known paper on the case (Freud, 1911/1958), the interpretation of Schreber's illness became a point of departure between them (Jung, 1914/1960a; see also Lothane, 1992, pp. 317–374), as did Jung's ongoing experience with psychotic patients which seemed to indicate the objective nature of mythological themes. Exploration of such themes reached a climax with Jung's 1911–1912 publication of *Transformations and Symbols of the Libido* which famously cemented his differences with Freud, but Jung's own engagement with autonomous mythical personalities in his *Red Book* experiences from 1913 to about 1917 served to verify the notion toward which he had been building: in addition to the personal unconscious there was a *collective* unconscious—an *objective* psyche—populated by *archetypes*, those "*a priori* determinants of all psychic processes," as he first defined them in 1919 (Jung, 1948/1969b, p. 133). It has been this concept that has proven most difficult to square with the early congruence of complex and complexity.

Emergent Archetypes: A Divergent Perspective

Two major developments in the English-speaking world of the 1980s contributed to the widespread introduction of complexity science across a variety of domains: the founding of the Santa Fe Institute in 1984 as an interdisciplinary research center for the study of complex systems, and the publication of James Gleick's *Chaos: Making a New Science* in 1987 (Gleick, 1987) which became a New York Times Bestseller and introduced a popular audience to the branch of complex systems studies known as *chaos theory*. It was Gleick's book which first made an impact on Jungian literature.

Ernest Rossi's 1989 article "Archetypes as Strange Attractors" (Rossi, 1989) and John Van Eenwyk's similarly titled 1991 paper "Archetypes: the Strange Attractors of the Psyche" (Van Eenwyk, 1991) represented two of the earliest efforts at applying the new science to Jung's thought. Both quoted from Gleick's *Chaos* and both pondered whether Jung's concept of the archetype might be understood as a *strange attractor*: a far more complicated type than the fixed-point attractor illustrated above (Fig. 4.2) but one which exhibits the same peculiar "gravity" that attracts a system toward a particular configuration over time. Indeed, strange attractors seem remarkably well suited as a description of those deep structures of the unconscious that Jung termed archetypes, and Rossi pointed out that they have even been called "psychoanalytically suggestive" by certain outsiders.

Though these early papers were cursory overviews which teased a more exhaustive translation of Jung's ideas into the language of complexity, in raising the question of archetypes-as-attractors, Rossi and Van Eenwyk were also broaching the issue of whether Jung's insistence on the a priori nature of the archetype was sustainable. Referring to Jung's method of archetypal amplification in *Transformations and Symbols of the Libido*, David Tresan (1996) captured the essence of the dilemma:

> The reductionism Jung employed was phylogenetic, or, in other words, historical-evolutionary, and presupposes that psychological material, such as portions of Miss Miller's fantasies, may be seen as a residue of behavioural and thought patterns originating during the course of development of the human psyche. Present behaviours or unconscious productions thus explained may be said to have been reduced through their identification with prototypical events. On its surface, phylogenetic reductionism resembles archetypal amplification because both involve mythological language, but by definition reductionism is always non-ampliative, rational in its explanatory intent, flat in its feel, and tautological in the sense that it offers nothing truly new. ... In contrast to phylogenetic reduction, archetypal elaboration is an expression that denotes emergent activity constitutionally imbued with a spirit of novelty and creativeness. Although couched in mythological language, archetypal activity that emerges in an analysis lends itself to an experience of insight that is more one of discovering than of uncovering. In this light, archetypes are seen to recreate themselves de novo, and behaviours and unconscious productions in the present are brought forward as ever new and unpredictable patternings instead of recrudescent old truths. (p. 408)

In essence, Tresan questioned whether archetypal situations *conform* to pre-existing patterns, as Jung unequivocally suggested, or *emerge* as novel responses to current conditions. Subsequent relevant literature weighed in decisively for the latter.

In 2001, Peter Saunders and Patricia Skar published their paper "Archetypes, Complexes, and Self-Organization" which, in a similar manner as above, defined complexes as self-organizing psychic properties. Following Jung's comments that the existence of archetypes was evident given that complexes tended to form around typical themes, for example, "inferiority complex, power complex, father complex, mother complex, anxiety complex, and all the rest" (Jung, 1957/1976a, p. 532), Saunders and Skar (2001) defined archetypes as *classes* of autonomous complexes falling into the same general category, though they made no descriptive claims as to what these classes are nor normative ones as to how they are determined. From their perspective, archetypes are not *structures* of the unconscious, and certainly not a priori, as they represent the *dynamic properties* of a class of self-organizing complexes (see the update given in Skar, 2025).

Though they did not fully treat the distinction, Saunders and Skar, by rejecting the a priori existence of an archetypal structure, were rejecting Jung's notable differentiation between the *archetype-as-such* and the *archetypal image* first mentioned in his essay "On the Nature of the Psyche." There, Jung (1954/1969d) employed the analogy of the light spectrum to contrast the "dynamism" of instinct—the infrared pole—with the "numinosity" of archetype—the ultraviolet pole. Each in themselves is unknowable but is represented in what lies between—the visible spectrum. "The archetypal representations (images and ideas) mediated to us by the unconscious," Jung stated, "should not be confused with the archetype as such ...[which] is a psychoid factor that belongs, as it were, to the invisible, ultraviolet end of the psychic spectrum" (p. 213). Although Jung qualified his use of the term *psychoid* in greater detail earlier in the essay, his most succinct definition came in his assessment that "the real nature of the archetype is not capable of being made conscious...it is transcendent, on which account I call it psychoid" (p. 213). Similarly, he cautioned that, "we must...constantly bear in mind that what we mean by 'archetype' is in itself irrepresentable, but has effects which make visualizations of it possible, namely, the archetypal images and ideas" (p. 214).

Clearly, given the incompatibility of "transcendent," "irrepresentable," pre-existent forms with the notion of emergence, those adhering to a version of the latter would be forced to outright reject the archetype-as-such. Yet given the importance of this distinction for Jung's thought, some sought to retain the semblance of an a priori element, such as McDowell (2001) who called the archetype-as-such a "pre-existent principle of organization" along the lines of a mathematical axiom. But by far the most significant such effort was that of Jean Knox whose 2001 paper (Knox, 2001) and subsequent book (Knox, 2003) offered the most compelling synthesis of a priori elements and emergent structures. Knox's developmental model made use of the cognitive science concept of *image schemas*, or genetically encoded "pre-experiential potentialities" (Knox, 2001, p. 629), the achievement of which gives rise to experiences that could be considered archetypal. For example, Knox (2003) cited research concluding that the propensity of infants to spend more time attending to human faces than to other structures suggests that they possess genetic programs for seeking out and orienting to such faces. Importantly, however, there is no presumed *knowledge* of what a human face is nor an *image* of what it looks like. Rather, this type of preferential behavior operates at a primitive, perhaps even reflexive, level. By engaging with the caregiver by way of gaze, followed by communication, the infant "draws" the caregiver into an attachment pattern in which the image schema of "containment" is actualized. The phenomenal experience of being contained, when metaphorically elaborated, results in the emergence of the mother archetype as the primordial container. Although this is perhaps the paradigmatic example, it remains but one among many, and Knox cited others such as the way in which one metaphorically enters *into* a conversation in the same way that one might physically reach *into* a cupboard. But the main point is that Knox retained the a priori element of the archetype-as-such, by way of rudimentary genetic instructions, as well as the emergent archetypal image:

> The abstract pattern itself, the image schema, is never experienced directly, but acts as a foundation or ground plan that can be likened to the concept of the archetype-as-such. This provides the invisible scaffolding for a whole range of metaphorical extensions that can be expressed in conscious imagery and language and that would therefore seem to correspond to the archetypal image. These metaphorical elaborations are always based on the Gestalt of the image schema from which they are derived. (p. 61)

Though ostensibly less mathematical than the applications before her, Knox traded some of the precision of *dynamical* systems theory for the biological sophistication of *developmental* systems theory, such as that offered by Oyama (2000). Though Knox did not refer to this research by name, she in effect championed this approach which recognizes, in a nuanced and elegant way, the contributions of both genes *and* environment in shaping development. Her concession to both biology and culture represented an attractive alternative to the then-debate as to whether archetypes were biologically determined (Stevens, 1982, 1998; see also Swogger, 2024 for a fuller account of Stevens' role in the archetype debate) or culturally formed (Pietikäinen, 1998a, 1998b, 1999). It was this debate which first drew in George Hogenson, who highlighted the holes in both sides of the argument (Hogenson, 1998; see also his debate with Stevens in Hogenson, Stevens, & Ramos, 2003) and published a paper demonstrating that Jung's reception of the evolutionary theories of C. L. Morgan and J. M. Baldwin—the so-called Baldwin effect—accounted for psychological factors influencing human evolution, including those resulting from cultural innovations, and therefore represented a kind of "*culturally driven* natural selection" (Hogenson, 2001, p. 597). Joined by Australian analyst John Merchant (2006), who explicitly drew out the at-that-time only implicit connections between archetype theory and Developmental Systems Theory, the trio of Merchant, Knox, and Hogenson led the charge of what became the developmental/emergentist approach to the archetype.

Yet despite Knox's efforts at preserving the archetype-as-such, its relevance for the developmental/emergentist approach soon waned. Writing on the implications of Knox's model, Merchant (2009) declared:

> If this reading is correct, then I believe the implications are…that there are no such things as pre-existent, innate archetypal structures which direct psychological life and which are at the core of complex development. Rather, there would be developmentally produced mind/brain structures (image schemas) underpinning a later scaffolding through various processes of emergence and self-organization… The ramifications are substantial, for the very existence of archetypes as Jung conceived them is called into question. (p. 342)

Indeed, later in that same paper, Merchant issued the call: "If contemporary neuroscience does ultimately reveal that the archetype-as-such is not innate as originally conceived, then the question arises – is the word 'archetype' itself too suffused with innatism and preformationism meanings to prevent confusion?" (p. 355). As if in response to Merchant's challenge to evaluate contemporary neuroscience, Hogenson (2009) expressed a similar concern and went even further. "Just as theoretical robotics, complex dynamic systems theories of development, and the discovery of mirror neurons have concluded that it is possible to develop complex behavioural patterns without the cognitive processor embedded somewhere in the brain/mind," he provocatively suggested, "we may be in a position to do without the dynamic unconscious as an explanatory hypothesis" (p. 334).

Given this seismic shift in understanding regarding such a foundational concept of Jung's psychology, several implications needed drawing out including issues of synchronicity (Cambray, 2002, 2009; Hogenson, 2014), the analytic field (Cambray, 2011b), and Self and symbolism (Cambray, 2010; Hogenson, 2004, 2005, 2018). But from all this it became apparent that consonant with the lack of necessity of an a priori archetype, *meaning itself* was to be understood as an emergent quality of patterns that are, in themselves, *not* meaningful. François Martin-Vallas, who had since joined the emergentist movement, captured this sentiment well:

> Emergence opens the way to an approach that is not driven by magical causality, nor by hermeneutics, nor by final causes in the sense of creationism, which then allows the Jungian model of synchronicity, as an acausal principle, to become an example of the emergence of meaning arising simply from what occurs, that is, 'ordinary' coincidence. (Martin-Vallas, 2018, p. 63)

As this quotation demonstrates, along with those by Hogenson and Merchant above, to interpret Jung's ideas in light of the emergentist model is to move away from his original theorizing. For while psychological complexes can easily be construed as self-organizing structures, when it comes to archetypes, Jung wrote not of *emergent* forms but *a priori* ones. And though, as has been shown, the absence of such ideas as a priori archetypes and intrinsic meaningfulness poses no hindrance to the explanation of complicated psychological phenomena, the situation is reminiscent of that outlined by Roderick Main (2004), whose authoritative book on synchronicity instructively showed that, amidst all the alternative models put forward to explain coincidence phenomena including statistical, causal, and psychological understandings—which are, indeed, all up for the task—what makes Jung's theory distinctive is, most importantly, his openness to the possibility of spiritual or transpersonal involvement. In this respect, Main concluded that "only Jung's theory of synchronicity comfortably includes all three qualities of scientific grounding, psychological sophistication and spiritual openness" (p. 34). Similarly, the following section argues that, more than any other model, the recently elaborated Pauli-Jung conjecture put forth by Atmanspacher and colleagues includes the same three qualities: scientific grounding (including incorporation of advancements made by complexity science), psychological sophistication, and spiritual openness.

The Pauli-Jung Conjecture

Taking as their point of departure Jung's correspondence with Austrian physicist Wolfgang Pauli, Atmanspacher and colleagues have refined the Pauli-Jung dialogue into a coherent and elegant understanding of mind-matter correlations based on the metaphysical premise of dual-aspect monism. Called the Pauli-Jung conjecture (Atmanspacher & Fuchs, 2014), this position posits that mind and matter are manifestations of some more basic underlying reality. This fundamental reality is psychophysically neutral (PPN) and decomposes into mental (M) and physical (P) aspects. The analogy here is to an entangled quantum state, but Atmanspacher and Rickles (2022) point out that this is not to suggest that the mind-matter problem is predicated exclusively on quantum theory but that quantum entanglement serves as a "conceptual metaphor" allowing for unfamiliar territory to be explored in a familiar way. In this example, measuring a property, such as spin, of an entangled quantum state yields a pair of entangled particles which are precisely yet *nonlocally* correlated, meaning that a certain spin will be instantaneously realized by one particle at the moment of measuring the spin of the other particle—regardless of their physical distance apart. At first incomprehensible, the situation renders itself intelligible when one considers the pair not as two separate particles but as *two aspects of the same state*. Similarly, by virtue of deriving from the same singular reality, M and P are necessarily correlated. This correlation is *acausal* since it is not caused by an influence between M and P, and neither is it chance. In this way, the loop is completed, as it were, since the bifurcation of the psychophysically neutral realm into mental and physical domains is then "connected" through acausal correlation (Fig. 4.3).

The Pauli-Jung conjecture abounds with technicalities well beyond the scope of this chapter; suffice it here to highlight the three qualities of

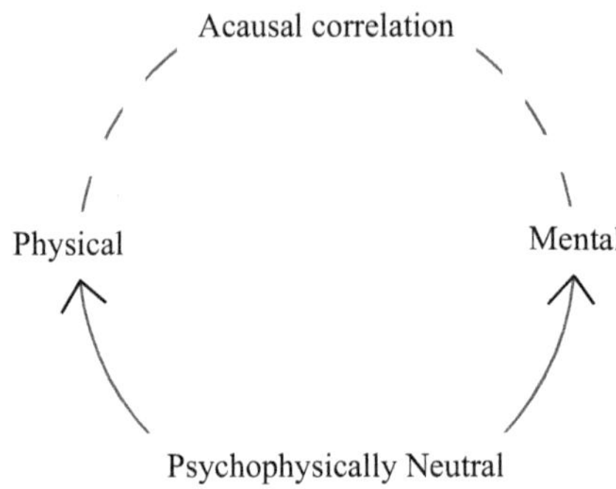

Fig. 4.3 A simplistic diagram of the Pauli-Jung conjecture. (Note: Decomposition of the psychophysically neutral domain into physical and mental aspects, like an entangled quantum state, necessarily results in acausal correlations between the aspects)

scientific grounding, psychological sophistication, and spiritual openness that make it the most comprehensive post-Jungian model of the psyche.

First, in addition to its support from quantum physics, the Pauli-Jung conjecture remains capable of incorporating emergent phenomena including the many examples discussed above. Atmanspacher and Rickles (2022) point out that bifurcation of PPN into dual aspects M and P results in three types of correlations: those between all three domains; those between any two domains such as M-P but also between M-PPN and P-PPN; and intradomain correlations, or those within each domain separately. The implication of this last type of intradomain correlation is that known causal laws in physical and mental domains are accounted for. In other words, physical and mental causation still have a place within this framework, and by extrapolation, so do circularly causal self-organizational phenomena like that depicted in Fig. 4.1. And, since both M and P ultimately derive from the same domain, it is logical to suspect that the same self-organizational behavior observable in the physical world is also operative in the mental world. It therefore seems justified to hypothesize, as above, that the formation of autonomous psychological complexes follows the same organizational principles as physical matter. The difference is that instead of positing archetypes as resulting from the process of emergence, *emergence itself is viewed as an archetype.*[3]

[3]This seems so both *cosmogonically*, as a "contemporary scientific creation myth" (Cambray, 2016, 2017) and *cosmologically* as part of the unfolding of known physical laws from the primordial unity immediately following the Big Bang (Cambray, 2011a).

The basis for this was given by Atmanspacher and Fach (2013) who distinguished two types of correlations between M and P: *structural* and *induced*. Structural correlations form the "persistent baseline" of M-P correlations responsible for psychosomatic reactions including such pairings as mental states and neural activity and psychical and physical stress. However, given that M and P derive from disaggregated archetypal states, even these most fundamental correlations are, by definition, manifestations of an archetype. As Atmanspacher and Rickles (2022) state, the archetypes from which these structural correlations originate are "always and ubiquitously constellated across time and irrespective of individual or societal differences" (p. 54).

The possibility of acausal correlation as the rule rather than the exception was one that Jung recognized in his Synchronicity essay where he conceded in a footnote: "should this conjecture ever be proved, my present view that synchronicity is a relatively rare phenomenon would have to be corrected" (Jung, 1952/1969e, p. 500).[4] Some paragraphs later, in the conclusion to that essay, he gave credence to the plausibility of a ubiquitous, mundane archetype by defining the archetype as "the introspectively recognizable form of *a priori* psychic orderedness" (p. 516). Naturally, Jung inclined toward the mental, but in the Pauli-Jung framework, archetypal orderedness applies just as well to the physical, as Pauli understood when he considered that that archetypes "condition anything law-like in the behaviour of the corporeal world," adding that "the laws of this world would then be the physical manifestations of the archetypes [emphasis omitted]" (as cited in Atmanspacher & Rickles, 2022, p. 187). From all this, it becomes apparent that, within this perspective, archetypes include the most fundamental aspects of physical and mental experience including space, time, causality, and, by extension, principles of self-organization and emergence. From this perspective, considering archetypes as emergent structures is insufficient since the very *process* of emergence is archetypal, that is, conditioned by an archetype. This view is consistent with Jung (1958/1976b) who, when describing the Self, wrote: "the original chaos of multiple gods evolves into a sort of monarchy, and the archetype

[4] Further evidence that Jung remained open to the possibility that synchronicity could be axiomatic can be found in his 1957 letter to Stephen Abrams in which he wrote that synchronicity, "though in practice a relatively rare phenomenon, is an all-pervading factor or principle in the universe" (Jung, 1975, pp. 399–400).

of the self slowly asserts its central position as *the archetype of order in chaos* [emphasis added]" (p. 734).[5]

Second, psychological sophistication of the model is evident both conceptually and empirically. Conceptually, the PPN domain resonates strongly with the elusive nature of the collective unconscious that Jung was at pains to describe in various ways, ranging from his early descriptions of the "undifferentiated archaic psyche" (Jung, 1952/1967) to his mature conception of the "one world" *unus mundus* (Jung, 1955–56/1970b). It also preserves Jung's notion of the archetype-as-such since, in the Pauli-Jung conjecture, archetypes are the populating structures of the PPN. Atmanspacher and Rickles (2022) clarify:

> Undivided and psychophysically neutral are not the same. There may be entities that arise by decomposition of the undivided reality and yet are psychophysically neutral, so that they have no physical or mental properties. Pauli and Jung refer to these as archetypes, culturally invariant patterns that exist prior to the mental-physical split but serve as ordering factors for M and P once those become separated. (p. 156)

This positions the archetype-as-such as a priori insofar as it exists *prior to* bifurcation into archetypal images, and although archetypes are neutral with respect to M and P, they are *not* indistinguishable. The Pauli-Jung conjecture therefore recognizes Jung's differentiation of various archetypal images in their personified (e.g., magician, crone, orphan) and transformational (e.g., nekyia, rebirth) forms and suggests that these images owe their origin to a less differentiated but nonetheless distinct ordering principle within the PPN. Moreover, Atmanspacher and Rickles suggest that the PPN is layered, such that approaching it from the physical side yields entangled quantum states and approaching it from the mental side passes through the personal unconscious (thus preserving classical psychodynamics) into the collective unconscious where successive layers lead to less differentiation concluding, ostensibly, with the archetype of the Self before passing into complete and utter invariance with no distinctions whatsoever—the *unus mundus.* Insofar as the Self indeed represents the most undifferentiated structure of the unconscious, the implication is that *the very process of individuation may be entropic.* That is, just as complex,

[5] Here it must be recognized that Jung was subscribing to a monotheistic psychology which may not be acceptable to all (see, e.g., Hillman, 1981). With thanks to Joe Cambray for drawing my attention to this important distinction.

higher-ordered life forms develop in the physical world in service of an overall increase in entropy (entailing so-called *negentropic* or *dissipative structures*, see Fig. 4.1; see also Schwartz-Salant, 2017), complex, ordered, archetypal structures manifesting mentally (e.g., personifications) might analogously be leading the psychic system toward the highest-entropy state of realization of the Self.[6]

But while this connection remains speculative for now, the Pauli-Jung conjecture has demonstrated empirical success elsewhere. The taxonomy yielded by the dual-aspect monist position has proven to be the most robust and generalizable model in the evaluation of a sample of 3000 exceptional experiences collected by the Institute for Frontier Areas of Psychology in Freiburg (Atmanspacher, 2020). These include synchronicities but also such phenomena as out-of-body experiences and sleep paralysis. Given that these results were achieved using a variety of mathematical procedures including factor, cluster, item, and scale analyses, the Pauli-Jung conjecture therefore demonstrates an impressive combination of theoretical and statistical power.

Third, the Pauli-Jung framework remains open to—in fact, incorporates—a spiritual dimension in the form of the PPN. For although not directly addressed in this fashion, it is clear that what Atmanspacher has in mind with this realm is something spiritual; PPN could just as easily—in a manner similar to Whitehead—be called *God*, though Atmanspacher understandably does not do so. Jung, however, was clear that he viewed the synchronicity problem as inextricably bound to the spiritual one. In a 1953 letter to Pauli, he wrote:

> I pressed for [Answer to Job] and [Synchronicity: An Acausal Connecting Principle] to be published at the same time, for in the latter I attempted to open up a new path to the 'state of spiritualization' of matter by making the assumption that 'being is endowed with meaning' (i.e., extension of the archetype in the object). (Pauli & Jung, 1992/2001, p. 98)

In that same letter he clarified that the archetype is the "feature that imbues [matter] with meaning," (p. 101) precisely because "it can be express itself [*sic*] *both psychically and physically*" (p. 98). Therefore, the

[6] See footnote 5; this necessarily entails a monotheistic perspective on the psyche. With thanks to Mike Steder for making the connection between the Self, entropy, and individuation clear to me.

Pauli-Jung conjecture does not face the issue of a lack of intrinsic meaningfulness since this dual manifestation of the archetype creates a situation whereby, in addition to a surface structure of meaning between M and P (as *reference* or *intentionality* in the phenomenological sense), there exists *a deep structure of meaning*, referring to the archetypal structures of the PPN underpinning M and P experiences irrespective of whether or not this meaning is recognized. Recalling the above quotation from Martin-Vallas (2018), the emergentist position acknowledges the subjective meaning attributed to a physical and mental coincidence in an instance of synchronicity, but the events themselves are arbitrary—stochastic, in the parlance of dynamic systems theory. In other words, the archetypal nature of the situation in which one finds oneself is emergent as a result of personal, social, and environmental factors. But in the Pauli-Jung conjecture, the archetypal nature of the situation derives from the constellation of the archetype in the undivided realm which then bifurcates into the meaningfully correlated mental and physical aspects. In this way, the correlation of M and P is experienced as meaningful, but so too are the M and P aspects themselves meaningfully related to the PPN. As Atmanspacher and Rickles (2022) put it: "the attribution of meaning is always subjective—but it is never arbitrary" (p. 55).

Moreover, aside from bolstering the emergentist position by supplying the deep structure of meaning, the Pauli-Jung conjecture remains compatible with emergence in other important ways. An example given by Atmanspacher and Rickles (2022) is that of an individual experiencing significant personal loss. The situation is associated with the archetypal constellation of loss which manifests itself mentally and physically as grief (the former as mental states; the latter as brain states, hormonal states, etc.). But as aspects of the archetype, M and P are thus *constrained* by it. Recalling the language of Synergetics, grief represents the order parameter of the system, constraining the parts M and P which make up the qualitative pattern of the experience. One can therefore still model archetypal scenarios such as this one using attractor landscapes like that depicted in Fig. 4.2 while staying truer to Jung's original theorizing.

To summarize, the Pauli-Jung conjecture represents a way forward that is (a) compatible with contemporary ideas regarding self-organization and emergence; (b) resonant with Jung's descriptions of the collective unconscious while exhibiting a high degree of empirical validity; and (c) supportive of experiences of reality that are intrinsically meaningful by incorporating what is, in effect, a spiritual dimension. Though much research is still to be done, it represents a promising way forward toward the unification of clinical and theoretical observations.

Future Directions

In a recent report to the International Association for Analytical Psychology, Christian Roesler (2022b, 2024) attempts to "deconstruct" archetype theory by evaluating Jung's ideas in light of the scientific state-of-the-art across a variety of fields. Despite, however, devoting considerable attention to post-Jungian formulations of the archetype, including the emergentist perspective, Roesler mentions Atmanspacher's work only once, immediately dismissing it on grounds that since it is "not part of the field of normal science, it can therefore not be tested in the [empirical] sense and will not be dealt with further" (p. 83). This is all the more curious given that the stated problem of the investigation is the "lack of consensual definition for the concept archetype," (p. 12) while in Roesler's earlier work, he calls Atmanspacher's explanation "theoretically the most coherent" (Roesler, 2016/2022a, p. 118). Roesler's dismissal of Atmanspacher on *empirical* grounds in a report otherwise predicated on the search for *conceptual* clarity is therefore puzzling—though Roesler perhaps tips his hand with his conclusion that "archetype theory…is part of cultural psychology" (p. 243).

Nonetheless, Atmanspacher's work has generally met with critical acclaim (e.g., Main, 2023) including, most recently, from the staunchest supporter of the emergentist position, George Hogenson (2024), who recognizes the aforementioned compatibility between the Pauli-Jung conjecture and emergence, including his own work on symbolic density, and who points to the theoretical coherence that Roesler alludes to when he (Hogenson) writes that "the introduction of Pauli's understanding of quantum theory…finally provided Jung with the worldview needed to explore his long-held intuition fully" (p. 11). In this way, the various guises of archetype theory throughout Jung's work, including the four disparate theories that Roesler (2022b) identifies, can—in fact, *do*—cohere when one works backward from Jung's final position arrived at with Pauli. What Atmanspacher and colleagues bring to the table in the form of the Pauli-Jung conjecture is an elaboration of this position based on more recent advancements in quantum theory as well as considerations mentioned by Pauli and Jung separately. As a result, the Pauli-Jung conjecture accounts for the most advanced aspects of Jung's theorizing including the psychoid, *unus mundus*, and synchronicity—"aspects," Hogenson (2024) suggests, "that are too easily overlooked in discussions of archetypes as developmental or biological in origin" (p. 12). That this statement comes from such an early and ardent proponent of the developmental/emergentist model speaks to the comprehensiveness of the Pauli-Jung conjecture. Indeed, by contending that beyond "the argument's scientific, philosophical, and psychological foundations, there is an almost mystical dimensional as well," (p. 12) Hogenson seemingly concurs with the argument put forward here for the scientific grounding, psychological sophistication, and spiritual openness of this approach, which in its scope has set a standard for future research such that "any subsequent work on archetypes will have to match [the] analysis [of Atmanspacher and Rickles] in terms of structure and depth" (p. 12).

Regarding future research, Atmanspacher and Rickles (2022) list many possibilities in their penultimate chapter including examples from mathematics, physics, biology, and psychology, but for now, the path forward may, in fact, be *backward* in the form of historical analyses—the kind that Roesler (2022b) calls for when he proposes that "a historical-critical investigation into the works of Jung, which would include a critical commentary on how the texts came about, what were the influences etc., is highly needed" (p. 12). Though Roesler's report purports to be such an investigation, the degree to which it fails to account for the important advancements made by Atmanspacher and colleagues raises serious questions as to its utility. More careful analyses are therefore necessary, including an examination of the extent to which Jung's dialogue with Pauli supplies the theoretical foundation that coheres his otherwise disparate statements about archetypes. Such an endeavor would go a long way toward a more accurate and decisive evaluation of Jung's relevance to contemporary times.

Competing Interests The author has no conflicts of interest to declare that are relevant to the content of this chapter.

References

Atmanspacher, H. (2020). The Pauli-Jung conjecture and its relatives: A formally augmented outline. *Open Philosophy, 3*(1), 527–549.

Atmanspacher, H., & Fach, W. (2013). A structural-phenomenological typology of mind-matter correlations. *Journal of Analytical Psychology, 58*(2), 219–244.

Atmanspacher, H., & Fuchs, C. A. (2014). Introduction. In H. Atmanspacher & C. A. Fuchs (Eds.), *The Pauli-Jung conjecture and its impact today* (pp. 1–6). Imprint Academic.

Atmanspacher, H., & Rickles, D. (2022). *Dual-aspect monism and the deep structure of meaning*. Routledge.

Blau, J. J. C., & Wagman, J. B. (2023). *Introduction to ecological psychology: A lawful approach to perceiving, acting, and cognizing*. Routledge.

Cambray, J. (2002). Synchronicity and emergence. *American Imago, 59*(4), 409–434.

Cambray, J. (2009). *Synchronicity: Nature and psyche in an interconnected universe*. Texas A&M University Press.

Cambray, J. (2010). Emergence and the self. In M. Stein (Ed.), *Jungian psychoanalysis: Working in the spirit of C.G. Jung* (pp. 53–66). Open Court.

Cambray, J. (2011a). Cosmos and culture in the play of synchronicity. In S. Wirth et al. (Eds.), *The playful psyche: Entering chaos, coincidence, creation* (pp. 133–147). Daimon Verlag.

Cambray, J. (2011b). Moments of complexity and enigmatic action: A Jungian view of the therapeutic field. *Journal of Analytical Psychology, 56*(3), 296–309.

Cambray, J. (2016). Darkness in the contemporary scientific imagination and its implications. *International Journal of Transpersonal Studies, 35*(2), 75–87.

Cambray, J. (2017). The emergence of the ecological mind in *Hua-Yen/Kegon* Buddhism and Jungian psychology. *Journal of Analytical Psychology, 62*(1), 20–31.

Dieckmann, H. (1999). *Complexes: Diagnosis and therapy in analytical psychology* (B. Matthews, Trans.). Chiron Publications.

Frank, T. (2019). *Determination and self-organization of human perception and performance*. Springer.

Freud, S. (1958). Psycho-analytic notes on an autobiographical account of a case of paranoia (dementia praecox). In J. Strachey (Ed. & Trans.), *The standard edition of the complete psychological works of Sigmund Freud: Vol. 12 (1911–1913). The case of Schreber, papers on technique, and other works* (pp. 1-82). Hogarth. (Original work published 1911).

Gleick, J. (1987). *Chaos: Making a new science*. Viking.

Green, C. D. (1997). *Classics in the history of psychology*. York University. https://psychclassics.yorku.ca/author.htm

Hillman, J. (1981). Psychology: Monotheistic or polytheistic. In D. L. Miller (Ed.), *The new polytheism: Rebirth of the gods and goddesses* (pp. 109–142). Spring Publications.

Hogenson, G. B. (1998). Response to Pietikäinen and Stevens. *Journal of Analytical Psychology, 43*(3), 357–372.

Hogenson, G. B. (2001). The Baldwin effect: A neglected influence on C. G. Jung's evolutionary thinking. *Journal of Analytical Psychology, 46*(4), 591–611.

Hogenson, G. B. (2004). What are symbols of? Situated action, mythological bootstrapping, and the emergence of the Self. *Journal of Analytical Psychology, 49*(1), 67–81.

Hogenson, G. B. (2005). The self, the symbolic, and synchronicity: Virtual realities and the emergence of the psyche. *Journal of Analytical Psychology, 50*(3), 271–284.

Hogenson, G. B. (2009). Archetypes as action patterns. *Journal of Analytical Psychology, 54*(3), 325–337.

Hogenson, G. B. (2014). Are synchronicities really dragon kings? In H. Atmanspacher & C. A. Fuchs (Eds.), *The Pauli-Jung conjecture and its impact today* (pp. 201–215). Imprint Academic.

Hogenson, G. B. (2018). The Tibetan book of the dead needs work: A proposal for research into the geometry of individuation. In J. Cambray & L. Sawin (Eds.), *Research in analytical psychology: Applications from scientific, historical, and cross-cultural research* (pp. 173–193). Routledge.

Hogenson, G. B. (2024). Review of the book Dual-aspect monism and the deep structure of meaning, by H. Atmanspacher & D. Rickles. *International Journal of Jungian Studies, 16*(1), 1–12.

Hogenson, G. B., Stevens, A., & Ramos, D. (2003). Debate: Psychology and biology. In *Cambridge 2001: Proceedings of the fifteenth international congress for analytical psychology* (pp. 367–377). Daimon Verlag.

Jung, C. G. (1920). The psychology of the unconscious processes. In C. E. Long (Ed. & Trans.), *Collected papers on analytical psychology* (2nd ed., pp. 354–444). Baillière, Tindall and Cox. (Original work published 1917).

Jung, C. G. (1960a). On psychological understanding (R. F. C. Hull, Trans.). In H. Read et al. (Eds.), *The collected works of C. G. Jung: Vol. 3. Psychogenesis of mental disease* (pp. 179–193). Princeton University Press. (Original work published 1914).

Jung, C. G. (1960b). The psychology of dementia praecox (R. F. C. Hull, Trans.). In H. Read et al. (Eds.), *The collected works of C. G. Jung: Vol. 3. Psychogenesis of mental disease* (pp. 1–151). Princeton University Press. (Original work published 1907).

Jung, C. G. (1967). *The collected works of C. G. Jung: Vol. 5. Symbols of transformation* (R. F. C. Hull, Trans. and H. Read et al., Eds.). Princeton University Press. (Original work published 1952).

Jung, C. G. (1969a). Analytic psychology and *Weltanschauung* (R. F. C. Hull, Trans.). In H. Read et al. (Eds.), *The collected works of C. G. Jung: Vol. 8. Structure and dynamics of the psyche* (2nd ed., pp. 358–381). Princeton University Press. (Original work published 1931).

Jung, C. G. (1969b). Instinct and the unconscious (R. F. C. Hull, Trans.). In H. Read et al. (Eds.), *The collected works of C. G. Jung: Vol. 8. Structure and dynamics of the psyche* (2nd ed., pp. 129–138). Princeton University Press. (Original work published 1948).

Jung, C. G. (1969c). On psychic energy (R. F. C. Hull, Trans.). In H. Read et al. (Eds.), *The collected works of C. G. Jung: Vol. 8. Structure and dynamics of the psyche* (2nd ed., pp. 3–66). Princeton University Press. (Original work published 1928).

Jung, C. G. (1969d). On the nature of the psyche (R. F. C. Hull, Trans.). In H. Read et al. (Eds.), *The collected works of C. G. Jung: Vol. 8. Structure and dynamics of the psyche* (2nd ed., pp. 159–234). Princeton University Press. (Original work published 1954).

Jung, C. G. (1969e). Synchronicity: An acausal connecting principle (R. F. C. Hull, Trans.). In H. Read et al. (Eds.), *The collected works of C. G. Jung: Vol. 8. Structure and dynamics of the psyche* (2nd ed., pp. 417–519). Princeton University Press. (Original work published 1952).

Jung, C. G. (1970a). On the psychology and pathology of so-called occult phenomena (R. F. C. Hull, Trans.). In H. Read et al. (Eds.), *The collected works of C. G. Jung: Vol. 1. Psychiatric studies* (2nd ed., pp. 3–88). Princeton University Press. (Original work published 1902).

Jung, C. G. (1970b). *The collected works of C. G. Jung: Vol. 14. Mysterium coniunctionis* (R. F. C. Hull, Trans. and H. Read et al., Eds.). Princeton University Press. (Original work published 1955–56).

Jung, C. G. (1973). On the doctrine of complexes. In H. Read et al. (Eds.), *The collected works of C. G. Jung: Vol. 2. Experimental researches* (pp. 598–604). Princeton University Press. (Original work published 1913).

Jung, C. G. (1975). *Letters volume 2: 1951–1961* (G. Adler, Ed.; R. F. C. Hull, Trans.). Princeton University Press.

Jung, C. G. (1976a). Forward to Jacobi: "Complex/archetype/symbol" (R. F. C. Hull, Trans.). In H. Read et al. (Eds.), *The collected works of C. G. Jung: Vol. 18. The symbolic life* (pp. 532–533). Princeton University Press. (Original work published 1957).

Jung, C. G. (1976b). Jung and religious belief. In H. Read et al. (Eds.), *The collected works of C. G. Jung: Vol. 18. The symbolic life* (pp. 702–744). Princeton University Press. (Original work published 1958).

Jung, C. G. (1983). The border zones of exact science (J. van Heurck, Trans.). In W. McGuire (Ed.), *The collected works of C. G. Jung: Supplementary volume A. The Zofingia lectures* (pp. 1–19). Princeton University Press.

Jung, C. G. (1991). *The collected works of C. G. Jung: Supplementary volume B. The psychology of the unconscious: A study of the transformations and symbolisms of the libido. A contribution to the history of the evolution of thought* (B. M. Hinkle, Trans. and W. McGuire, Ed.). Princeton University Press. (Original work published 1911–1912).

Jung, C. G. (2009). *The red book: Liber novus* (M. Kyburz, J. Peck, & S. Shamdasani, Trans. and S. Shamdasani, Ed.). W. W. Norton.

Jung, C. G., & Riklin, F. (1973). The associations of normal subjects (D. Riviere & L. Stein, Trans.). In H. Read et al. (Eds.), *The collected works of C. G. Jung: Vol. 2. Experimental researches* (pp. 3–196). Princeton University Press. (Original work published 1904).

Kelso, J. A. S. (1995). *Dynamic patterns: The self-organization of brain and behavior*. MIT Press.

Knox, J. (2001). Memories, fantasies, archetypes: An exploration of some connections between cognitive science and analytical psychology. *Journal of Analytical Psychology, 46*(4), 613–635.

Knox, J. (2003). *Archetype, attachment, analysis: Jungian psychology and the emergent mind*. Routledge.

Kondepudi, D., Kay, B., & Dixon, J. (2015). End-directed evolution and the emergence of energy-seeking behavior in a complex system. *Physical Review E, 91*(5), 050902.

Krieger, N. M. (2014). *Bridges to consciousness: Complexes and complexity*. Routledge.

Lothane, Z. (1992). *In defense of Schreber: Soul murder and psychiatry*. The Analytic Press.

Main, R. (2004). *The rupture of time: Synchronicity and Jung's critique of modern western culture*. Brunner-Routledge.

Main, R. (2023). Jung among the physicists: A review essay of Dual-aspect monism and the deep structure of meaning. *Journal of Analytical Psychology, 68*(3), 534–547.

Martin-Vallas, F. (2018). Some remarks concerning archetypal theory and its epistemology (A. Kutek, Trans.). In J. Cambray & L. Sawin (Eds.) *Research in analytical psychology: Applications from scientific, historical, and cross-cultural research* (pp. 49-68). Routledge.

McDowell, M. J. (2001). Principle of organization: A dynamic-systems view of the archetype-as-such. *Journal of Analytical Psychology, 46*(4), 637–654.

Merchant, J. (2006). The developmental/emergent model of archetype, its implications and its application to shamanism. *Journal of Analytical Psychology, 51*(2), 125–144.

Merchant, J. (2009). A reappraisal of classical archetype theory and its implications for theory and practice. *Journal of Analytical Psychology, 54*(3), 339–358.

Noll, R. (1997). *Jung's concept of die Dominanten (the dominants)*. Academia. https://www.academia.edu/6789277/Jungs_concept_of_die_Dominanten_the_Dominants_1997_

Oyama, S. (2000). *The ontogeny of information: Developmental systems and evolution* (2nd ed.). Duke University Press.

Pauli, W., & Jung, C. G. (2001). *Atom and archetype: The Pauli-Jung letters, 1932–1958* (C. A. Meier, Ed. and D. Roscoe, Trans.). Princeton University Press.
Pietikäinen, P. (1998a). Archetypes as symbolic forms. *Journal of Analytical Psychology, 43*(3), 325–343.
Pietikäinen, P. (1998b). Response to Hester McFarland Solomon, George B. Hogenson, and Anthony Stevens. *Journal of Analytical Psychology, 43*(3), 379–388.
Pietikäinen, P. (1999). *C.G. Jung and the psychology of symbolic forms*. Academia Scientiarum Fennica.
Roesler, C. (2022a). *C. G. Jung's archetype concept: Theory, research, and applications*. Routledge. (Original work published 2016).
Roesler, C. (2022b). *Development of a reconceptualization of archetype theory: Report to the IAAP*. International Association for Analytical Psychology. https://iaap.org/wp-content/uploads/2023/04/Report-Archetype-Theory-Roesler-1-3.pdf
Roesler, C. (2024). *Deconstructing archetype theory: A critical analysis of Jungian ideas*. Routledge.
Rossi, E. L. (1989). Archetypes as strange attractors. *Psychological Perspectives: A Quarterly Journal of Jungian Thought, 20*(1), 4–15.
Saunders, P., & Skar, P. (2001). Archetypes, complexes, and self-organization. *Journal of Analytical Psychology, 46*(2), 305–323.
Schwartz-Salant, N. (2017). *The order-disorder paradox: Understanding the hidden side of change in self and society*. North Atlantic Books.
Shamdasani, S. (2003). *Jung and the making of modern psychology: The dream of a science*. Cambridge University Press.
Shamdasani, S. (2021). *Descensus ad infernos*: Jung's 'season in hell'. *Phanês, 4*, 152–176. https://doi.org/10.32724/phanes.2021.Shamdasani
Skar, P. (2025). What sort of thing is an archetype? Archetypes, complexes and self-organization revisited. *Journal of Analytical Psychology, 70*(1), 69–92.
Stevens, A. (1982). *Archetypes: A natural history of the self*. .
Stevens, A. (1998). Response to P. Pietikäinen. *Journal of Analytical Psychology, 43*(3), 345–355.
Swogger, B. J. (2024). In memory of Anthony Stevens: A career retrospective with emphasis on his formative role in the archetype debate. *Journal of Analytical Psychology, 69*(1), 1–16.
Swogger, B. J., & Dillon, J. J. (2023). Historical foundations of affectivity and learning research: C. G. Jung's word-association experiments. In P. Fossa & C. Cortés-Rivera (Eds.), *Affectivity and learning: Bridging the gap between neurosciences, cultural and cognitive psychology* (pp. 587–603). Springer.
Thelen, E., & Smith, L. B. (1994). *A dynamic systems approach to the development of cognition and action*. MIT Press.

Tresan, D. (1996). Jungian metapsychology and neurobiological theory. *Journal of Analytical Psychology, 41*(3), 399–436.

Tschacher, W., & Haken, H. (2019). *The process of psychotherapy: Causation and chance*. Springer.

Van Eenwyk, J. R. (1991). Archetypes: The strange attractors of the psyche. *Journal of Analytical Psychology, 36*(1), 1–25.

von Franz, M.-L. (1983). Introduction (J. van Heurck, Trans.). In W. McGuire (Ed.), *The collected works of C. G. Jung: Supplementary volume A. The Zofingia lectures* (pp. xiii–xxv). Princeton University Press.

Yates, F. E. (Ed.). (1987). *Self-organizing systems: The emergence of order*. Plenum Press.

PART II

Jungian Psycho-Social Case Analyses

CHAPTER 5

Pop-Culture Pantheon: Cultural Figures as Archetypal Expressions

Noah W. Cochran

I begin by introducing the terminology and the psycho-social method I use in this chapter. Specifically, I present the terms *cultural figure* and *pop-culture pantheon*. The term *cultural figure* refers to significant historical figures who are either fictional or non-fictional. Cultural figures are people and characters, real or imaginal, who have materialized and are referenced within a culture and are imbued with varying degrees of significance (Cochran, 2018). I define *pop-culture pantheon* as the cast of cultural figures who come to define different eras and dimensions of the culture itself. Historically, a pantheon is understood as a temple dedicated to the gods. The most notable example of this is found in Roman culture (Gauthier, 2021). Extending this idea to modern culture, the spirit of the pantheon lives on less in physical space, and more in the collective psyche of Western culture as psychic forces. The notion of a pop-culture pantheon can be understood as being the iconic or defining individuals of a particular place, time, and/or areas of interest.

Similar to Jung et al.'s (1976) distinction between "big dreams" and "little dreams," the pop-culture pantheon can be understood on both individual and collective levels. Little dreams are restricted to personal

N. W. Cochran (✉)
University of West Georgia, School of Social Sciences, Carrollton, GA, USA

J. J. Dillon (ed.), *Complex and Archetype*,
https://doi.org/10.1007/978-3-032-02609-5_5

meanings. Similarly, an *individual's* pantheon is developed based on their preferences and experiences, constituted by their personal associations and selection of cultural figures. As Jung et al. (1976) write, "a personal image has neither archaic character nor collective significance, but expresses contents of the personal unconscious" (p. 443). Big dreams, on the other hand, have "a sense that something more than their personal experiences was involved, something of either social or cosmic significance (and often both)" (Progoff, 1953, p. 189). The *collective* pop-culture pantheon is constituted by those figures who gain prominence and notoriety by becoming a culturally shared representation, a position that is beyond the control of the individual.

In Western culture, historical eras are often organized by decades. Each decade contains its distinctive roster of notable figures to the ambient popular culture that most people are familiar with. Each decade expands the fabric of the culture in which we find ourselves irreducibly entangled. Each decade contributes artists, athletes, politicians, intellectuals, and sex-symbols who become icons of the respective era. These icons become the content and artifacts of future discussions while shaping the structures of intra- and interpersonal engagements. The high-profile nature of these defining individuals presents a shared cultural access to meaningful patterns of behavior and understanding. In her outline of archetypes, Jacobi (1959) writes,

> The basic structure is laid down, but its individual spatiotemporal concretizations are imprinted by the time and environmental constellation in which they appear. As in the genealogies of the gods, these archetypes are 'children' removed from the 'primordial family,' and accordingly they disclose the most diverse aspects. The primordial, essentially unchanging needs, the typical eternally recurrent, basic experiences of mankind perpetuate the archetypes, and at the same time create those 'magnetic tensions' within the psyche, which cause them to be manifested forever anew, in the most diverse variations and guises. (p. 52)

The archetypes that become part and parcel of an era contribute semiotic material for subsequent events and eras, and this recurs throughout the annals of history. Within this framework, the "magnetic tensions" engage the collective consciousness, collective unconscious, and the ever-evolving cultural forces which pull certain individuals into cultural prominence over others.

Popular culture presents a carousel of personalities who are woven into the fabric of contemporary society. For as long as there have been forms of media, celebrities have come and gone through meteoric rises and precipitous falls in popularity. For example, Charlie Chaplin, Henry Ford, and Einstein are notably iconic personalities of American culture from the 1920s. In the 1950s, figures such as John "The Duke" Wayne, Elvis Presley, and Marilyn Monroe emerged as cultural icons. The 1980s produced Michael Jordan, Ronald Reagan, and Madonna. Iconic personalities become significant sources and representations of dynamics that speak both to and from a given era. The popularity of a personality is a response to some cultural need that commands the attention of many. The resonance of one personality over another is an unconscious centripetal force that weaves the cultural fabric which then becomes the medium through which we come to understand ourselves and communicate with others. While each era and decade has a cast of characters that represent categories of widespread interest, since the turn of the 2000s, the modern era has been characterized by technological advancements which have given rise to a digital world of social media platforms and personalized algorithms that are curated based on demographics and online engagement.

Connecting the Collective and Individual

There are many useful approaches to investigating cultural patterns that constitute archetypes within a culture. The aim of these approaches is to provide a method for expanding our understanding of how the collective both consciously and unconsciously interacts with and shapes individual behaviors and personality development. Progoff (1953) discusses the confusion around Jung's notion of the "collective unconscious." He argues that the term "collective" means that individuals have a "...psychic reality which, is prior to personal experience. This is to say, these materials are present *in potentia* because they are inherent in the psychic structure of the individual, from both a biological and an historical point of view" (p. 54). Progoff (1953) outlines how Jung described the psyche as having three basic layers which can be understood as something akin to geological formations. The topmost layer is described as a general notion of consciousness, and this layer is understood to be the most fragile due to the attitudes that guide an individual's interactions with their external environment. The second layer below consciousness is constituted by the *personal unconscious* which consists of the contents that have been repressed and shape desires and drives. The bottom layer consists of the *collective unconscious*, the source of material that percolates "come into consciousness and as the point of contact between the individual and the greater-than-individual forces in life" (Progoff, 1953, p. 67).

Progoff notes that archetypes are, "expressed in the individual in dream and fantasy, just as they are expressed in the group via myth, collective delusion, and so on" (Progoff, 1953, p. 72). Furthermore, the "psyche carries with it certain necessary psychic processes, which take the form of spontaneously recurring patterns by which the psychic energies within the individual seek expression. These inherently-contained psychic processes come forth in the form of the archetypal motifs." (Progoff, 1953, p. 72). I understand the relationship between the individual and the collective bi-directional reciprocating dynamic where individuals shape culture and culture shapes the individual. On the one hand, culture provides the semiotic resources that individuals psychologically assimilate as a "form of spontaneously recurring patterns" (Progoff, 1953, p. 72) through which they come to understand experiences. On the other hand, the actions of individuals will continually reinforce, modify, and negotiate cultural norms that become redefined over time through interpretations, behaviors, and perceived demands of social interactions. Creative expressions of individuals must take a form, and forms become the "nodal points" of shared meaning. Archetypes are primordial images that process pent-up psychological energy by transforming instinct into thought and linking experiences to meaning through recognizable dynamics. They are psychic tools that structure and connect inner experiences with the outside world.

Cambray and Sawin (2018) summarize the history and methods of social analysis become more complex and evolve over time. In an age of information technology, new ways of gathering information arise and present new opportunities to explore how the self and mind develop. On the development of mind, Cambray and Sawin (2018) write,

> We can also look at mind as ecological emergent from interactions with caregivers and the world. Mind is not generated in a vacuum but gradually forms and comes into being from internal pressures meeting a receptive metabolizing environment which gives articulate meaning to the internal urges and reactions. Our minds are thus formed in the interactive field of engagement with caretakers who are in turn impacted by their engagements with those in their care. Mind emerges in a bidirectional field of interactions embedded within natural and cultural worlds. (p. 263)

This passage suggests that the collective and individual are intertwined in a dynamic process that shapes psychological development. It is the collective which provides the contents and influential forces from which the individual mind emerges.

Midgley et al. (2023) offer an archetypal perspective which attempts to identify universal patterns and themes. They provide a quantitative approach to analyzing culturally held values based on varying compositions of four archetypes: secular versus sacred, and obedient versus emancipatory. They suggest that individuals and cultures include all four but are composed of varying proportions of each, thus preserving individuality and distinguishing cultural traits. Their investigation is aimed at understanding unity and diversity of values within and across different cultures, providing "a powerful lens on culture" (Midgley et al., 2023, p. 3). They describe archetypes as "universal pattern of values which we hold in our minds and can recognize examples of in real people, even though these examples may be variants of this universal" (p. 4). While Midgley et al. (2023) provide a powerful lens through which we can substantiate and view the historical and future directions of cultures, their approach requires a specialized knowledge of complex statistical methods to provide a description of the general socio-cultural forces that shape individuals of the societies in question. They offer a comprehensive and detailed approach to exploring the notable archetypes on the collective level, but do not directly address how this is presented on the individual level. The complexity and application of sophisticated statistical methods and models means that this type of analysis is not within the grasp of most researchers' skillsets or available tools. This necessitates an approach which is more widely accessible and can be applied to identifying prominent socio-cultural motifs which are connected and embodied by cultural figures that influence the norms and ideals that guide individual development.

As discussed in the Foreword, Lu and Yeoman's (2024) Archetypal Thematic Analysis (ATA) is the culmination of a range of qualitative methods. ATA offers a flexible framework that emphasizes culturally meaningful coincidences (synchronicity) and can provide insights into the collective unconscious through deductive analysis of prominent cultural patterns. Their approach is both deductive and inductive. It is deductive in the sense they have established their primary coding from Jung's descriptions of the archetype of the child. It is inductive in the sense their coding is flexible enough to accommodate themes that emerge from their analysis. ATA offers a rigorous psycho-social qualitative approach that "not only enhance the selection of data and codifying practices, but also extend and enrich the interpretation of datasets" (Lu & Yeoman, 2024, p. 108). In summary, ATA emphasizes the importance of intuition in addition to deductive and inductive coding when pursuing the synchronicities that symbolize the interplay between individuals and collective unconscious motifs that arise within the culture.

From these reviewed approaches, I highlight the need to connect the collective to the individual. This is achieved through a mixture of qualitative and quantitative methods which provide a means to substantiate and strengthen claims that connect the collective to the individual. Cambray and Sawin (2018) point out how methods of social analysis continue to become more complex, and in an age of information technology there have been new ways of gathering information which help illustrate how the self and mind develop. In his search for adequate tools with which we can explore and analyze the self, Progoff (1953) places emphasis on connecting Jung's notion of individual personality to culture, history, and religion, dimensions of the self that are treated as being interrelated and from which we construct social meaning for exploring the "principles of knowledge capable of interpreting to us all the aspects and implications of our situation, our past, our present, our potentialities" (p. 3).

Drawing from Midgley et al. (2023), identifying archetypes can be strengthened through quantitative empirical methods and provide a means to track and illustrate socio-cultural forces that shape societies and the individuals within them. To do this, it is helpful to have access to data on the socio-cultural trends, specific cultural figures, the social weight, and significance of the values which shape the development of individuals. Taking a wide societal approach in conjunction with Lu and Yeoman's (2024) flexible method of ATA, I provide an approach which strengthens claims about societal attitudes and cultural figures who constellate synchronicities while also providing a thematic analysis of the cultural figures' archetypal qualities. I draw on the intuitive dimension of this approach by (a) identifying synchronicities, (b) connecting figures to historical anchors, and (c) applying Jungian themes relevant to collective attitudes and cultural figures that embody contemporary values.

Procedure

To investigate prominent archetypes embodied in contemporary cultural figures, I began by selecting two polarizing cultural figures with whom I had been recently and frequently exposed: Kim Kardashian and Elon Musk. I then identified my initial impulses which were prompted by this unsolicited frequent exposure. This involved recognizing a) that Kim Kardashian is regarded as a contemporary embodiment of sensuality and attraction, that is the Sex-symbol archetype, and b) that Elon Musk is widely considered and presented as the face of innovative technology associated with transportation and space exploration, that is the Creator-Innovator archetype. I should note that my exposure to Musk occurred before his recent and well-publicized American political involvement. The following analysis operates according to his pre-political image of a technological savant. The extent to which his recent political behavior is an expression of another aspect of the Creator-Innovator archetype is beyond the scope of this chapter but represents a future area of research.

After identifying these two cultural figures, I then turned to researching synchronistic events around the time they began to gain notoriety. To substantiate cultural relevance, I looked for reliable metrics of popularity and settled on a two-pronged approach to minimize personal bias of my exposure and selection. I investigated each cultural figure using the MIT *Pantheon* (Collective Learning group at MIT Media Lab, 2025) database to establish what they are known for, to gauge their popularity, and identify other cultural figures with whom they are associated. Additionally, I searched in Google Trends to help identify notable shifts in their popularity. Making note of these points of interest, I performed Google searches for significant popular culture events that occurred within the proximity of the two cultural figures points of higher interest to identify moments of synchronicity. While not an exact formula, the combination of Google Trends and MIT *Pantheon* provide quantified data which allows for a reasonable triangulation of the popularity and cultural-historical impact of each cultural figures, while also making shifts in popularity easier to identify and triangulate with synchronistic events.

I provide historical anchoring to strengthen the archetype claim that these figures embody archetypes by comparing Kardashian and Musk to historical figures with whom their behaviors are aligned. Jung refers to archetypal images as "nodal points" (Jacobi, 1959, p. 33), the total constellation of which constitutes the collective unconscious. I understand each cultural figure as constituting a nodal point in this Jungian sense. A historical perspective highlights the archetypal qualities of these contemporary cultural figures. With the popularity index and historical anchoring as a foundation for substantiating my claims, I explore how Kardashian and Musk embody archetypal roles, particularly within the areas of entertainment and technology.

Kim Kardashian and Elon Musk are commonly understood as figures representing the structural institutions of the socio-cultural landscape which includes entertainment, technological advancement, and more recently in Musk's case, politics. Using the *Lover (Sex-Symbol)* and *Visionary/Innovator* archetypes as thematic codes, I collected and analyzed online magazine and blog articles, interviews, images, and video clips which address the archetypal characteristics of the two cultural figures. I coded each article and interview for themes of each archetype.

MIT's *Pantheon* (Collective Learning group at MIT Media Lab, 2025) database uses Historical Popularity Index (HPI) as a metric constructed to assess biographical information on Wikipedia and combines information of the number of languages, time since birth, and page-views (Yu et al., 2016). This information is correlated with individual accomplishments which measures the historical impact of that individual. For example, the highest ranked individual is Muhammad, a religious figure, has an HPI of 100 in part due to having a Wikipedia page in 210 different languages. The second highest ranked individual is Isaac Newton, a physicist, with an HPI of 98.73 with Wikipedia page in 225 languages. Looking at Carl Jung's historical impact, with an HPI of 82.95 with Wikipedia page in 107 languages, he is the second highest ranked psychologist in Wikipedia, following Freud and preceding Piaget. This database provides a metric that helps to ensure cultural relevance.

In order to understand how these two cultural figures embody the archetypes that propelled their popularity and influence, I analyze a few of many viral instances where they exemplify patterns of behavior which have come to define them as cultural figures. A composed pantheon of icons is a collection of cultural figures that tell the stories that are essential dynamics for the structure of the psyche. These figures play prominent roles that tell archetypical stories and cultural myths that resonate with individuals. This means that the icons of each era are the semiotic and archetypal resources through and with which people *individuate*. As Jacobi (1959) states, "every archetype is capable of infinite development and differentiation; like a robust tree it can put forth branches and thousands of magnificent blossoms" (p. 55). In this sense, cultural icons evolve and embody contemporary iterations of archetypes which adapt to the demands of their era.

In the remainder of the chapter, I present my findings and analysis of both figures in three sections. The first section establishes the findings of popularity through the *Pantheon* database, including their classification, current HPI, and the archetype they embody. In the second section, I use Google Trends to explore the cultural figures' connections to notable events taking place around the same time (synchronicity). In the third section, I explore the cultural significance of the cultural figure's archetypal expressions.

Kim Kardashian: Popularity, Historical Anchoring, and Synchronicity

Popularity. Kim Kardashian's popularity, as measured on the *Pantheon* database, is 68.18 HPI. Her Wikipedia page has 70 million views across 94 languages. Of the people born in 1980, she is ranked the third most popular. As a celebrity, she is ranked twenty-fourth; of the people born in the United States, she is ranked 955; and, of celebrities born in the United States, she is ranked tenth (Collective Learning group at MIT Media Lab, 2025). Assessing Google Trends (Google, n.d.), searches for Kardashian increased markedly in February and November of 2007. Her search trend steadily increased from 2007 and hit its highest point to date in November 2014. Notable spikes for Kardashian include 2007, 2011, 2013, 2014, and 2016 (Google, n.d.).

Historical Anchoring. In linking Kardashian to other historical expressions of the sex-symbol archetype, very few celebrities have achieved the same level of iconic status as Marilyn Monroe. When considering historical sex-symbols, Monroe can be identified as the quintessential archetype who presents a blend of glamour, seduction, and femininity that became iconic and era-defining. Among others, Monroe's historically significant moments that have contributed to her becoming a sex-symbol include being the first *Playboy* centerfold in 1953, the famous photo of her holding her white dress down while standing over a subway vent, and singing a seductive interpretation of "Happy Birthday" to John F. Kennedy in 1962. Searching the term "sex-symbol" on Wikipedia leads one to the description of a person that is widely considered as sexually attractive along with a picture of Marilyn Monroe with the caption "most enduring sex symbol" (Sex Symbol, 2025). Within Western culture, Monroe is synonymous with the notion of "sex symbol." She symbolizes a Western ideal of "blond bombshell" or "buxom blonde" that is widely regarded as a Western idealized object-of-desire, often presented as attractiveness and sexual appeal in cultural myths. Yang et al. (2022) suggests that, prior to the rise of cultural figures like Kardashian, "a well-proportioned and natural body like Marilyn Monroe's was considered the sexiest. If the girls want the same sexy body, they just need to control their diet properly or exercise" (p. 580). While this may have been a beauty standard for previous generations, celebrities and social influencers like Kardashian have shifted this standard over time by tethering their image to Marilyn's while also normalizing exaggeration of the features that have been historically held up as ideal. An example of Kardashian intentionally connecting to Monroe occurred at the 2022 Met Gala where she was embroiled in controversy when she donned and damaged Marilyn's iconic dress worn at President Kennedy's 1962 birthday celebration (Englund, 2024). Other celebrities have also attempted to tether themselves to Monroe's image. A prominent example of how Monroe has inspired generations of women imitate her sensuality was Anna Nicole Smith.

Synchronicity. In the case of Kim Kardashian, the constellating synchronistic events that point to the emergence and evolution of the contemporary sex-symbol is arguably the death of Anna Nicole Smith. Smith's death occurred in February, one month prior to Kardashian's infamous sex-tape that launched her career (NZ Herald, 2017). The tragic death of Anna Nicole Smith and Kardashian's rise in popularity is synchronistic in the sense that Smith embodied Monroe through imitation. Symbolically, Smith's death left a cultural vacancy to be filled. Kardashian filled this vacancy through reality television, social media, personal commodification, and branding. This presents a shift of cultural values and aesthetics that contrast with previous Monroe-inspired sex-symbols. Among the various connections that can be made between Kardashian and Monroe, a comparison of some of their most iconic photoshoots provides valuable insights into how the sex-symbol archetype is shaped by culture. Anna Nicole, Kim, and Marilyn all famously posed for *Playboy* (Englund, 2024). Their *Playboy* features, each embodying ideals of their respective eras, provide key markers for understanding how sex-symbols evolve over time.

Corey (2022) notes that "alignment to a historic icon like Marilyn accelerates Kim's virality on the social media algorithms and expands the dimension of her own mythology." In examining the construction of the celebrity myth that connects Kim to Marilyn Monroe, Englund (2024) finds that the propagation of fame has changed over time with the introduction of modern technologies as a means to access media and exposure to celebrities. Exposure to celebrities has become more immediate because of social media, reality shows, and on-demand streaming services such as Netflix and Hulu. Additionally, social media provides unprecedented and more personalized ways to engage with celebrities that were not possible for Marilyn Monroe. This gives Kardashian the ability to curate her personal persona and narrative in ways previous cultural figures could not.

There is no shortage of biopics investigating and attempting to explain exactly why Kardashian is famous. She is no stranger to being the target of controversy and criticism. Central to her brand is the notion of "being famous for being famous" (Hochman, 2007, p. 156). This is an observation of her seemingly unfounded and mysterious widespread notoriety and often a criticism that implies connotations of superficiality, lack of merit, and unworthy of high social status. As far as her being "famous for being famous," Kardashian has a mystique about her in that her fame and influence is a result of her high-profile sexuality which she has turned into a billion-dollar beauty brand. Kardashian is, in part, famous for the sheer amount of praise *and* criticism she generates. Meredith Jones questions the criticisms of the Kardashians by stating, "when people devote time and space to condemnation, it immediately makes me wonder what social fears or cultural desires might lie beneath the aggression" (cited in Corey, 2022, para. 17). When reflecting on the hype that surrounds Kim Kardashian, a few exceptional examples of culturally significant moments contribute to her sex-symbol status. First, it is necessary to acknowledge that her rise to fame initially built momentum from a "leaked" 2007 sex-tape that featured her and her former boyfriend, Ray J, that was filmed in 2003 when she was 23 years old. After gaining notoriety from the sex-tape scandal, she propelled her popularity by launching the reality show *Keeping Up with the Kardashians* (henceforth KUWK) in October of the same year. Starting with the introduction of Kardashian and her family to mainstream culture, the debut of her KUWK reality show most memorable moments include Kim's mother and manager, Kris Jenner, critiquing Kim's body as she walked out of the room, and Kim being informed that she had been invited to appear on the daytime talk show, *Tyra* (Andaloro, 2023). As Kim and her sister speculate on what would be discussed when she goes on the show, her sister brings up Kardashian's infamous sex-tape. Notably, when asked why she made it, Kim casually and playfully responds, "Because

I was horny, and I felt like it" (Andaloro, 2023). Kim's embrace of such a taboo and controversial subject became a defining moment for her and evidence of her ownership of her sexuality and a shift in values regarding female sexuality. Her unflinching and playful attitude concerning what would have historically been considered a point of shame illustrated a reclaiming of sexuality while also using it as a means of engagement.

Another defining moment occurred in December of 2007 when she would go on to do her first *Playboy* shoot, landing on the cover, and cementing her sex-symbol status. In her 2007 *Playboy* interview regarding her sex-tape, Kardashian stated that "They [people] assume that I'm slutty…", and, regarding how her body is a popular topic of discussion, she went on to say "I always laugh when it says on the Internet that I have fake boobs or butt implants or injected lips, because it's so not true. I've never had plastic surgery" (Hochman, 2007, p. 176). Whether or not these statements were true at the time of the interview, they illustrate how her initial rise in popularity is tethered to her body, sexual appeal, and sex-tape.

Kardashian's peak moment of social interest is in 2014 when she "broke the internet" by, again, posing nude. The phrase "broke the internet" was coined after it was the headline for a nude photoshoot she did for the magazine *Paper*. She dressed (and undressed) in a formal ballroom sequined gown, and the series of pictures portrayed her turned away from the camera while looking over her shoulder and exposing her bare backside and balancing a champagne glass on her butt while opening an excited bottle of champagne that erupts in an arch and lands in the glass balanced on her backside. As much of an impressive display as this was, it further solidified and reaffirmed her status as a contemporary sex-symbol that has the power to capture the attention of a global audience through her sex appeal.

The motif which makes Kim Kardashian a contemporary expression of the Lover and sex-symbol archetypes is first and foremost her physical features that emphasize her exaggerated feminine figure. In the instance of her *Paper* photoshoot, her hair was tied in a neat knot atop her head. She bears a playful facial expression with her mouth smiling and agape, Her neck is adorned with stacked pearl chokers, and she is wearing a shimmery formal black dress and gloves. She poses with a side profile that exaggerates her figure, showing an erupting champagne bottle shooting over her head and landing on a glass that is balanced atop her butt. In a series of four pictures, she proceeds to reveal more of her body as the empty bottle and cocktail glass lay on the floor in puddles of champagne. This set of photos explicitly associates Kardashian with high social status and formal celebrations while simultaneously evoking symbolism of her emerging from dark waters. Jung (1934/1969) suggested that water, often dark water, is the most common symbol for the unconscious.

In my analysis of the *Paper* photo shoot, I noticed symbols representing a rebirth from the unconscious. Her black formal gown has a wetness quality, and in the series of four photos, she progressively sheds her clothes while posing sideways and backwards, culminating in almost full-frontal nudity with the gloves on the floor. This photo series also evokes associations of Sandro Botticelli's "The Birth of Venus" as Kardashian stands on a box with her dress down to her knees, body shining, and an excited facial expression with her mouth slightly open. Like Venus, Kardashian emerges nude from depths of the water or, in this case, champagne. With her dress held around her knees, she presents a siren or mermaid-like image. In Jung's (1934/1969) investigation of the *anima*, he describes nixies, sirens, and mermaids as forms "who infatuates young men and sucks the life out of them" that are "as much dreaded as adored so that their rather peculiar erotic charms were only one of their characteristics" (p. 25). Pearson (1991) argues that the rise in the pornographic is a response to devaluing of eroticism: "When Eros is banned, it goes underground, and is thus seen only in its shadow forms, which are depraved and destructive rather than life-giving and life-promoting. Banished to the unconscious, where it reigns in its shadow form…" (p. 155). Kardashian's prominence in media culture which focuses on her physical appearance and relationships can be understood as the psychological energy of eroticism being displaced, resulting in the commodification and idealization of desire and beauty.

Jung points out that while the nature of the collective unconscious remains obscure and directly unknowable, we become familiar with the collective unconscious indirectly through the effects produced and presented by archetypal images (Jacobi, 1959). Furthermore, he distinguishes between "archetype" as the latent psychoid dimension and "archetypal image" as the actualized psychic material that can be represented and perceived (Jacobi, 1959, p. 35). Archetypes are understood as,

> *inherited possibilities* of representation. They appear only in the finished or shaped material as the regulative principles that shape it. They are channels, predispositions, river-beds into which the water of life has dug deep. These

> 'channels' form a kind of psychic mesh with 'nodal points,' corresponding, as we have seen, to the complex structure of the psyche, with its 'nuclei of meaning.' (Jacobi, 1959, p. 52)

The perceivable forms of archetypes "persists throughout the ages and requires interpreting ever anew. Its 'fundamental pattern' is immutable, but its mode of manifestation is ever changing" (Jacobi, 1959, p. 53). In this sense, Kardashian symbolizes the projection of the *anima* and a sign of the contemporary sex-symbol archetype in how she presents herself as a high-profile celebrity reshaping and embodying contemporary standards of beauty, a business mogul, and partner in her relationships.

My analysis of Kardashian's prominence in culture shows the historical connections and comparisons, and viral moments where she has been defined by her sensuality, relationships, body image, and her ability to commodify these qualities through self-promotion. Her rise to fame in 2007 reflects a turning point in the way society views identity, sexuality, and fame by increasing the visibility of how women can embrace their femininity in ways that had historically been discouraged. Kardashian presents a normalization of women's sexuality, family drama, and interracial relationships, much of which aligns with experiences that were becoming more common for many young women. In her online and television presence, she is unabashedly transparent and candid about her controversies surrounding sex, relationships, and her body. Kardashian develops a high-profile status through her use of nascent social media platforms and reality television. She leverages these points of interest to build her personal brand and become a business mogul.

Like Marilyn Monroe, Kim Kardashian has been held up as an idealized expression of beauty. This can be understood as a projection of the anima in that they connect to powerful unconscious feminine ideals of beauty, seduction, and desirability, expressing collective fantasies. Both of their personas are shaped by a combination of personal agency and collective fantasies. This shapes how Kardashian curates her public persona, driven by unconscious notions of what she believes her audience or followers desire to see. This drive is intertwined with the "male gaze," one of the motivations for the sexually suggestive visuals that contribute to her maintaining her relevance and continue growing her brand. This reinforces how femininity and sexuality are commodified and produced for the consumption of the public, encouraging the objectification of women as sexual objects. The collective aspect of the anima can be observed as others are expected to present themselves in ways that align with conventional ideals.

Identifying synchronicities involves pinpointing moments when the culture is receptive to expressions of cultural change. The meaning constructed from these moments is tethered to *what* and *who* is being promoted over other possible alternatives, presenting new representations by filling the cultural vacancy with a contemporary iteration that embodies societal desires for different forms of beauty that have been proliferated through digital media. In 2007, the collective fascination with Kardashian represented a greater acceptance of interracial relationships, public displays of young women exploring their sexuality, and commodification of personal life. I observed the sex-symbol archetype is an amalgamation of the anima and the Lover archetypes responding to a consumeristic cultural environment where commodification is both consciously and unconsciously upheld as an essential value. From a psycho-social perspective, Kardashian is the embodiment of the collective unconscious adapting to the digital era and new media landscapes.

Elon Musk: Popularity, Historical Anchoring, and Synchronicity

Popularity. Elon Musk's popularity as measured by the *Pantheon* database is 84.81 HPI. His Wikipedia page has 170 million views across 143 languages. Of people born in 1971, he is the most popular inventor being ranked first; among inventors, he is ranked sixth; of the people born in South Africa, he is ranked third; and of inventors born in South Africa, he is ranked first (Collective Learning group at MIT Media Lab, 2025). In Google Trends (Google, n.d.), searches for Musk increased in January and March of 2007. His search trends increased modestly in 2007 and 2008, and then steadily increased until 2024 with notable spikes in 2018, 2020, 2022, and 2024 (Google, n.d.).

Historical Anchoring. In linking Musk to a historical anchor, he is often compared to Henry Ford and the fictional character of Tony Stark, also known as Ironman. Both comparisons evoke the qualities of the Creator or Innovator archetype. In comparing Musk to Tony Stark, the initial similarities involve massive wealth and innovation. The most obvious similarity of Henry Ford to Musk is the fact that both are successful in the car manufacturing business, although Ford is credited with commercializing gas-powered vehicles and Musk has expanded the commercialization of electric vehicles (EVs). Both men entered the transportation sector in their early 30s and solidified their place in transportation by their mid-30s (Hines, 2016). Ford revolutionized car manufacturing and made cars affordable to the masses; Musk is credited for doing the same for EVs. In addition to revolutionizing EV manufacturing, Musk has various other ventures that are advancing other technology industries such as Neuralink Corporation, The Boring Company, OpenAI, and SpaceX (Renz & Vogel, 2020). With all of Musk's technologically innovative ventures, it is understandable that he is seen as an embodiment of the Creator and Innovator.

A "creator" is often referred to as "inventor," someone who brings something new into existence. An "innovator" is someone who improves or transforms existing ideas or technologies. With this distinction in mind, the creator and innovator archetypes overlap in the sense that innovators expand upon what creators previously construct. Similarly, innovators invent new applications and should therefore be considered inventors. As a result of Musk's expanding and revolutionizing technologies, he is often considered an "inventor" (Collective Learning group at MIT Media Lab, 2025) even though it is more accurate to recognize him as more of an *innovator*. Because inventor and innovator share the same spirit, I hyphenate the archetype as "creator-innovator" to avoid conflating the two terms and to highlight the dynamic relationship that exists between them.

Synchronicity. The synchronicities which align with Musk's rise in notoriety is Steve Job's introduction of the iPhone and the release of Marvel Studio's *Iron Man* film which led to tech hero Tony Stark becoming the face of the Marvel franchise. These synchronicities, which involve themes of innovation and technological empowerment, suggest that the culture was hopeful for and receptive to technological innovations which could empower society to address large-scale problems and transform everyday life. Innovative technology presented a potential salvation from widely held concerns while also opening new possibilities in the world for society and individuals to explore. The release of the iPhone was a first step toward this new world of possibilities, and *Iron Man* presented a fictional world that captured the culture's imagination, spurred creativity, and was more feasible than ever before.

The iPhone marks the beginning of the smartphone era, an era where individuals have mobile pocket-size personal computers that have expanded access to the internet and social media. The iPhone, and smartphones in general, became a catalyst of the current digital age in the ways it reshaped how people engage with technology, consume media, interact, and participate in the digital world that distinguishes the modern era. *Iron*

Man was the first movie of the Marvel Cinematic Universe franchise which now has over 30 movies which have generated more than $29 billion (Clark et al., 2023). The commercial success of Marvel Studio's *Iron Man* (2008) is also a synchronicity that responded to the developmental state of the culture at that time. *Iron Man* is centered around Tony Stark, a billionaire genius, philanthropist, and celebrity, the heir to his father's lucrative weapons manufacturing and contracting company. After finding himself in a typical comic book conundrum, Stark develops the Iron Man suit with proprietary technology and becomes the hero with whom many people are familiar.

Another synchronicity coinciding with Musk's rise in popularity is the 2006 release of one of the top grossing documentaries of all time: Al Gore's *An Inconvenient Truth* (Guggenheim, 2006). This documentary follows Al Gore giving a series of lectures highlighting the dangers of the global climate crisis. The film raised awareness within mainstream culture about climate change and the urgent systemic need for change. In this sense, Gore can be seen as generating or perpetuating a societal demand for reducing reliance on fossil fuels and spurring collective desires for more renewable and sustainable energy sources. Musk, given his associations with Henry Ford and Tony Stark, can be understood as embodying the compensatory potential technological solutions for addressing a looming ominous crisis.

Elon Musk initially emerged as a Creator-Innovator archetype gaining notoriety by being the CEO of SpaceX and Tesla (Renz & Vogel, 2020). He represents pushing the limits of what is possible by campaigning for multiplanetary colonization, refining and popularizing EVs, and developing technologies such as reusable space rockets. The similarities between Musk and the fictional Tony Stark is apparent. Musk is widely referred to as the "real-life Iron Man" (Renz & Vogel, 2020). This comparison was prevalent enough that Musk, playing himself, had a cameo in the 2010's *Iron Man 2* where he had a brief conversation with Tony Stark at a public event. Musk and Tony Stark both mobilize resources, abilities, and technology which can change what is possible, reshape reality, and even redefine humanity's potential. In this sense, Musk can be compared to Prometheus who brings fire to humanity. In Jung's analysis of Goethe's Prometheus, he described Prometheus as "definitely creative for collective ends" (Jung et al., 1976, p. 182). Furthermore, he stated "Prometheus was the saviour who brought life and fire to mankind languishing in darkness" (Jung et al., 1976, p. 186). When considering the initial rise of

Musk's popularity, we can understand Musk as a personified symbol of the technology which holds the promise of saving humankind from the impending environmental crisis.

As Lu and Yeoman (2024) point out, collective concerns about climate change and clean energy come into focus as science, governments, and societies look to mitigate the negative impacts of pollution. The compensatory child-hero archetype emerges from this dilemma to demand and make change for the future. We can see Musk's rise in status and popularity as similarly compensatory in the sense that it is facilitated by many of the same concerns and needs to overcome a "monster of darkness" (Lu & Yeoman, 2024, p. 89). Musk's cultural association with Henry Ford and Tony Stark in addition to the synchronistic emergence and reception of new technology and the start of the Marvel franchise suggest that Musk was identified as the embodiment of potential for innovation and technological visionary. He embodied the creator-innovator archetype who would help avoid the dire consequences of a century of burning fossil fuels by transforming the transportation industry by making EVs affordable just as Henry Ford did in the beginning of the twentieth century.

Representation and Compensation

Jung provides an important distinction between a *sign* and a *symbol*. He argues that a "sign" is limited in its meaning because it denotes a definite known object, whereas a "symbol" presents connotations which point to something relatively unknown, intuitive representations that develop out of the depths of the unconscious and, for the individual, are "a living thing…pregnant with meaning" (Progoff, 1953, p. 186). Jung argues that the "alive" quality of the symbol emerges from the psyche. As symbols, cultural figures reflect collective values that evolve with the desires and anxieties of the culture concerning their respective landscapes as well as the culture at large. Drawing upon this distinction between a sign and a symbol, we can view Kim Kardashian's and Elon Musk's names are signs that denote them as an actual person, but their names do not speak to their symbolism and socio-cultural significance. Once they achieved significant notoriety, they became cultural symbols that point to something beyond themselves as individual people. They become representations and vestiges of collective compensation. Jung et al. (1976) define compensation as a "*balancing* or *supplementing*" (Jung et al., 1976, pp. 419–420). Jung et al. (1976) argue that the function of an archetype is "not just a vestige but a system functioning in the present whose purpose is to compensate or correct, in a meaningful manner, the inevitable one-sidednesses and extravagances of the conscious mind" (p. 162). Additionally, the autonomy of the collective unconscious is expressed through manifestations of the projected anima that can "display an unbearable independence" and spur states of fascination and erotic fantasies that emerge from illusions and seduction. This section will touch on some of the ways in which Kardashian and Musk can be understood as the embodiments of cultural representations and compensations.

Kim Kardashian

We can understand Kim Kardashian's rise in popularity from two perspectives. First, she represents a change in cultural attitudes and values concerning sexualized body types, racial appeal, and personal branding and commodification through various media. Second, she embodies of an unconscious compensatory reaction to the social movements such as the "purity movement" centered around women's sexuality, a historical focus of Western culture. In a sense, Kardashian is a symbolic representation of shifting contemporary values that are contrasted with historical sociocultural values. Being of Armenian descent, she is a racially ambiguous sex-symbol. She represents a modern multiracial family. Her relationships have been a wide point of interest for many, and these have included three marriages and a range of dating partners. She has dated and married a range of people of different races and occupations that include musicians, producers, and professional athletes. Her various romantic partners and frequent provocative media presence has become a common critique for not taking relationships seriously, which has subsequently become part of her personal branding. Kardashian's high-profile status represents and reinforces a collective shift in racial inclusivity and interracial relationships which become normalized through her media presence.

Kim Kardashian as a sex-symbol archetype is also a projection of the anima archetype. With over 322 million followers on Instagram, Kardashian is one of the most famous online "social influencers." She is often credited for ushering in a new beauty standard that is observed in beauty trends related to hair and makeup, clothing, photos and videos editing, and even plastic surgery (Yang et al., 2022). Yang et al. (2022) argue that the shift in idealized body types over the past few decades could be observed as "white women tended to idealize a slim body shape, but Kim Kardashian preferred to create a curvaceous body shape" (p. 579). For example, at the turn of the twenty-first century, celebrities such as Paris Hilton, Britney Spears, and Christina Aguilera were held up as examples of the beauty standard centered on slimmer or athletic body types. Shortly after the turn of the century, curvier, full-figured women such as Jennifer Lopez, Beyonce, and Kim Kardashian became examples of the evolving cultural beauty standards (Howard, 2018). The evolution of the standard was redefined, in part, thanks to the "combination of the power from social media platforms and the popularity of Kim Kardashian herself have led to a new era of beauty standards" (Yang et al., 2022, p. 579).

A central theme of Kardashian's online photos is the "male gaze," and this has led to a large-scale imitation by others, shaping gender performances on social media and self-perception and regard (Yang et al., 2022). Kardashian is admired by a wide range of people, but especially by teenage girls and men groups (Yang et al., 2022). Yang et al. (2022) observe that Kardashian is very good at engaging her audiences through the use of "the content being sex-related images. It is highly likely that this is the result of the male gaze view" (Yang et al., 2022, p. 577). In other words, "Kim Kardashian fulfilled the fantasies that males have on feminine beauty, and the highest numerical favorite rate confirms this view as well" (Yang et al., 2022, p. 578). The notions of the "male gaze" and anima are interrelated in the sense that the male gaze encourages women to embody the anima. The anticipation of the other's desire shapes the behaviors and thoughts of those attempting to make the appeal. It is worth noting that the "male gaze" is not restricted to only males, but rather this term applies to all people that have internalized the perspective that evaluates others from a patriarchal perspective, typically as sexual objects. Many of the sexually suggestive pictures of Kardashian can be described as seductive or flirtatious. Jung et al. (1976) thought of flirting as "the expression of an experimental attitude" and a "skill in self-expression, adaptation, and defense" (p. 110). For women, he cautions that "becoming a habitual flirt, shallow, frivolous, and heartless" turns "the girl a coquette, and a serious man instinctively feels that she is not to be taken seriously" (p. 110).

As a compensatory symbol, Kardashian can be understood as a reaction to the Christian "purity movement." The seeds of the evangelical Christian "purity movement" sprouted in the 1970s as a reaction to the social movements such as the free love movement that promoted promiscuity, pro-choice, and birth control. The purity movement gained in popularity among teenagers and young adults in the 1990s and 2000s. The movement promotes a strict biblical approach to abstinence until marriage, only endorsing heterosexual, monogamous relationships as legitimate unions (Natarajan et al., 2022, p. 317). While the view promoting abstinence and heterosexual monogamy is not limited to Christianity, the social movement that gained popularity in youth ministries was explicitly evangelical. Natarajan et al. (2022) pointed out that young women must act as "gatekeepers of sex without any urges or sexuality of their own while simultaneously shaming young women as temptresses" (p. 318). Furthermore, Natarajan et al. (2022) draw attention to the unconscious racial bias inherent to the purity movement that "focused on white womanhood" and "was created for white, able-bodied women" (Natarajan et al., 2022, p. 317). House and Moslener (2023) also note an underpinning of ethnocentricity within Christian purity movements in addition to the shaming strategies that are employed, stating that for "a particular generation of teenagers between 1994 and 2010 (and beyond), spiritual formation and lessons in sexual restraint and shame went hand in hand" (p. 83).

In response to the growing popularity of the purity movement, the cultural landscape shifted, and counter-movements emerged. Kardashian's emergence as a cultural figure offers alternative ways of being that are less rigid, constrained, and oppressive and more so recognized as unapologetically embracing sexuality, self-expression, and self-branding, a stark contrast to the restrictive purity movement. Kim Kardashian represents a confluence of contemporary values, extending to notions of consumerism, women's autonomy, and commodified sex appeal. Her curated online presence can be understood as the projection of the contrasexual anima in how beauty standards have been idealized and distorted, affecting social norms. She symbolizes the sex-symbol archetype changing form, and she has "affected people's perception of feminine beauty and reinforced the ideology of the male gaze by showing a sexualized performance of women in media productions" (Yang et al., 2022, pp. 578–579).

Elon Musk

Musk's rise in popularity can also be understood from two perspectives. First, he can be understood as a representation of our contemporary technological culture. Musk represents or symbolizes a cultural fascination with intelligence, technology, and innovation, all of which hold promises of alleviating existential anxieties, envisioning a more promising future, and potentially expanding human potential. Second, Musk can be understood as an expression of compensatory actions that emerge from the environmental crisis that is a prevalent cultural point of concern. For Musk, the prospective promises include rescuing humanity from the environmental crisis that has gained attention since the turn of the century. The promises of technology, particularly in the automotive and space exploration industries, are appealing by mitigating detrimental effects on the environment and the potential of becoming a multiplanetary species by colonizing Mars. These visionary and innovator qualities have contributed to Musk emerging as a social influencer and, eventually, the richest person in the world.

Cultural figures represent the potential promises and threats of their respective industries. For Kardashian, the promises include expanding the range of beauty standards by becoming more inclusive of racial and body acceptance while contributing to the normalization of interracial relationships. She is at the forefront of embracing feminine sensuality, unabashedly embracing the moments that propelled her popularity and provided the foundation on which she has built her brand. For Musk, the promises include a new era of technological progress by developing new technologies that can mitigate negative impacts on the environment and explore the unknown space frontier. He represents the potential to shift technological fantasies to reality. In this sense, he initially embodied a Promethean mythos that in which the "fire" is in the form of renewable energy, space exploration, and artificial intelligence. Like Kim Kardashian, he has used his cultural prominence to ambitiously expand wealth, fame, and influence. Both figures' rise in popularity can be understood as a reaction to and representation of shifting conscious and unconscious collective attitudes and values that influence how individuals understand both themselves and the world they inhabit.

Conclusion

My central aim in this chapter is to expand the accessible means of empirical Jungian research that contribute to investigating the ways in which individuals are shaped by emerging socio-cultural dynamics. This involves exploring how the archetypal patterns emerge, and how synchronicities are constellated through the collective expressions within media representations, public figures, and cultural motifs which come to define historical eras and social landscapes. Furthermore, I seek to demonstrate how the rising and sustained popularity of cultural figures comes to shape societal narratives, placing emphasis on the reciprocating dynamic that exists between culture and individuals. Individuals draw on the semiotic material available to construct the narratives and make sense of experiences, shaping their understandings and ways in which they respond to circumstances.

Jung et al. (1976) describe how the primordial image, or the archetype, is a fundamental symbol of the collective unconscious, providing something akin to a repository of collective memory formed through the psychological condensation of repeated psychic processes that form the basic patterns of human existence. "The primordial image (elsewhere also termed the 'archetype') is always collective, i.e. it is at least common to entire nations or epochs... the most important mythological motives are common to all times and races" (Jung et al., 1976, p. 443). These archetypes can be triggered by particular events and respond to the needs of individuals and cultures.

Wertsch (2002) draws a distinction between *reexperiencing* and *remembering*. Remembering presupposes a degree of separation, while reexperiencing "assumes that the individual or group merges with, or is a part of the past event. In its extreme form, this may be a way of representing the past that seems to involve no textual mediation" (p. 46). Wertsch (2002) outlines how collective memories simplify and reduce events to archetypes that embody certain dynamics, and these collective memories are textually mediated through the shared narratives and myths that present templates of understanding that shape collective and individual behaviors. Building on this idea, I argue the emergence of cultural figures is a *re-experiencing* of the archetypes which becomes assimilated into our shared narratives and myths, whereas we, as observers or witnesses, *remember* archetypal motifs that have been privileged and associated with certain distant eras and historically prominent cultural figures. Wertsch (2002) understands remembering on both the individual and collective levels as a more intentional activity in how memories must be reconstructed through thought and shared narratives that function as cultural tools while textually organizing individuals into communities or groups.

It may also be worth understanding popular culture as a parallel expression of the needs and desires that religious practices have tended to in culture for millennia. The "religiosity" of popular culture and individuals is observed through the narratives and symbols that organize shared meaning and purpose as well as a sense of belongingness across communities. Through various evolving forms of media, popular culture presents narratives that implicitly or explicitly express moral frameworks. Archetypes offer a means through which people develop a shared purpose by connecting them to causes that transcend individual experiences. Despite being often dismissed as superficial or insignificant, the label of "social influencer" suggests individuals that have the power to affect the thoughts and behaviors of large groups of people by establishing, amplifying, and propelling trends that mobilize large communities of followers by unconsciously connecting them to something beyond themselves (Guthrie, 2021). The need or desire to rejoin these realms is not always conscious and can simultaneously be expressed both consciously and unconsciously through the individual and collective movements that highlight a symbiotic relationship between the two.

On the collective level, whenever a dire need or significant social movement emerges, such as the climate crisis or purity culture, a collective response will arise simultaneously or shortly thereafter. The creative forms of the individual and the collective are giving expression to the primordial "greater-than-individual forces in life" (Progoff, 1953, p. 67). One level consists of conscious needs and demands whereas another level is constituted by primordial needs, desires, and patterns that lie below the threshold of consciousness and are discharged by way of available forms of expression. Individuals do not select which archetypes become part and parcel of the times. Jacobi (1959) emphasizes a collective dimension of cultural symbols, describing the collective unconscious as a "supra personal matrix" (p. 59) that shapes individual experiences. Jung's concept of archetypes highlights unconscious structures that guide perceptions, thoughts, and behaviors. As Jung et al. (1976) explain:

> The archetype is a symbolic formula which always begins to function when there are no conscious ideas present, or when conscious ideas are inhibited for internal or external reasons. The contents of the collective unconscious are represented in consciousness in the form of pronounced preferences and definite ways of looking at things. (p. 377)

This suggests that individuals inherit archetypes rather than consciously bring them into being. Individuals must learn to navigate how to relate to the world that features those archetypes. How people relate to the forms of archetypes, particularly as they are expressed in popular cultural figures, is crucial to the individual process of becoming and individuation. Cultural figures will certainly evolve over time—for better or for worse—changing with the socio-cultural landscape and their perceived needs and desires. The dynamic constellation of cultural figures who populate a pop-culture pantheon of a given era are psychologically significant threads that define the socio-cultural fabric with which we are inextricably and irreducibly intertwined.

Competing Interests The author has no conflicts of interest to declare that are relevant to the content of this chapter.

References

Andaloro, A. (2023, July 24). 16 years have brought so many changes to the Kardashians' lives, and the very first episode of *Keeping Up With the Kardashians* proves it. *BuzzFeed*. https://www.buzzfeed.com/angelaandaloro/i-rewatched-first-episode-keeping-up-with-the-kardashians

Cambray, J., & Sawin, L. (Eds.). (2018). *Research in analytical psychology: Applications from scientific, historical, and cross-cultural Research*. Routledge.

Clark, T., Delouya, S., Gendron, W., & Jackson, S. (2023, November 21). All 33 marvel cinematic universe movies, ranked by how much money they made at the global box office. *Business Insider*. https://www.businessinsider.com/marvel-movies-ranked-how-much-money-at-global-box-office-2021-11

Cochran, N. (2018) *Consulting characters* (Publication No. 10827156). Master's thesis, University of West Georgia. ProQuest Dissertations and Theses Global.

Collective Learning Group at MIT Media Lab. (2025). *Pantheon*. MIT Media Lab. https://pantheon.world/

Corey, M. (2022, May 6). I won't stop intellectualizing the Kardashians. *Refinery*. https://www.refinery29.com/en-us/2022/05/10970105/how-kardashians-influence-society

Englund, L. (2024). Celebrity myth-making: From Marilyn M. to Kim K. *Celebrity Studies, 15*(3), 367–381. https://doi.org/10.1080/19392397.2023.2173016

Gauthier, L. (2021). *Laws of divine power in the Greek pantheon*. HAL Working Papers. https://hal.archives-ouvertes.fr/hal-03289609

Google. (n.d.). *Google Trends*. Retrieved January 4, 2025, from https://trends.google.com

Guggenheim, D. (Dir.). (2006). *An inconvenient truth* [Film]. Paramount Classics.

Guthrie, S. (2021). Understanding influencers. In P. Harris, A. Bitonti, C. S. Fleisher, & A. Skorkjær Binderkrantz (Eds.), *The Palgrave encyclopedia of interest groups, lobbying and public affairs*. Palgrave Macmillan. https://doi.org/10.1007/978-3-030-13895-0_209-1

Hines, N. (2016, June 28). Elon Musk and Henry Ford at 45: Comparing the two on Musk's birthday. *Inverse*. https://www.inverse.com/article/17588-elon-musk-and-henry-ford-at-45-comparing-the-two-on-musk-s-birthday

Hochman, D. (2007, December). Crazy for Kim: The savvy star power of Kim Kardashian. *Playboy, 54*(12), 156, 176.

House, K., & Moslener, S. (2023). Evangelical purity culture and its discontents. *Theology & Sexuality, 29*(2-3), 83–91. https://doi.org/10.1080/13558358.2024.2332976

Howard, J. (2018, March 7). The history of the 'ideal' woman and where that has left us. *CNN*. https://edition.cnn.com/2018/03/07/health/body-image-history-of-beauty-explainer-intl/index.html

Jacobi, J. (1959). *Complex/archetype/symbol in the psychology of C. G. Jung* (R. Manheim, Trans.). Princeton University Press.

Jung, C. G. (1969). Archetypes of the collective unconscious (R. F. C. Hull, Trans.). In H. Read, M. Fordham, & G. Adler (Eds.), *The collected works of C.G. Jung: Vol. 9 (part 1). The archetypes and the collective unconscious* (2nd ed., pp. 3–72). Princeton University Press. (Original work published 1934).

Jung, C. G., Adler, G., & Hull, R. F. C. (1976). *The collected works of C. G. Jung: Vol. 6. Psychological types*. Princeton University Press. (Original work published 1921).

Lu, K., & Yeoman, A. (2024). Jungian psycho-social studies: Akira, Greta Thunberg, and archetypal thematic analysis (ATA). *International Journal of Jungian Studies, 16*, 77–112.

Midgley, D., Venaik, S., & Christopoulos, D. (2023). *A new theory of cultural archetypes*. Palgrave Macmillan. https://doi.org/10.1007/978-3-031-24482-7

Natarajan, M., Wilkins-Yel, K. G., Sista, A., & Anantharaman, A. (2022). Decolonizing purity culture: Gendered racism and white idealization in evangelical Christianity. *Psychology of Women Quarterly, 46*(3), 316–336. https://doi.org/10.1177/03616843221091116

NZ Herald. (2017, March 28). The real story behind the release of Kim Kardashian's sex tape. *NZ Herald*. https://www.nzherald.co.nz/entertainment/the-real-story-behind-the-release-of-kim-kardashians-sex-tape/EPTHTKKP4E75Z2WW5A5LRYS7A4/

Pearson, C. S. (1991). *Awakening the heroes within: Twelve archetypes to help us find ourselves and transform our world*. HarperOne.

Progoff, I. (1953). *Jung's psychology and its social meaning: An introductory statement of C. G. Jung's psychological theories and a first interpretation of their significance for the social sciences*. Grove Press.

Renz, F. M., & Vogel, J. U. N. (2020). Elon Musk: Leader or liability? *Journal of Case Research and Inquiry, 6*, 27–50.

Sex Symbol. (2025, April 2). In *Wikipedia*. https://en.wikipedia.org/wiki/Sex_symbol

Wertsch, J. V. (2002). *Voices of collective remembering*. Cambridge University Press. https://doi.org/10.1017/CBO9780511613715

Yang, S., Dang, Y., & Ma, Y. (2022). Social media opinion leaders who cater to the male gaze and their influence on beauty standards: A case study on Kim Kardashian's posts on Instagram. In G. Ali (Ed.), *Proceedings of the 2022 6th international seminar on education, management and social sciences* (pp. 574–583). https://doi.org/10.2991/978-2-494069-31-2_71

Yu, A., Ronen, S., Hu, K., Lu, T., & Hidalgo, C. (2016). Pantheon 1.0, a manually verified dataset of globally famous biographies. *Scientific Data, 3*, 150075. https://doi.org/10.1038/sdata.2015.75

CHAPTER 6

Archetypal Play: Contemporary Video Gaming as a Playground for Interactive Individuation

Louise Grann

Introduction: The Legend Begins

> In a realm beyond sight,
> The sky shines gold, not blue.
> There, the Triforce's might
> Makes mortal dreams come true.
> —Excerpt from the Book of Mudra, *A Link to the Past* (1993).

Jung describes in his autobiography *Memories, Dreams, and Reflections* (1963) that it was a modality of child-like play and imaginal engagement with archetypal figures that helped Jung to heal during his deepest depression and later led to the development of his approach to depth psychology and the Jungian concepts we know today. The act of play and imaginative engagement can have a profound role in self-reflection and inner growth. It can take on a more direct approach, utilizing Jung's technique of active

L. Grann (✉)
University of West Georgia, School of Social Sciences, Carrollton, GA, USA

J. J. Dillon (ed.), *Complex and Archetype*,
https://doi.org/10.1007/978-3-032-02609-5_6

imagination (Jung, 1916/1969h), or it can happen spontaneously in our daily lives. As a modern medium, video gaming is like an alchemical amalgamation of technology and human imagination. It can offer the player a playground in which to become the mythic hero and move through the archetypal hero's journey in symbolically significant ways. As Bean (2019) notes, when it comes to video gaming and symbolic play,

> By symbolically playing as and projecting onto these characters, the player is in fact engaging their own personal self-discovery of moral choices, gaining experience as to how others act, and learning to think in critical terms about the world around them. (p. 94)

For the purposes of my discussion, I have opted to focus exclusively on a single video game franchise, *The Legend of Zelda*. For those not already familiar with the *Zelda* franchise and its lore, it is a fantastical video game series originally created by Japanese game designers Shigeru Miyamoto and Takashi Tezuka of Nintendo fame. The narrative is primarily set in the Kingdom of Hyrule, a land created by the three Golden Goddesses Din (Goddess of Power), Naryu (Goddess of Wisdom), and Farore (Goddess of Courage). After creating the world, the three Goddesses assemble a powerful artifact known as the Triforce. The Triforce is composed of three pieces, The Triforce of Power, Wisdom, and Courage. Once all three pieces of the Triforce have been gathered, it will grant a single wish, no matter if the heart of the wisher is pure or corrupted. If separated from its unified whole, each corner of the Triforce will choose a bearer, someone who best exemplifies the qualities of power, wisdom, and courage: the villainous and power-hungry Ganon/Ganondorf, the ever-wise Princess Zelda, and heroic-hearted protagonist Link, respectively. The structure of the *Zelda* series is unique in that it is one of reincarnation. Each character, with exceptions, is effectively rebirthed as a new Link, Zelda, or Ganondorf. In other words, Link has the core qualities of a *hero* in each game, but he is not the same Link in each adventure.

The mainline[1] titles in *the Zelda* series include: *The Legend of Zelda* (1987, Nintendo), *The Adventure of Link* (1988, Nintendo), *A Link to the Past* (1992, Super Nintendo), *Link's Awakening* (1993, Gameboy), *Ocarina of Time* (1998, Nintendo 64), *Majora's Mask* (2000, Nintendo

[1] By "mainline" I mean titles which are not considered spin-offs or remasters of previously released titles.

64), *Oracle of Seasons* (2001, Game Boy Color) and *Oracle of Ages* (2001, Game Boy Color), *Four Swords* (2002, Game Boy Advance), *The Windwaker* (2002, Gamecube), *Four Swords Adventures* (2004, Gamecube), *Minish Cap* (2004, Gameboy Advance), *Twilight Princess* (2006, Wii), *Phantom Hourglass* (2007, Nintendo DS), *Spirit Tracks* (2009, Nintendo DS), *Skyward Sword* (2011, Nintendo Wii), *A Link Between Worlds* (2013, Nintendo DS), *Triforce Heroes* (2015, Nintendo 3DS), *Breath of the Wild* (2017, Switch), *Tears of the Kingdom* (2023, Switch), and, most recently, *Echoes of Wisdom* (2024, Switch). There are some titles I refer to sparingly and others from which I pull numerous illustrative gameplay examples. The reason I have chosen to focus on this series is because of its symbolically rich material and because it is one of the most beloved and enduring video gaming series worldwide. This popularity is due in no small part to the meaningful resonance it has with audiences both young and old (Howe, 2022), from its archetypically rich world, characters, and masterful use of the hero's journey structure (see Campbell, 1949; Vogler, 2007). In his work exploring the hero's journey presented in *the Zelda* franchise, Kuniak (2019) writes,

> The Legend of Zelda was one of the first fully realized heroic stories on which players could embark...The continued success of the Zelda franchise exemplifies the strength of its ability to create a bond with us... has enlivened and inspired gamers for over thirty years, allowing generations of players, through Link's Adventures in Hyrule the opportunity to become heroes. (p. 57)

This is not to say that all video games have the potential to inspire organic in-the-moment self-reflection or out-of-game change. Additionally, I do not suggest that *The Legend of Zelda* games are the only ones that can inspire such experiences.

For this chapter, I pull illustrative examples across the *Zelda* games which strongly exemplify a series of archetypes which follow a hero's journey structure from beginning to end. For this component, I rely upon the monomythic threads from Joseph Campbell (1949) as well as Vogler's (2007) 12-stage contemporary iteration of the hero's journey. I will highlight archetypes that are most likely to appear in a particular stage. The archetypes I focus on are the Hero, the Orphan, the Child, the Persona, the Mentor/Wise Old Man/Woman, the Villain, the Temple, the Shadow, and the Self. Not every archetype I list will fit neatly into each stage, but I highlight the symbolic importance of each stage and, in turn, why playing the game can potentially inspire reflection and change outside the game gap. Echoing my conceptualization of ***transcendent play*** (Grann, 2021), my aim is to show how engaged video gameplay can potentially inspire self-discovery and, in turn, grow outside the game-space. This chapter also serves as a continuation and expansion of my earlier work in which I explored how the shadow archetype appears and is engaged within the *Zelda* series. Now, it is time to play with some archetypes.

Stage I: The Ordinary World

> Open your eyes… wake up, Link. You are the light that must shine upon Hyrule once again.
> —Princess Zelda, *Breath of the Wild* (2017).

The hero's journey often begins in the Ordinary World, that is, the mundane world one has known and become routinely accustomed to (Vogler, 2007, p. 15). Depending on the soon-to-be hero's perspective, it could be a world that is welcoming and comfortable, or dreadfully boring. Symbolically, the archetype of the Hero represents the evolution of the Self, or individuation (Jung, 1933/1969a). In other words, the hero personifies the Self, the unified personality with all its strength and power (Campbell, 1949). At its heart, the quest of the *hero* is the ego's quest for identity and wholeness (Vogler, 2007, p. 35). Many hero's stories have humble beginnings and Link, in his many incarnations, is no exception.

I turn now to introduce Link, the hero upon whom I will direct my focus throughout this chapter. Link is a Hylian, a race in the world of Hyrule which is analogous to humans. Compared to the many more fantastical races, such as the massive rock-munching Gorons or the elegantly aquatic Zora or the minute Minish, Hylians are similar to humans in their overall physical appearance and inherent abilities, aside from their pointed elf-life ears. Link is intentionally designed to evoke youth, androgyny, and invite projection on the part of the player. His form is relatively small, lithe, and not characterized by hypermasculine traits such as visible muscles or gruff features. He can also be considered a silent protagonist. Aside from occasional noises such as shouts, grunts, or laughter, he is primarily mute. Sensing his kind and courageous heart, the Triforce of Courage always chooses him as its bearer across his many incarnations. Additionally,

Link begins his story in nearly all his incarnations as a literal child. There are a few exceptions such as *Twilight Princess*, 2006, *Skyward Sword*, 2011, *Breath of the Wild*, 2017, and *Tears of the Kingdom*, 2023, but even in those special instances, he is more so an adolescent than an adult man. This is consistent with Jung's (1940/1969g) description of the archetype of the child which symbolizes someone or something growing towards independence (p. 168). The child is the Deku seed that will later grow into a mighty Deku tree. Across all his incarnations, Link is eventually dressed in a tunic of bright green, symbolizing newness and growth. Bean (2019) writes,

> The Hero is defined not only by their noble aims, but by their sacrifice of who and what they were before in order to become a greater version of themselves. They must face—with courage—adversity and danger, while accepting the possibility of being killed in exchange for salvation of their self or the land they wish to save. Usually a heroic figure starts out weak and becomes stronger the more they give themselves over to the archetypal hero's journey. (p. 94)

While the player may be a child themselves while playing these games, those who are teenagers or even adults can still empathize with Link's struggles since we were all once small and unsure of ourselves and the world around us. This inclination to empathize and identify with Link is also be amplified by his tendency to contain qualities of the archetype of the Orphan, which Jung (1948/1969f, p. 225) describes as someone without parents who is at times ostracized for being in some way different, such as when Link is picked on for being a "fairy-less boy" among the Kokiri he grew up with (*Ocarina of Time*, 1998). As a Hylian, Link likely saw himself as unlike the rest of his village and thought himself lacking or strange. In this instance, the social expectations imposed onto him, the various "masks" he wears become the persona (Jung, 1934/1969b, p. 20), clashes with his lived experience and his truest, heroic Self under neath it all.

Stage II: The Call to Adventure

> As I thought, you are the legendary Hero.
> —Princess Zelda, *A Link to the Past* (1991).

Before the hero's journey can begin, the hero must first answer the call to adventure. Following Campbell (1949), we can consider this call to be an "awakening of the self" (p. 42). There are many *Zelda* installments that begin with Link quite literally being woken up, usually in a place of familiarity and comfort, such as in *The Wind Waker* (2002) when his little sister Aryll wakes him up from a lazy nap, or Link's Loftwing delivering a letter from Zelda by dropping it on his head while he was still in bed (*Skyward Sword*, 2011), or reawakening after sleeping for 100 years in the Tower of Resurrection, awakened by Zelda's voice in a prophetic dream (*Breath of the Wild*, 2017) without the memories of his experiences of the Great Calamity, effectively reawakening him anew. The journey may begin with a message, a blunder, or a twist of fate. Link tends to be chosen by destiny to save the world. In other instances, such as in *The Wind Waker* (2002), he is a boy who freely chooses to take up the green tunic of the hero presented to him. Regardless of how, the hero is quickly presented with a problem, challenge, or adventure to undertake (Vogler, 2007, p. 15). This call to action can be seen and felt in the first few hours of gameplay in *Twilight Princess* (2006). Sitting on the bank of spring with his adult mentor, Rusl, he asks young Link to deliver something to the Royal Family of Hyrule in his stead. Rusl himself notes that Link has never been to the bustling Kingdom of Hyrule or ever left his small village of Ordon, so this would be a new experience for him. The matter is put on hold for the time being, and the player/Link then spends an extended amount of time in Ordon Village surrounded by friendly neighbors and tasked with relatively mundane farm tasks and chores, such as rounding up goats and looking for a lost kitten. It is one of the longest prologues in a *Zelda* game. Aptly designed, the player can simultaneously feel the comfort, and at times the slight boredom, of remaining in Ordon for an extended period. This calm is later broken when Link's childhood friend Ilia is suddenly attacked and kidnapped by a group of Bulbins. While trying to save her, he is transported into the Twilight Realm and transformed into a wolf. While Link/the player is initially called by Rusl to go to Hyrule, the loudest call is when Link's friend is in danger, and he is pulled from his warmly colored, welcoming village into the dark, disorienting Twilight Realm. In terms of immersion, the sudden shift from normalcy to a call to action is stark and effective.

Once the call has been issued, the hero must respond either by accepting it and taking up the master sword or by refusing it by allowing it to slumber forever inside the Temple of Time. A choice must be made. In a literal sense, the player can choose to continue playing the game or turn it off right away, leaving Link in limbo. As in our own daily lives, we are presented with many choices that we can choose to take up or ignore. We may accept an invitation to a party to try to make new friends or ignore the summons and choose solitude. Echoing another classic fantastical tale, Tolkien's (1937) mild-mannered hobbit Bilbo Baggins could choose to stay home in his comfortable hobbit-hole stocked with good foods and books, or choose to answer Gandalf the Wizard's invitation to go on an adventure to face down trolls, giant spiders, and a gold-hoarding dragon as a burglar. Which will the player choose? Which would you choose?

Stage III: Refusal of the Call

Hey, listen!
—Navi, *The Legend of Zelda: Ocarina of Time* (1998).

At the crossroads of destiny, the hero can make the choice to refuse the call to adventure and shirk the path of the hero. As described by Campbell (1949), "refusal of the summons converts the adventure into its negative. Walled in boredom, hard work, or 'culture,' the subject loses the power of significant affirmative action" (p. 49). This is the part of the hero's journey process where the persona, much like how Majora's Mask ensnares the previously impish yet innocent Skull Kid, latches on tightly and can cause its wearer to become a puppet to its whims of safety and the status quo. The chosen hero has now become the victim in need of rescuing instead of the hero rescuing others or the world. It is a choice born from fear, especially of the unknown. For the player, they could choose to turn the game off before the heroic narrative has a chance to begin and never return to it. To point to a few examples of refusal from the game, Link could have listened to his uncle and not left the house when Hyrule Castle was under attack (*A Link to the Past*, 1991) or Link/the player via an in-game dialogue choice could have refused the King of Hyrule's request for help (*The Minish Cap*, 2004), or chosen to never leave Kokiri Village (*Ocarina of Time*, 1998) despite the Great Deku Trees and his childhood friend Saria's expressing that his origins as a Hylian, and destiny as The Hero of Time, lie beyond their little village. For one to know oneself and grow, the hero and the player must leave what they have known before or else risk stagnation. Developmentally speaking, to remain in one's comfort zone is to stifle growth and potential. As Jung writes, "We cannot change anything unless we accept it" (1955, p. 234), or more famously, "there is no coming to consciousness without pain" (Jung, 1928, p. 193). To resist and refuse is to retreat and regress. It is, effectively, a game without progression. In other words, the acceptance of the call to move through struggle is part of the process of individuation. An aspiring swordsman who does not pick up the blade for fear it is too sharp or unwieldy cannot learn to master it. Jung (1912/1976) writes,

> For the hero, fear is a challenge and a task, because only boldness can deliver from fear. And if the risk is not taken, the meaning of life is somehow violated, and the whole future is condemned to hopeless staleness, to a drab grey lit only by will-o'-the-wisps. (p. 354)

In our own lives outside of Hyrule, we can choose to accept a promising job opportunity or turn it down because it seems like it would be too difficult or risky to leave the comfort of what we already know. During times when the call is not immediately answered, a guiding figure appears (Campbell, 1949, p. 57), much like Gandalf for Bilbo, to help give the hesitant hero in training a swift Moblin spear whack in the right direction.

Stage IV: Meeting the Mentor

> It's dangerous to go alone! Take this.
> —The Old Man, *The Legend of Zelda* (1987).

As the hero begins their journey, they are likely unsure of exactly what to do or where to go. When the newly initiated hero needs guidance, a wise mentor is sure to find them. Jung describes this guiding archetype, as originally coined as the Wise Old Man, in the following excerpt:

> The wise old man appears…in the guise of a magician, doctor, priest, teacher, professor, grandfather, or any person possessing authority…appears in a situation where insight, understanding, good advice, determination, planning, etc., are needed but cannot be mustered on one's own resources. (Jung, 1948/1969f, p. 216)

While many stories do have a literal elderly male figure filling this role, it does not mean that a mentor cannot be female or younger in age. More so than anything, it is a bond between two people like that of a parent to a child or a teacher to a student (Vogler, 2007, p. 17). Throughout his many adventures, Link has many mentors such as Impa of the Sheikah tribe. Intriguingly, she appears to Link as a literal old woman in numerous titles (e.g., *Legend of Zelda*, 1987, *The Adventure of Link*, 1988, *Ocarina of Time* 1998, *Skyward Sword*, 2011, *Link Between Worlds*, 2013, and *Breath of the Wild*, 2017) and occationally as a younger woman. In other games, Link's guide is a younger, more mischievous figure such as the faeries Navi (*Ocarina of Time*, 1998), Tael (*Majora's Mask*, 2000), or Midna (*Twilight Princess*, 2006). Princess Zelda herself can also be considered a wise, guiding figure for Link despite her assigned archetype as the Maiden, Damsel, and the Princess. As the reader may already know, many of the quotes of wisdom and guidance I have chosen to include in this chapter are spoken by Zelda herself. Although her role is switched for Link's in the newly released *The Legend of Zelda: Echoes of Wisdom* (2024), in which she is the protagonist on a quest to rescue Link, her role as an invaluable teacher and supportive figure of guidance throughout the series cannot be understated.

I highlight here Link's mentorship with the King of Red Lions to illustrate the mentorship dynamic. During the opening hours of *The Wind Waker* (2002), the player is introduced to Link and his humble, peaceful life on a small island with his grandmother and little sister, Aryll. Link is portrayed as an easy-going, somewhat lazy, if good-natured youth who is given a set of green clothes by his grandmother—effectively a costume of tales long passed—for him to wear as part of a coming-of-age ritual. Not long after this, Aryll is scooped up and kidnapped by a huge bird called the Helmaroc King. Unable to save his sister, Link joins up with a group of rag-tag, but gold-hearted, pirates to save her. After reaching the Forsaken Fortress where Aryll was taken, despite his best efforts, Link is knocked off the uppermost rampart and into the ocean below. The scene then fades to black. Link soon awakens to the morning light laying inside of a bright red boat. A voice can be heard speaking to the unconscious boy and both he and the player soon discover that the boat is speaking. The dragon figurehead turns and introduces himself as the King of Red Lions. It was he who saved Link when he fell into the ocean that night. Without him, Link cannot continue his journey across the many oceans that cover this world or brave its unknowns. The King of Red Lions, from this moment forward, acts as a fatherly figure to Link. While he does guide him, he cannot always accompany Link. There are many instances in which the King of Red Lions quite literally must be left on the shore when reaching a new island or fortress. The King can guide and advise Link, along with the player, but he/they must still walk on their own, equipped with the knowledge and resources given to them by their mentor.

According to Jung, the old man and boy mentorship represents the "spiritual factor" and plays a considerable alchemical role (Jung, 1948/1969f, p. 215). The player is new to this world, just as Link is, so someone more knowledgeable is needed to introduce and guide them through it. In our own lives, we can likely think of at least one instance when someone older and more knowledgeable than ourselves guided us when we felt as callow as a newly hatched Rito, or flopping around like an Octorok out of water; times when someone woke us up during a state of ennui or depression, inspired us, or gave us a needed nudge out the door. This guiding figure could be a parent, grandparent, friend, teacher, or even a stranger. They can come in many forms, but typically they are already knowledgeable about the stages of life, or the places and experiences we are now entering ourselves for the first time. Alchemically, the mentor helps to facilitate a change within the child, or would-be hero, like the potions skillfully brewed by the Witch (*A Link Between Worlds*, 2013). Developmentally, we all must go through stages of transition to change and grow, a shift from the old into the new. "Leveling up" takes place both inside and outside the game the player is engaged in, and the lessons learned in this fantastical space could inspire them to take on new challenges in daily life. The crossing of the threshold into the Special World is on the starboard bow. The greenhorn hero is now at the helm.

Stage V: Crossing the Threshold

> Time passes, people move. Like a river's flow, it never ends…
> A childish mind will turn to noble ambition…
> Young love will become deep affection…
> The clear water's surface reflects growth…
> —Sheik, *Ocarina of Time* (1998).

The Threshold can be considered, symbolically and developmentally, as the shore of change. To enter these unknown waters submerges the hero into its depths to be baptized and reemerge anew. For the player, crossing this Threshold into the fantastical world of Hyrule and into the larger narrative of the game, is palpable. This shift is especially apparent during the initial gameplay of *Breath of the Wild* (2017). The game's narrative begins by showing a cinematic cutscene of Link waking up half naked and alone from a magically suspended sleep inside the Shrine of Resurrection. He, as well as the player, does not know where he is or why he is there. Upon venturing outside of the dark, atmospheric shrine, Link runs to a cliffside and the lush land of Hyrule is before him. The sight is breathtaking and lets the player know that there is a vast world in front of them. However, Link and the player cannot venture out into the wild unknown just yet, as Link finds himself on the Grand Plateau, a self-contained and walled-in region which will serve as a training ground for Link and the player to learn basic gameplay mechanics.

Apropos of the hero's journey, not long after leaving the shrine, a mysterious "Old Man," as he appears and calls himself, greets the newly awakened youth. He offers introductory lore of the kingdom, as well as survival advice such as arming oneself against monstrous enemies and cooking. As the only other human found inside the Grand Plateau, he is Link's only guide. The Old Man not long after informs Link that the walls surrounding the Great Plateau are high and if he brings spirit orbs from the nearby shrines which serve as puzzling tutorials, The Old Man will give Link a paraglider to glide over the massive walls. Once Link's and the player's training is complete, the moment of gliding over the walls and into a new world accelerates at a daunting pace. *Breath of the Wild's* (2017) rendering of Hyrule is the largest and most open-ended to date. From this point forward, the player can explore in whichever direction they desire. The hero has now traveled into the Special World and their journey can truly begin (Vogler, 2007, p. 18). Once the hero has crossed the first threshold and taken that important step away from their previous everyday life, there is no turning back. The player, and Link by proxy, are on their way. They will face many challenges ahead, along with meeting new friends and foes. The tutorial is now over. Whether it is by officially leaving the safety of Kokiri Forest (*Ocarina of Time*, 1998), or jumping from Skyloft to the mysterious lands below (*Skyward Sword*, 2011), the game, and the hero's journey, have officially begun.

Stage VI: Tests, Allies, Enemies

> It is something that grows over time… a true friendship. A feeling in the heart that becomes even stronger over time… The passion of friendship will soon blossom into a righteous power and through it, you will know which way to go…
>
> —Sheik, *Ocarina of Time* (1998).

The hero's journey is now fully underway. The road ahead, also known monomythically as the Road of Trials (Campbell, 1949), will not be an easy one. Quests, both main and minor, will assess the hero's courage, resistance, intelligence, and resourcefulness through a series of Tests. As Link/the player travels across the overworld of Hyrule, they are presented with tasks to complete, such as collecting and retrieving missing items, or helping a local race to reclaim their home, ravaged by monsters and miasmas, from the dark forces set loose upon Hyrule. Although the hero's journey is one only the hero themselves can see through to the end, they should and cannot do it on their own. Along the way, Link meets with and joins up with allies who help him by providing information, useful items, or clearing the way forward in ways he cannot do alone. These friendships become more than a matter of convenience, but turn into bonds that Link and the player cherish. One such ally is Sidon, the endearingly positive Zora Prince, who always cheers Link/the player on in *Breath of the Wild* (2017) when so many others in the game are less welcoming. Another example of an ally is Princess Zelda herself across her many incarnations. Conversely, while Allies embrace the hero, Enemies stand against them. These enemies can be dark creatures scattered across the land, grunts working under Ganon, or Ganon himself. Embodying the evildoer Villain archetype (Bean, 2019), and to a degree the Trickster archetype (Jung, 1948/1969f; Vogler, 2007), Ganon is like Link, but corrupted. While Link is a humble, true-hearted Knight archetype seeking to protect and save the world, Ganondorf is the inverse: an all-powerful, iron-fisted King archetype seeking to enforce his will upon the world. In another world, another timeline, Ganondorf could have used his power to help his people prosper as he is by the very nature of his birth destined for greatness. As one of the Gerudo Elders (*Four Swords Adventures*, 2004) tells Link,

> Once every 100 years, a special child is born unto my people. That child is destined to be the mighty guardian of the Gerudo and the desert. But this

> child, its heart grew twisted with every passing year. The child became a man who hungered for power at any price.

It is Ganon's hunger for power that corrupts his purpose and condemns him to become the beastly king. Echoing the trickster, Ganondorf longs to change the world, but for dark purposes. This voracious desire for power quite literally turns him into a beastly boar, his own shadow which consumes his more human persona, "Ganondorf," whole. As wisely spoken by The Great Dragon Lanaryu (*Skyward Sword*, 2011), "Those who do not know the danger of wielding power will, before long, be ruled by it." Ganon's is a warning to all that every calling or profession brings with it its own characteristic persona (Jung, 1939/1969c, pp. 122–123) and its own dangers if we are consumed by it. In our own lives, we are often faced with many tests which we must overcome, and while antagonistic individuals may impede us, we have friends who can help and guide us along the way. For it is not power alone that makes a hero, but the wisdom and courage to wield it mindfully.

Stage VII: Approach to the Innermost Cave

> Your trial in the desert has made you stronger. The blood of the Hero must be in your veins...
> —Agniah, *A Link to the Past* (1991).

There comes a point in the hero's journey where they reach the deepest, darkest, and most dangerous place they have yet encountered. Sometimes this is a literal underground cave, dungeon, or fortress into which the hero must descend. Other times it is the headquarters of their greatest enemy or the location where the quest item is hidden. In short, "[The] Approach covers all the preparations for entering the Inmost Cave and confronting death or supreme danger" (Vogler, 2007, p. 21). In the *Zelda* series, dungeons, caves, and especially temples tend to be designed to not only test the player but also serve as an archetype unto itself. Bean (2019) notes,

> These temples often play a significant role in how Link progresses in the game and contribute significantly to the challenge and arduousness of his journey. But there are also, individually and collectively, powerful archetypes

> the serve as barriers to Link's personal growth, and which he must overcome in order to become the Hero. (p. 88)

Many temples explored throughout the series are symbolic of where Link is on his journey and what he must learn to progress and become the destined hero. They are also considered spiritual and sacred places in lore. It is in the darkest dungeon where the hero encounters their own darkness, their personal shadow. Jung (1939/1969d) writes, "the shadow personifies everything that the subject refuses to acknowledge about himself and yet is always thrusting itself upon him directly or indirectly—for instance, inferior traits of character or other incomparable tendencies" (p. 285). The personal shadow is ever amorphous and unique to each person, but a few forms it can take are low self-esteem, unchecked anger, or boastful pride. Whether they are aware of it or not, the player enters these gaming spaces with their own shadow in tow. We all possess this shadow, and the hero is no exception. The hero's battle consists of not only externalized challenges in the world around them, but also from within by facing their hidden, inner weaknesses and darkness. As Jung (1934/1969b) writes,

> The meeting with oneself is, at first, the meeting with one's own shadow. The shadow is a tight passage, a narrow door, whose painful constriction no one is spared who goes down to the deep well. But one must learn to know oneself in order to know who one is. (p. 21)

According to Jung, A battle with one's own shadow "is the first test of courage on the inner way" and a test "sufficient to frighten off most people" (1934/1969b, p. 20). For the hero, the innermost cave along with the dragon dwelling therein, is symbolically their own Shadow.

Stage VIII: Ordeal

> Shadow and Light are two sides of the same coin…one cannot exist without the other.
>
> —Princess Zelda, *The Legend of Zelda: Twilight Princess* (2006).

The ordeal is described by Vogler as a key moment in the story in which the hero must die, or appear to die, so they can be reborn again (2007, p. 22). It is a moment that shakes the hero to their core. Themes of literally facing and battling one's own darkness, as well as the darkness reflected in the world itself, are relatively common throughout the *Zelda* franchise. An example is from *A Link Between Worlds* (2013) when Ganon corrupts the Sacred Realm by attempting to steal the guarded Triforce. Because of his transgression, the realm turns into Lorule, a dark, distorted reflection of the beautiful, bountiful land of Hyrule. This design, both visually and narratively, is an apt representation of Jung's conceptualized structuring of the psyche in terms of the persona represented by the Surface World and the shadow being the Dark World underneath. However, for the purposes of this discussion, I focus on moments in which Link must face a dark doppelgänger of himself known as Dark Link or Link's Shadow. I will also pull a few examples more fully explored in my previous work (Grann, 2019) which focuses on the archetype of the shadow within the *Zelda* franchise.

The first notable appearance of Dark Link occurs in *The Adventures of Link* (1998). Appropriately, we encounter him at the lowest level of The Great Palace. Dark Link's power levels and heart container number are the same as Link's own. He quite literally mirrors his movements sword swing for swing, albeit a bit more aggressively. Link's shadow becoming its own relatively autonomous character is an appropriate symbol of the personal shadow (Jung, 1954/1969e, p. 270). The player must effectively outwit themselves if they are to win this final battle. As I write,

> Facing down one's shadow is no easy feat. It is a true challenge not only for Link, but for the player as well. Aptly, the dual with Dark Link...is the most difficult battle in the game and one of the notoriously difficult boss battles in the entire series...the personal shadow is a foe that must be directly challenged...The path to victory lies in self-understanding and in using this knowledge of one's shadowy unconscious to counter the dark double. To master one's shadow is to master oneself. (Grann, 2019, p. 66)

Another encounter with Dark Link arises during Link's/the player's traversal of the Water Temple in *Ocarina of Time* (1998). This setting is symbolically powerful since water has long been used for self-reflection and for diving deeper inside one's own unconscious. After unlocking The Room of Illusions, the player finds the floor covered in water as Link walks into the room. In the center of the room is a single barren tree. At its base is a single shadowy figure: Dark Link. Dark Link does not immediately attack but instead stands and watches. The door, however, will not unlock unless Dark Link is defeated. It is not until Link/the player initiates the first attack that his shadow will respond in kind. Calling back to my previous work, "this [moment] is symbolically significant as it requires Link to choose to confront his shadow, as we all must in order to overcome our personal shadows" (Grann, 2019, p. 67). One's shadow cannot be ignored, but must be faced head-on (Jung, 1934/1969b, p. 20). Much like his previous incarnation, Dark Link mimics the player's movements and attacks. At one point, if the player continues to perform the same attacks over and over without attempting a new strategy, Dark Link will leap unto Link's outstretched sword and stand on it, taunting him and the player by proxy. However, if Dark Link's moves are parried instead of repeated, he will become more visibly opaque. After he is fully visible, Dark Link's attacks will become increasingly aggressive until the final blow is struck, and he disappears. However, I argue that Dark Link does not vanish entirely, but rather, becomes reintegrated into Link. Link, by battling his shadow, moves through his own concealed pain and struggles.

Harkening back to his time in Kokiri village, I argue the wilted tree symbolizes Link's lingering feelings about his previous home and that his destined role as The Hero of Time not only pulled him away from it, but has caused him much pain and grief (Grann, 2019). The player can absorb this meaning, and it can become a moment of reflection and processing for them. While this experience does not occur for all players, some may vicariously observe and play out Link's struggles and bring a moment of reflection upon themselves. What is holding me back in my own life? What does my own personal shadow look like and how might I face and accept it? Developmentally, according to Jung, one cannot move through the process of individuation if they do not face and accept *all* of themselves, including the "darker" parts they might rather bury in a sunken chest and throw away the key. Jung (1963, 1977) writes,

> In myths the hero is the one who conquers the dragon, not the one who is devoured by it...only one who has risked the fight with the dragon and is not overcome by it wins the hoard, the 'treasure hard to attain.' He alone has a genuine claim to self-confidence, for he has faced the dark ground of his self and thereby has gained himself...He has acquired the right to believe that he will be able to overcome all future threats by the same means. (p. 531)

To ignore one's shadow is like trying to keep wild Wolfos locked away in your bedroom closet. It will make a lot of noise and break down the door, eventually causing havoc in your house and life in ways both big and small. Learning to understand one's shadow and live with it, even learning how to harness its previously unforeseen strengths, is invaluable and necessary for individuation. Because the hero has conquered themselves, they are now ready to take on future challenges unencumbered by their past pains or personas.

Stage IX: Reward/Seizing the Sword

> A sword wields no strength unless the hand that holds it has courage.
> —The Hero's Spirit, *Twilight Princess* (2006).

After many hours of grinding and puzzle-solving, along with overcoming their inner battles, the hero has effectively found what they were looking for and reached their final form: their Apotheosis. This Reward, Sword, or Ultimate Boon can come in a physical form, such as a literal blade of power or power artifact, or it can be something intangible such as knowledge or experience (Vogler, 2007, p. 22). Throughout the *Zelda* series, one of the most iconic items is the sword, either the Magical Sword (*The Legend of Zelda*, 1987, and *The Adventure of Link*, 1988), The Ultimate Sword (*Link's Awakening*, 1993), The Master Sword (*Ocarina of Time*, 1998, *Oracle of Seasons/Ages*, 2002, *Wind Waker*, 2002, *Twilight Princess*, 2006, *Skyward Sword*, 2011, *Link Between Worlds*, 2013, *Breath of the Wild*, 2017, and *Tears of the Kingdom*, 2023), The Great Fairy's Sword (*Majora's Mask*, 2000), The Four Sword (*Four Swords*, 2002, *Four Swords Adventures*, 2004, *and Minish Cap*, 2004), The Phantom Sword (*Phantom Hourglass*, 2009), or The Lokomo Sword (*Spirit Tracks*, 2009). Appropriately enough, Child Link becomes an adult after pulling the Master Sword from the altar of the Temple of Time. Sometimes this blade of evil's bane is found at the very end of Link's journey such as when Link acquires the Master Sword after defeating Zant, one of the main antagonists in *Twilight Princess* (2006), or after acquiring the collective strength to finally put the Master Sword from its resting place in *Breath of the Wild* (2017). The player, along with Link, acquires the long sought-after blade of power or golden treasure. It represents the culmination of Link's/the player's experiences throughout their adventure. For the player, there is most likely an immediate, intangible sense of accomplishment and victory, the sense that the hours of work and time they have invested have paid off.

This feeling of achievement can bolster self-confidence, which can be invaluable to young and old players alike. Relating this to everyday life, there are times when one decides to take a risk and take on a difficult project. Their "Sword" is the completed projector, at the very least, what they have learned while pursuing and working on it. One can still win without literally "winning," but a victory does not necessarily mean that the journey is over just yet. There is still a bit more road to travel.

Stage X: The Road Back

> It will be time for us to say good-bye… Now, go home, Link.
> —Princess Zelda, *Ocarina of Time* (1998).

With sword, or sought after treasure/item in hand, the hero needs to return to the ordinary world. Vogler (2007) notes that there comes a time when, "the hero realized that the Special World must eventually be left behind, and there are still dangers, temptations, and tests ahead" (p. 24). In terms of gameplay, there are instances in which the player can backtrack across Hyrule or Termina, to complete lingering quests or collect elusive treasures before it is time to make the trip towards the conclusion of the game's overarching narrative. For example, despite the looming threat of Termina's moon falling in *Majora's Mask* (2000), Link and the player can still help solve the problems of others across the land and put their minds, spirits, and memories at peace. This can be a trying endeavor as several quests require precise timing and the 72-hour countdown and horrific moon fall cycle can make it feel like an unrelenting cyclical nightmare. Despite the time-bending trials and existential dread Link and the player must face, time and care can be taken to help the troubled denizens of Termina before choosing to face off in a final boss duel with the manifestation of Majora's Wrath. By helping villagers solve their problems, such as breaking a curse set on Kafei by Skull Kid which caused him to look like a child and helping him recover his stolen Moon wedding mask, or more comically, reuniting a quartet of frogs so that they can sing together again in their frog choir. Regardless of the side quest, many of them yield a unique, wearable mask that may have a helpful or more mundane purpose. If gathered together before the end and facing the wicked spirit of Majora's mask, these masks can be exchanged for the ultimate mask: The Fierce Deity's Mask. This mask contains the powers of a warrior god by the same name. Wearing it transforms Link into a combination of his adult form, which we had not seen until this moment, as well as the formattable Fierce Deity. Link/the player can then face their final test not only well equipped, but also assured that they have helped everyone they can before the curtain falls on the tale and they find their own happily ever after. But the darkness must first be defeated and the land freed once more in a final test I describe in the next section.

Stage XI: Resurrection

> Do not look away. You witness a king's revival, and the birth of his new world!
> —Ganondorf, *Tears of the Kingdom* (2023).

The Resurrection acts as a "final test" for the hero, a test of what they have learned while on their journey, facing their Ordeal, and transforming moments of death into rebirth and new life (Vogler, 2007, p. 24). While in some instances the hero quite literally dies, more often the hero survives, but is forever transformed. In the case of the *Zelda* narratives, the final battle with the villain Ganon/Ganondorf marks this moment for both Link and the player (Kuniak, 2019, p. 37). This moment in the narrative is often presented as a great cataclysm. The world darkens and it is not immediately clear whether Link will survive his final encounter with the self-appointed Dark King. Aligning with the noble, self-sacrificial qualities of the hero archetype, Link/the player chooses to fight despite the dangers before him. In *Ocarina of Time* (1998), should Link fall in battle to Ganon's blade, a new timeline will branch off into what is known as the "Fallen Hero" timeline, leading to him becoming the "Hero's Shade" in *Twilight Princess* (2006), shamed for his failure and disgraced by the world in legends told thereafter. While the medium of gameplay does not pose a direct mortal threat to players themselves, they can still feel the magnitude and importance of this moment. They worry for Link, the Kingdom of Hyrule, and its many innocent inhabitants should he fail. Conversely, Ganon seeks to destroy and reform the world into one of his own visions of himself as the rightful ruler, holding fast to a corrupted persona rather than go on his own adventure of genuine self-actualization. Unlike Link, Ganon is selfish and self-ignorant, often leading to his own downfall.

The final clash is intense and world-shaking, but the battle is won, and light returns to the Kingdom of Hyrule once more. Link is no longer the weak, orphaned child he was when he began this quest. Regardless of the story told, at its conclusion Link becomes an actualized version of himself, thus marking his successful journey through individuation. This change might be presented literally through his transformation from a child into an adult, or given a new form via the previously discussed Fierce Deity transformation (*Majora's Mask*, 2000). The player is not the same as before either, but is changed by the adventure in their own unique ways from guiding Link along his way.

Stage XII: Return with the Elixir

> Courage need not be remembered, for it is never forgotten.
> —Princess Zelda, *Breath of the Wild* (2017).

Once the hero has returned, they have now become a Master of Two Worlds: The Ordinary and the Special World (Campbell, 1949, p. 196). Unless they bring back an Elixir, it can be said that the journey was meaningless. This Elixir can be love, wisdom, knowledge, a healing potion with which to restore the land, a greater understanding of oneself, or a story to tell (Vogler, 2007, p. 25). For Link, depending upon his respective adventure, the Elixir can come in a variety of forms. Often, Link's goal is defeating Ganon and stopping his dark forces in order to return peace to the land of Hyrule and save Princess Zelda. Link has collected many treasures and friendships along the way. He has grown and changed. The player has also gone on an adventure, one in which the boons of their time in Hyrule, Termina, or wherever they find themselves in Zelda's universe, can potentially be taken back into their daily life. They gather not literal Rupees, or the Master sword, but lessons they have learned about themselves and other aspects of life through immersive Archetypal Play. It is conceivable that the player can take the experiences of their time in Zelda rich game-space and bring it with them into their own out-of-game lives (see Grann, 2021). The fantastical and other-worldly narratives found in interactive video games are immensely powerful vehicles for conveying human experiences and ideas. While a fair percentage of players are not playing mindfully in this way, but instead seek an escape from their comparatively more dull and stressful lives, they could be integrating their experiences on a more unconscious level. These shoots of growth may later present themselves like Deku Sprout popping out of the ground. As the medium of gaming continues to rapidly evolve along with their players, it is an exciting time to consider what kind of experiences may be imaginatively invited and engaged through archetypal play.

Conclusion: The Hero's Never-Ending Journey

> I lack sufficient data to be sure of my conclusion, but I believe this feeling correlates closest to what your people call…happiness.
> —Fi, *Skyward Sword* (2011).

Throughout this chapter, I have taken you along with me and our hero, Link, on a journey during which we explored the archetypically rich materials offered within the *Legend of Zelda* video game series. We used Campbell's monomythic structure (1949) and Vogler's (2007) 12-stage hero's journey as a map to guide us during our introductions to and encounters with a colorful cast of playful archetypes. Whether you are a player or a newcomer, it is my sincerest hope and ambition that this playful chapter of mine entertained and enlightened you about how developmentally enriching this medium has the power and potential to be, both inside and outside of the vibrant virtual world of Hyrule. As with any heroic tale, it too must come to an end. But much like Link in his own cycles of reincarnation, as we traverse the hero's journey which is our own life, we are always reborn into a new stage of life, presented with a new calling to answer, challenges to face, friends to meet, and adversaries to overcome. I see this exploration of transformative play arising with future games, players, and technological advancements. While digital media evolves rapidly, the mythopoetic and archetypal can still be found in them, and therein invite individuation.

Competing Interests The author has no conflicts of interest to declare that are relevant to the content of this chapter.

References

Bean, T. M. (2019). The archetypal attraction. In A. M. Bean (Ed.), *The psychology of Zelda: Linking our world to the legend of Zelda series* (pp. 79–102). BenBella Books, Inc.

Campbell, J. (1949). *The hero with a thousand faces.* Princeton University Press.

Grann, L. (2019). The nocturne of (personal) shadow. In A. M. Bean (Ed.), *The psychology of Zelda: Linking our world to the legend of Zelda series* (pp. 61–78). BenBella Books, Inc.

Grann, L. (2021). *Transcendent play: An empirical exploration into how character creation and imaginative role-play in online and offline video games can facilitate self-discovery* (Publication No. 28775368). Doctoral dissertation, University of West Georgia, ProQuest Dissertations and Theses Global.

Howe, A. J. (2022). Active imagination and the legend of Zelda: An unlikely source of modern mythology. *Psychological Perspectives, 65*(3-4), 436–445.

Jung, C. G. (1928). *Contributions to analytical psychology* (H. G. Baynes & C. F. Baynes, Trans.). Harcourt, Brace.

Jung, C. G. (1955). *Modern man in search of a soul* (W. S. Dell & C. F. Baynes, Trans.). Harcourt Publishers Group.

Jung, C. G. (1963). *Memories, dreams, reflections.* Crown Publishing Group/ Random House.

Jung, C. G. (1969a). A study in the process of individuation (R. F. C. Hull, Trans.). In H. Read, M. Fordham, & G. Adler (Eds.), *The collected works of C.G. Jung: Vol. 9 (part 1). The archetypes and the collective unconscious* (2nd ed., pp. 290–354). Princeton University Press. (Original work published 1933).

Jung, C. G. (1969b). Archetypes of the collective unconscious (R. F. C. Hull, Trans.). In H. Read, M. Fordham, & G. Adler (Eds.), *The collected works of C.G. Jung: Vol. 9 (part 1). The archetypes and the collective unconscious* (2nd ed., pp. 3–72). Princeton University Press. (Original work published 1934).

Jung, C. G. (1969c). Concerning rebirth (R. F. C. Hull, Trans.). In H. Read et al. (Eds.), *The Collected works of C. G. Jung: Vol. 9 (part 1). The archetypes and the Collective Unconscious* (2nd ed., pp. 113–147). Princeton University Press. (Original work published 1939).

Jung, C. G. (1969d). Conscious, unconscious, and individuation (R. F. C. Hull, Trans.). In H. Read et al. (Eds.), *The Collected works of C. G. Jung: Vol. 9 (part 1). The archetypes and the Collective Unconscious* (2nd ed., pp. 275–289). Princeton University Press. (Original work published 1939).

Jung, C. G. (1969e). On the psychology of the trickster figure (R.F.C Hull, Trans.). In H. Read, M. Fordham, G. Adler, & W. McGuire (Eds.), *The collected works of C.G. Jung: Vol. 9 (part 1). The archetypes and the collective unconscious* (2nd ed., pp. 255–272). Princeton University Press. (Original work published 1954).

Jung, C. G. (1969f). The phenomenology of the spirit in fairy tales (R. F. C. Hull, Trans.). In H. Read et al. (Eds.), *The Collected works of C. G. Jung: Vol. 9 (part 1). The archetypes and the Collective Unconscious* (2nd ed., pp. 207–254). Princeton University Press. (Original work published 1948).

Jung, C. G. (1969g). The psychology of the child archetype (R.F.C Hull, Trans.). In H. Read, M. Fordham, G. Adler, & W. McGuire (Eds.), *The collected works of C.G. Jung: Vol. 9 (part 1). The archetypes and the collective unconscious* (2nd ed., pp. 151–203). Princeton University Press. (Original work published 1940).

Jung, C. G. (1969h). The transcendent function (G. Adler, & R.F.C. Hull, Trans.). In G. Adler & R. F. C. Hull (Eds.), *The collected works of C.G. Jung: Vol. 8. Structure & dynamics of the psyche* (2nd ed., pp. 67–91). Princeton University Press. (Original work published 1916).

Jung, C. G. (1976). *The collected works of C.G. Jung: Vol. 5. Symbols of transformation* (G. Adler & R. F. C. Hull, Trans.). Princeton University Press. (Original work published 1912).

Jung, C. G. (1977). The conjunction (G. Adler & R. F. C. Hull, Trans.). In H. Read, M. Fordham, G. Adler, & W. McGuire (Eds.), *The collected works of C.G. Jung: Vol. 14. Mysterium coniunctionis* (2nd ed., pp. 457–553). Princeton University Press. (Original work published 1963).

Kuniak, S. F. (2019). It's dangerous to go alone: The hero's journey in the legend of Zelda. In A. M. Bean (Ed.), *The psychology of Zelda: Linking our world to the legend of Zelda series* (pp. 23–60). BenBella Books, Inc.

The legend of Zelda. (1987). [Nintendo]. Nintendo of America.

The legend of Zelda: A link between worlds. (2013). [Nintendo DS]. Nintendo of America.

The legend of Zelda: A link to the past. (1992). [Nintendo]. Nintendo of America.

The legend of Zelda: Breath of the wild. (2017). [Nintendo Switch]. Nintendo of America.

The legend of Zelda: Echoes of wisdom. (2024). [Nintendo Switch]. Nintendo of America.

The legend of Zelda: Four swords. (2002). [Nintendo Gameboy Advance]. Nintendo of America.

The legend of Zelda: Four swords adventures. (2004). [Nintendo Gamecube]. Nintendo of America.

The legend of Zelda: Link's awakening. (1993). [Nintendo Gameboy]. Nintendo of America.

The legend of Zelda: Majora's mask. (2000). [Nintendo 64]. Nintendo of America.

The legend of Zelda: Ocarina of time. (1998). [Nintendo 64]. Nintendo of America.

The legend of Zelda: Oracle of ages. (2001). [Nintendo Gameboy Color]. Nintendo of America.

The legend of Zelda: Oracle of seasons. (2001). [Nintendo Gameboy Color]. Nintendo of America.

The legend of Zelda: Phantom hourglass. (2007). [Nintendo DS]. Nintendo of America.

The legend of Zelda: Skyward sword. (2011). [Nintendo Wii]. Nintendo of America.

The legend of Zelda: Spirit tracks. (2009). [Nintendo DS]. Nintendo of America.

The legend of Zelda: Tears of the kingdom. (2023). [Nintendo Switch]. Nintendo of America.

The legend of Zelda: The adventure of Link. (1988). [Nintendo]. Nintendo of America.

The legend of Zelda: The minish cap. (2004). [Nintendo Gameboy Advance]. Nintendo of America.

The legend of Zelda: Triforce heroes. (2015). [Nintendo 3DS]. Nintendo of America.

The legend of Zelda: Twilight princess. (2006). [Nintendo Wii]. Nintendo of America.

The legend of Zelda: Wind waker. (2002). [Nintendo Gamecube]. Nintendo of America.

Tolkien, J. R. R. (1937). *The hobbit, or there and back again.* George Allen & Unwin.

Vogler, C. (2007). *The writer's journey: Mythic structures for writers.* Micheal Wiese Productions.

CHAPTER 7

Seeking a Soulmate as a Path Toward Individuation

Andrea M. Stover

It is no secret that marriage in America is undergoing a major shift. According to the US Census Bureau in 2022, 34% of people ages 15 and over had never been married, up from 23% in 1950. Further, the estimated median age for a first-time marriage in 2022 was 30.1 for men and 28.2 for women, up from ages 23.7 and 20.5 respectively, in 1947. People are choosing to marry later in life, if at all. This shift is most evident beginning with Millennials, given a 2019 *Pew Research Poll* found the majority (56%) of this generation to be unmarried (Barroso, et al., 2020). Twenge (2023) notes that for Millennials, "individual freedom is valued over the tight social bonds of institutions like marriage and religion" (p. 339). As society shifts, so too do the patterns of partnering. The rise of individualism has surely influenced these partnering trends, but perhaps things are not so black-and-white. It is unknown how many people would like to find a special someone to share their life with, but for one reason or another this just has not happened for them. Are fewer people getting married because they don't want to, or is it because they have not yet found the *right* mate for themselves? I refer to those who are seeking a specific person or perhaps the experience of finding "the love of their life"

A. M. Stover (✉)
Licensed Marriage & Family Therapist, Kansas City, MO, USA

J. J. Dillon (ed.), *Complex and Archetype*,
https://doi.org/10.1007/978-3-032-02609-5_7

as *Romantics*. I would venture to guess a solid percentage of those who are unmarried are in this category: open to marriage but have not yet found the right partner for themselves. In these cases, being unmarried is not so much due to choice or preference for remaining single.

Throughout this chapter I explore Romantics and discuss how the quest to find a soulmate relationship can inform the process of *individuation*. Embedded within this exploration of a Romantic's quest to find their beloved, I discuss the purpose of marriage from a Jungian perspective, key archetypes involved in romantic love (i.e. the *Self*, *anima/animus*, and *syzygy*), and common experiences Romantics confront when seeking a soulmate (i.e. "the one," synchronicity and fated encounters, and heartbreak).

What Is a Romantic?

Knee (1998) discusses implicit theories of relationships and identifies *growth belief* and *destiny belief* as two implicit approaches people take in their romantic relationships. *Growth belief* suggests a relationship can be developed through time, while *destiny belief* holds a relationship is either "meant to be" or not and looks for signs to support this. A person can hold both beliefs simultaneously or predominantly fall into one category or the other. I will refer to those who subscribe to destiny belief as *Romantics* from here forward. Romantics come in all shapes and sizes, but the one thing that separates them from non-Romantics is their belief in the power of love and the belief in destined partnership with a specific Other (a *soulmate*). Knee (1998) states the key to a satisfying relationship for those who hold a destiny belief is believing one is with their ideal partner (p. 369). I argue that Romantics can hold *both* a destiny belief and a growth belief, whereby through relationship with the right partner, romantic love can unlock deeper dimensions of each other's personalities, as well as a shared space for discovering the possibilities of all that love can do. Romantics long to feel deeply and intimately connected to another person and derive a greater sense of meaning and purpose in their lives from romantic love. Therefore, it is incredibly important for Romantics to feel they have chosen the *right* partner for themselves if they are to marry.

Jungian analyst, Edward G. Whitmont (1978) suggests having a relationship based on personally meaningful connection with another is a recent phenomenon. He suggests things have complexified, as people are now looking for far more from relationships and have no frame of reference for how to be successful in them:

> One may conclude from the scarcity of true relatedness symbolism in mythology that the urge toward such a conscious personal I-Thou relatedness may have been constellated by the objective psyche as a pressing human problem only in relatively recent times, that it is truly a pioneering task of modern generations, without precedent in the historical past of mankind. In the past, personal interrelations were initiated by spontaneous emotions such as love and hate, and they were regulated by collective rather than personal standards. Today we find ourselves increasingly pressed to work out interpersonal connections, to come to terms with one another, on the basis of personal, individual—hence unpredictable—feelings not subject to normative regulation. (pp. 176–177)

Without having some type of model or understanding for how relationships have changed, and therefore, what needs to change in one's approach to them, many are left dissatisfied and longing to actualize the impossible. Perhaps this gives insight into why some people are more hesitant to commit to marriage or are looking for alternative ways to explore what feels like a better fit for them (e.g. consensual non-monogamy), as it is unclear what exactly they would be committing to.

Jungian analyst Robert Johnson (1983) sees romantic love as a necessity for the evolution of the Western psyche (p. 3). He states we must learn to live consciously with romantic love if we want to be able to advance to the next evolution of our consciousness (p. 3). For Johnson, living consciously with romantic love means living with "the vast psychological forces that it represents" (p. 3). Though romantic love seems quite a personal endeavor, we are reminded there is something larger unfolding in the tapestry of the collective unconscious. With this ever-shifting picture of partnership, it seems there is an attempt to work out how to both use romantic partnership and marriage as a vehicle to grow and develop one's personality and consciousness, as well as evolve the consciousness of the species, society, and human endeavor.

The Function of Marriage from a Depth Psychological Perspective

Jung (1925/1974b) views marriage as a psychological relationship, one where the opportunity to discover more about oneself is readily available through the relationship with the Other. For Jung, the commitment that comes with marriage allows for the safety, containment, and foundation necessary for psychological growth to occur. This concept is quite a contrast to the marriages of Jung's day and before, which were largely based on external factors such as social standing, religious doctrine, and were generally more transactional. With contemporary marriage being on a downward trend, and to accommodate reasons for a delay in getting married, it is important to question what happens to those who do not or have not yet become married. Following Jung, it seems a shift in focus to one's personal journey to seeking a partner might hold some of the psychological value perhaps seemingly lost if marriage does not come to fruition for the individual.

Peck (1978) states, "Whether it be shallow or not, commitment is the foundation, the bedrock of any genuinely loving relationship" (p. 140). Without the commitment, there is no container. Without the container, it is all too easy to simply decide to end a relationship or to never fully face the heat from the transformative flames of conviction. Jungian analyst James Hollis (1998) states, "One of the implicit demands of marriage is that issues are to be faced and worked through, rather than evaded" (p. 13). Through the container provided by marriage, both individuals within the partnership are forced to confront themselves. It is the mutual commitment to working things through, the commitment to something greater than oneself, and the commitment to bravely face the unknown which allows for the personal challenges and hardships to be faced, endured, surmounted, and integrated. Perhaps a reframing of the value of commitment to the journey of self-discovery brought about by *the pursuit of a meaningful relationship* is a way to accommodate those who are not married but are in search of a mate.

Jungian analyst Liz Greene (1977) discusses relationships as consisting of more than personal satisfaction of one kind or another. Rather, she says, they also exist "for the growth of consciousness and the individual's understanding" of themselves (p. 2). Partners serve as a mirror and allow for individuals to see things about themselves they cannot see without having someone reflect these aspects of their personalities back to them.

Here again we see how the individual consciousness can be expanded by and be more deeply known through relationships. All relationships consist of unconscious components, and though the contents of the unconscious can never be fully exhausted, by growing one's own consciousness, a relationship can become freer from the burden of unconscious projections onto one another. There is no reason why the quest to find (rather than have) a partner, and the many trials and tribulations on this path, could not also serve as a catalyst for the growth of the individual as well.

Hendrix (1988) describes how to make a marriage conscious and lists ten characteristics of such partnerships. These are summarized as follows:

1. Realizing your love relationship has a hidden purpose of healing childhood wounds;
2. Creating a more accurate image of your partner;
3. Taking responsibility for communicating your needs and desires to your partner;
4. Becoming intentional in your interactions;
5. Learning to value your partner's needs and wishes as highly as your own;
6. Embracing the dark side of your personality;
7. Learning new techniques to satisfy your basic needs and desires;
8. Searching within yourself for the strengths and abilities you lack;
9. Becoming aware of your drive to be loving, whole, and united with the universe;
10. Accepting the difficulty of creating a good marriage (pp. 90–92).

Attempting to embody these characteristics is bound to lead to a great challenge, as projections onto the partner must be retracted, which is a difficult feat. Hendrix (1988) also emphasizes the importance of commitment as a part of this growth process for both members of the couple. Again, it seems easy to stretch these same characteristics to be inclusive of one's relationship with themselves as they are seeking a satisfying and meaningful partnership.

Jung's work is sometimes criticized for being too individualistic. For example, does the actual Other (a real person unto themselves) even matter, or instead, is the Other objectified as the key to unlocking hidden parts within oneself without holding their own subjective importance to their partner? Obviously, the individuality of one's partner is just as important a factor in the growth and development of each person in the partnership. Would Jung be who he came to be were it not for the influence of Toni Wolff or Emma Jung, both women who stood on their own in their own right? I would remind critics that Jung developed original theories and often used his personal experiences to inform them. Therefore, much of his working through relationships with the actual Others are embedded within Jungian psychology. In *The Psychology of the Transference*, Jung (1946/1966) himself states the following:

> The process of psychological differentiation is no light work; … a radical understanding of this kind is impossible without a human partner. A general and merely academic 'insight into one's mistakes' is ineffectual, for then the mistakes are not really seen at all, only the idea of them. But they show up acutely when a human relationship brings them to the fore and when they are noticed by the other person as well as by oneself. Then and only then can they be really felt and their true nature recognized. Similarly, confessions made to one's secret self generally have little or no effect, whereas confessions made to another are much more promising. (p. 294)

Additionally, someone who offers this critique does not understand the multi-faceted dimensions of Jung's analytical psychology, as it pertains not only to the personal, but also the social and collective aspects of human existence. By being in a relationship with another person, we belong to something larger than ourselves which leads to a sense of transcendence from the individual nature of our personal consciousness. Jungian analyst Robert Johnson (1983) puts forth the aim of romantic love is to taste the divine:

> Romantic love has always been inextricably tied to spiritual aspiration. This is so obvious that it would seem unnecessary to say it, yet we all avert our gaze and miss the obvious. It is a truth too close to see. We only need to look at the love stories, the poetry, the songs that came from our romantic era, and we find that man-in-love has made of woman a symbol of something universal, something inward, eternal, and transcendent. What he sees in woman makes him feel that he has finally realized himself, that he sees all the meaning of life. He sees a special reality revealed in her; he feels completed, ennobled, refined, spiritualized, uplifted, transformed into a new, better, and whole man. (p. 54)

The aim for a marriage or committed romantic partnership is determined by one's personal relationship with themselves and by the level of consciousness from which they operate. It is from this highly personal and unique perspective that potential mates are selected. A good match is made when both partners can serve as a carrier of the Other's unconsciously projected contents. Even if partners share a mutual aim of growing their consciousness through the relationship, it does not mean the couple is working out the same contents with one another, nor does it mean they are going to be successful in their pursuits long-term. It is important to have some type of structure or articulated way of approaching relationships to give them the greatest chance of success. Hollis (1998) emphasizes a common adage about one not being able to achieve any higher or better self with the Other than they have attained with themselves. He writes of four principles of relationship: 1. What we do not know about ourselves (the unconscious project), or will not face in ourselves (the shadow), will be projected onto the Other; 2. We project our personal childhood wounding (personal pathology), our infantile longing (the narcissistic going home agenda), and our individuation imperative onto the Other; 3. Since the Other cannot, and should not, bear responsibility for our wounds, our narcissism or our individuation, the projection gives way to resentment and the problem of power; and 4. The only way to heal a faltering relationship is to render our going home project conscious and take personal responsibility for our individuation (p. 74).

The idea of having a conscious marriage or partnership, even when things do not work out long term, does appear to be growing within the collective. For example, Marriage & Family Therapist Katherine Woodward Thomas (2016) wrote a *New York Times* bestseller entitled *Conscious Uncoupling: 5 Steps to Living Happily Even After*. Woodward Thomas' work skyrocketed to common vernacular after celebrity couple Gwyneth Paltrow and Chris Martin went through a divorce and cited her as an aid in the process. Whether or not a marriage or relationship lasts, its goal remains the same: an attempt to advance the consciousness of each individual within the partnership. In doing so, it works to connect the individual to the larger narrative arch of both their personal myth, as well as their place on the collective stage of humanity. With these principles in mind, I now shift the focus more specifically to how Romantics can use their quest to find a partner to advance along Jung's process of individuation.

In Search of a Soulmate: Individuation and Archetypes Related to Romantic Love

When one hears the word *soulmate*, there are several different associations which may come to mind. Some say belief in soulmates is a myth (Peck, 1978). Others say the romance industry commodifies the utopian fantasy of romantic love (Illouz, 1997). Still a great many people believe soulmates exist. According to a YouGov poll in 2021, it is estimated 60% of Americans believe in soulmates (Ballard, 2021). If this is so, it begs the question: What is a soulmate? Plato's (2003/380 B.C.E.) *Symposium* suggests there was once a time when human beings were whole—two people fused together, having four arms, four legs, and two faces. This was before they were separated into two. As a result, each person exists as half of a whole and is seeking to be reunited with their other half to regain wholeness and a sense of completion. This feels to be the underlying motif in many soulmate stories and fantasies about finding one's "missing half": the sense of being found, put back together, and all loneliness dissipating forevermore. It appears the desire to return to wholeness and find a sense of union with something that is the same as oneself is at the heart of soulmate ideology.

Thomas Moore (1994) focuses on the *soul* aspect of relationships and emphasizes how this shifts the focus from "interpersonal mechanics," thereby allowing different values of relationship to emerge such as fantasy and imagination. Relationships become a space where *soul* works out its destiny (p. xii). Moore (1994) also emphasizes the mysteries of the heart and how the soul is not interested in perfection (p. xv). Culturally speaking, though, a soulmate is often thought of as one's "perfect match" or the one who enables a person to live out their very own storybook romance. The soulmate is often perceived as an act of divine ordination, as the two lovers cannot imagine someone more rightly suited for them than this beloved. Whether looking at the classic Jane Austen love story between Mr. Darcy and Elizabeth Bennet or a modern, pop culture couple such as Travis Kelce and Taylor Swift (who have swept the nation by storm at the time of this writing), it is obvious people have a strong reaction to the power that certain couples bring forth in their pairing with one another. It is interesting to see what observers project onto couples such as these (fictitious or not), as these projections can help both individuals and society clarify what it is they value in romantic love.

Embedded within a love story is who the two people were prior to their meeting. How did their personalities change or emerge once they partnered with one another? For example, rough and tumble Travis Kelce is now revered as the epitome of a gentleman, while Taylor Swift is exercising more public displays of her devotion for her partner than is typical of her in previous relationships (thereby exercising influence on an entire industry—the National Football League (NFL) —and exposing herself to an unprecedented level of scrutiny). As an outsider, I can project a soulmate love story onto them and believe this is all coming about because of their love for one another. However, the line gets quite blurry between a celebrity couple who exudes an air of mystery for the general masses vs. the mysterious forces drawing the couple together in the first place.

In the fictitious couple example, Elizabeth Bennet and Mr. Darcy both must confront inborn stereotypes for their love to prevail. Both are changed by their confrontation with themselves because of their feelings for one another. In this way (if we classify this couple as soulmates), a soulmate is a bridge and a mirror, serving to take a person deeper into themselves and offer the experience of transformation through a transcendent, romantic relationship which is lived out *both internally and externally*. Jungian analyst Benig Mauger (2008) sees soulmates as the mirror of the Self. Mauger (2008) puts forth soulmates are split off parts of ourselves, and when we unite with them, we become more conscious and more whole:

> Our search for union and for wholeness guides us to our 'other half,' to our soul mate. In essence, we are being guided to become more conscious, and to become more whole within ourselves. Inner union is essential to the spiritual well being of every individual, which makes the desire for relationship so compelling. (Mauger, 2008, p. 204)

Using *individuation* as a framework for Romantics' seeking to find this type of union allows for personal exploration of one's own experiences of the *Self*, *anima/animus*, and *syzygy* archetypes. The journey to finding a partner such as this can involve many twists and turns, and there are no guarantees. Some people may find a relationship like this early in their life, but I reckon a great many people kiss a lot of toads before they find their prince(ss). It can take a fair bit of psychological work to get to this type of relationship, as it requires a level of psychological maturity and self-development which may not be available to all from an early age. The establishment of a solid individual sense-of-self can be both the condition for and the outcome of a soul union such as this.

Individuation

Individuation is a term Jung (1939/1969c) uses to describe the process by which a person becomes a psychological individual who can stand on their own as a separate yet connected part of the whole of life (p. 275). This process is forever unfolding, and the aim is not about reaching a static place or destination. Rather, a person is challenged throughout their life to come into greater wholeness by developing their ego, strengthening their relationship with the archetypal dimension wherein they have a relationship with the collective unconscious, and integrating parts of the unconscious into their conscious personality. The process of individuation "…is a process or course of development arising out of the conflict between the two fundamental psychic facts," the existence of both consciousness and the unconscious (Jung, 1969c, p. 288). Jung (2009) also writes of "the spirit of the times" and "the spirit of the depths." When it comes to romantic love, we are now entering a time where the "spirit of the times" is in flux, and this flavors the way partnership is conceptualized and sought. Regardless of the backdrop of a particular time in history, it is important to remember the archetypal dimensions of the depths remain constant. Put differently, the archetypal core does not change through time, though its valence might shift to fit the cultural norms and societal conventions of the particular times.

Greene (1977) discusses a shift of consciousness represented by the dawn of a new age in the coming centuries which many refer to as the *Aquarian Age*. One of its motifs is a striving toward inner knowledge (p. 3). Perhaps this shift is part of what underlies society's curiosity, a desire to push beyond the bounds of what is known, and seek a variety of experiences to learn more about oneself when it comes to partnership (e.g. polyamory, open relationships, and non-committal relationships). For Romantics, I find it valuable to use individuation as the frame to ground the relational experiences, rather than attempting to fit them into any type of relational label or box (e.g. traditional relationships or married couples). I now present a non-exhaustive list of archetypes involved in a Romantic's quest to find a soulmate.

Self. Individuation is guided by the archetype of the *Self*. The *Self* is the sum total of the psyche, both the conscious and unconscious parts. It is the driving force behind life itself. As Whitmont (1978) writes,

> This archetype expresses itself in the form of predestined wholeness, not however of general human wholeness but of the specific wholeness of an individual life, which seeks fulfillment. It may be viewed as an archetype of a central authority, a unitary field, which governs conscious as well as unconscious functioning, outer as well as inner reality; and it manifests itself in both realms in ways which appear to be governed by the correspondence rather than by the laws of cause and effect. (p. 219)

We could speculate that the *Self* is the archetype which both sets the path for the Romantic and pushes them to develop themselves as they undertake the often-difficult task of finding and maintaining love, both for themselves and for their partner. Not everyone's path to growth is through romantic love and partnership, but for Romantics, they are unable to imagine a life well-lived without meaningful relationship. Through their quest to find this type of partnership, they are able to grow their personality by developing the ego, facing the shadow, and getting to know the *anima/animus*. The inner drive to find a soulmate is brought on by the *Self*'s quest to find wholeness and bring these parts of the psyche into consciousness.

Anima/Animus. Traditionally speaking, *anima/animus* are archetypes which represent the inner image of "woman" for a man and the inner image of "man" for a woman, respectively (Jung, 1925/1974b). Some argue that a few of Jung's theories are dated and antiquated to the time he developed them, that this pair of archetypes is offensive to some in our modern times. For purposes of this chapter and for simplicity's sake, I speak of *anima* and *animus* in a classical Jungian sense (see Samuels, 1985), but as Lu and Yeoman (2023) note, classical does not mean uncritical (p. 86). A big part of individuation is confronting these archetypes within one's own psyche. Much of romantic love centers around these two forces, as partners are able to project these unconscious aspects onto one another. Through time, the projections break down and each member of the couple is tasked to take responsibility for the disowned parts of themselves. The *anima/animus* represents a contrasexual other, and therefore, they feel more foreign to the man/woman. By being in a relationship and having a partner carry one's *anima/animus*, one can learn to relate to this aspect of themselves on the outside.

Jung (1951/1974a) emphasizes these archetypes can never be fully known or integrated, and so he implores people to constantly bear them in mind (p. 159). *Anima* and *animus* are extremely important in romantic relationships and should be approached with respect, caution, and responsibility. Their archetypal roots show they have been around since time immemorial, though the personal preferences, experiences, and tastes of these archetypes take a personal bent given a variety of factors including: the spirit of the times, the imago of partnership put forth by the parents' relationship, and previous relationships from the past. One may easily succumb to possession by any archetype, and this is especially evident in cases of the *anima/animus*. Jung (1925/1974b) states,

> Just as the animus projection of a woman can often pick on a man of real significance who is not recognized by the mass, and can actually help him achieve his true destiny with her moral support, so a man can create for himself a *femme inspiratrice* by his anima projection. But more often it turns out to be an illusion with destructive consequences, a failure because his faith was not sufficiently strong. To the pessimists I would say that these primordial psychic images have an extraordinarily positive value, but I must warn the optimists against blinding fantasies and the likelihood of the most absurd aberrations. (p. 175)

As Swogger notes in the next chapter, theoretically speaking, the masculine (*animus*) and feminine (*anima*) are opposite sides of the same coin. Through the process of individuation, they are capable of coming into greater balance and promoting a sense of psychological wholeness.

Syzygy. When we experience this contrasexual balance, which occurs when opposites unite a divine pair), we are in the realm of the *syzygy* archetype. This archetype does not always have to do with sexual union, but it does relate to the "masculine" and "feminine" energies coming together in perfect harmony and balance. As archetypes appear as instincts with form, the *syzygy* is the impulse which arises within individuals to form partnership and shows there is something innately divine within each of us that is pulling us into something greater than ourselves. In the case of marriage and soulmate partnership, the act of coming together with another and creating wholeness through the personal, relational, and archetypal dimensions, the *syzygy* represents an attempt at realizing the *Self*. This is what the process of individuation is all about, and it helps immensely to have this archetype to draw from as an image/figure for Romantics, rather than feeling as though one should be a self-contained individual that shouldn't long for union with another.

Jung (1936/1969b) states that archetypes, "…are found in every individual, and their effect is always strongest, that is, they anthropomorphize reality most, where consciousness is weakest and most restricted, and where fantasy can overrun the facts of the outer world" (p. 67). He discusses this condition being most present in a young child's first years of life and associates the divine *syzygy* archetype as being cast upon the parents, only to later leave the child feeling disillusioned and disappointed to realize their real parents are, in fact, not gods. There are innumerable combinations of parental imagoes a child might perceive or infer from their parents' relationship when the human cracks begin to show. These individual nuances and particularities are most certainly bound to show up in the psychology of a Romantic and what they are driven to work out on their path to finding a soulmate. Hendrix's (1988) work is developed to help people clarify just this sort of thing.

A final point on these types of relationships is that they are uniquely defined by the two people in them. Moore (1994) suggests every relationship where soul is involved is individual and unique. There are various archetypes involved in these relationships (*Self*, *anima/animus*, and *syzygy*), but the archetypes alone do not indicate the particular flavor of the individual expression of what each person is looking for in a soulmate. Jung (1939/1969c) discusses the archetypes as being more like fragmentary personalities (p. 286). He writes, "There is nothing in their behaviour to suggest that they have an ego-consciousness as we know it" (p. 286). Given the rise of individualism, perhaps it makes sense why modern people are in a place unknown to previous generations. Moore (1994) states our problem in relationships is,

> how to have an ongoing, intimate life with another person at the same time as we invite this completely unpredictable depth to have a significant place in our lives. It isn't easy to live with the power and mystery of another person's soulful personality. (p. 235)

The task of today is to find a way to allow for *soul* to authentically exist, express, and animate our lives and relationships, whereby we can become more wholly ourselves by and through the exchange with another. With this in mind, I turn now to common experiences Romantics bump into on their path to seeking a soulmate and how these archetypes might express themselves through lived experience to further advance individuation.

Experiences Related to Seeking the Soulmate

"Ever since I can remember I've longed for a soulmate" (Schierse-Leonard, 1986, p. 1). These are words most Romantics relate to, as the longing to find their special person is often the very drumbeat of a Romantic's heart. While psychoanalysis might offer valid explanations and interpretations for what this longing stems from (e.g. unfulfilled childhood needs, a reaction based on the parental imago one carries, an attempt to regress back to the "Garden of Eden," or a form of archetypal possession of some form or another), Jung (1934/1969a) states:

> In dealing with the shadow or anima it is not sufficient just to know about these concepts and to reflect on them. Nor can we ever experience their content by feeling our way into them or by appropriating other people's feelings. It is no use at all to learn a list of archetypes by heart. Archetypes are complexes of experience that come upon us like fate, and their effects are felt in our most personal life. (p. 30)

Attempting to solve matters of the heart with head knowledge is only going to go so far. I now explore three different types of experiences Romantics may encounter on the path to seeking soulmate love and how these inform the process of individuation accordingly. In doing so, I loosely hold the frame offered by Lu & Yeoman (2023) to introduce archetypal thematic analysis (ATA) as a psycho-social method for understanding specific qualitative phenomena. It is my hope to present a balance of the head and the heart as I explore the following phenomena: seeking "the one," synchronicities, and heartbreak.

The One

I defined a soulmate from a Jungian perspective in the previous section, but it is now important to do more exploration as it pertains to "the one" who so many seem to be seeking. From a Jungian perspective, when people speak of "the one," they speak about something far deeper than they realize: they convey the specific nature of their inner *anima/animus* figure. What a profound moment for a Romantic to feel they have just met their life companion, their beloved soulmate, "the one" whom they have been waiting to meet their entire life! If the *anima/animus* carries the coding of the soulmate they are so ardently seeking as their partner, it makes sense that the experience of finding "the one" occurs when an outer manifestation of an inner phenomenon, only privately carried up until now, is concretized into material form. Schierse-Leonard (1986) speaks of "imaginal companions" being the psyche's way of "wedding the divine." The longing for a soulmate comes as a natural prelude on the way to the wedding (pp. 1–3). Many Romantics have rich, inner lives and report feeling the presence of another living within themselves. Whether this fantasy figure fits neatly and squarely into the human form of another person or not, there does appear to be an inner knowing of a specific Other one is in search of.

When looking at how this experience shapes individuation, it is important to acknowledge that a Romantic is *expecting* to find a soulmate and shows up to each new relational encounter with the hope that this person is their beloved soulmate. This expectation may be the very thing which constellates the archetypes into their conscious experience. Further, this expectation results in a great deal of projection and skews the lens of perception between who the actual Other is vs. who the Romantic hopes them to be. If, for example, a Romantic quickly declares, "I have found the one!" without really knowing who the person is who carries their projection, there will inevitably be disillusionment and perhaps an ending of the relationship altogether. An experience such as this is a wonderful opportunity for a Romantic to reflect upon just who they projected onto the Other, and start to question the nature of the personal qualities of their inner *anima/animus*. This realization opens the doorway to greater maturity and self-development, as the Romantic can tolerate the discord between the inner and outer realities. Hendrix (1988) offers many exercises to help people discover these inner figures.

If a Romantic is inflexible and only tolerates a mate who fits their exact fantasy, then it is possible they are in the grips of archetypal possession where the *anima/animus* is having its way with them. Schierse-Leonard (1986) details many couples and figures a Romantic meets on the way to the wedding: Prince Charming and the Special Princess, the Ghostly Lover, the Bewitchment, the Demon Lover, Beauty and the Beast, and various others. In instances such as these, Romantics are unable to grow or make progress in their aim for soulmate love until they are willing to surrender the projection and allow for the humanness of an actual Other. Jung says of a female patient, "At least she is trying to work on her animus and that is the most meritorious thing that anyone can do" (cited in Hannah, 2011, p. 161). It is safe to assume this also applies to a man working on his *anima*. By holding the tension between these two experiences, something new is bound to emerge. *Anima/animus* work is not easy, but it is necessary to progress along the path of individuation.

A second point about how the search for "the one" relates to individuation is the necessity of having real life experiences to better inform oneself what type of partner is the best match. It is a popular practice in dating advice and self-help culture for those seeking love to make a list of all the qualities and characteristics they are looking for in a partner. Many "Law of Attraction" practices also suggest a person "act as if" they already are living in the reality of being with their beloved before they ever meet in the flesh. This is yet another example of how a Romantic may literally feel they are drawing their mate into their conscious reality, giving them a sense of being in touch with the divine orchestration for their own soul's "perfect" match. I have known many people who have engaged in these types of practices and ended up meeting someone who matched their wish list of preferred qualities and characteristics. Interestingly, I have seen many people become disappointed and even confused when they realize they want something very different from what they put on their list. What these practices often exclude is reflection on why these qualities or characteristics are important to the person doing the exercise and where these qualities come from. Engaging in Jung's *active imagination*, for example, might lead a person to contact the inner *anima/animus* and better connect with this "inner other." Once contact is made, it is important to venture out into the dating world and do some reality testing on whether these constructs hold true in real world encounters. Without doing a bit of reality-testing and putting oneself into various situations, it is impossible to get the self-knowledge and awareness to better inform the partner selection process moving forward. By learning more about oneself and by becoming more oneself through the process of individuation, Romantics learn the journey to seeking the right partner for themselves is equally a journey of becoming a "one" unto themselves.

Similarly, a third point related to seeking "the one" for Romantics is the importance of finding value in the times when they are wrong in their assertions. It is possible, for example, for a Romantic to meet many "false ones" on their journey to seeking soulmate love. It is through these multiple "ones" that the Romantic is better able to come to know the "inner other" within themselves (*anima/animus*). Further, a person may be "the one" for the Romantic during a certain period of life, but this may not translate across the lifespan. The experience of a high school sweetheart comes to mind in this context. It is difficult to get through to any teenager who is madly in love for the first time that the likelihood of their relationship lasting much beyond high school is low. Even though this is statistically true, the experience of being so deeply enamored with their high school flame does not allow for any openness to a contrary reality. If the relationship does not last for the rest of their adult life, it likely still holds a special place in the person's heart and personal development. Who is to say they were not with "the one" they were meant to be with during that chapter of their life? Given that they were with the right person for them at the time, does it mean they will never meet another "one?" Of course not. So, there is value in having a variety of experiences and allowing for each individual relationship to be what it is/was for a Romantic. Even if a Romantic allows their hopes for who the person is to overshadow the reality of the not-so-great-match in front of them, there is much to be learned and gained from these types of experiences. Rather than throw their hands up in the air and give up the search for a quality love partnership when they are wrong about the relationship's longevity (so as not to be humiliated or heartbroken again), Romantics can integrate what was previously unknown to them and use these disappointing experiences to inform their future search.

Synchronicity and Fated Encounters

The next Jungian concept I explore related to Romantics is *synchronicity*. Jung (1952/1974c) defines synchronicity as an acausal correlation between two meaningful coincidences, particularly when an inner psychological event is linked to an external event. Jungian scholar Roderick Main (2004) writes of synchronicity, "Although he does not say so, Jung's whole presentation implies that it promotes individuation" (p. 22). From an archetypal perspective, the mysterious workings of the *Self* are at play in synchronicity. I have found the belief in synchronicity to be inextricably linked to the psychology of a Romantic and a real catalyst for psychic transformation. Romantics *expect* synchronicities, as they are always on a quest to find greater meaning and believe in the miraculous and seemingly irrational ways things can unfold or develop. Perhaps this expectation is what actively constellates the archetypes of romantic love into the conscious, waking life of the Romantic.

When it comes to any good love story, part of the intrigue is the series of events that lead the two lovers to find one another. Getting lost in the story and trails of synchronicities is one way Romantics can both get lost and be found on their quest to find a soulmate. To illustrate, I return to the example of Taylor Swift and Travis Kelce. Taylor's fanbase is referred to as the "Swifties." Since Taylor and Travis have become a couple, many of the Swifties have been busy connecting lyrics to some of her songs written prior to meeting Travis to their relationship today. Their belief is that Taylor *manifested* Travis as a partner. For example, in Taylor's song "Mary's Song," one of the lyrics is "I'll be 87; you'll be 89." Travis' football jersey number is 87, Taylor has an album released called 1989, and both of them were born in 1989. Another example is from Taylor's song "Ready for It?" in which she says, "Knew he was a killer, first time that I saw him." Travis' Instagram username is "killatrav." Finally, another lyrical example brought forth by the Swifties is from Taylor's song "Fifteen" in which she says, "In your life you'll do things greater than dating a boy on the football team." Taylor is currently on one of the highest grossing world tours ever while she is dating Travis (a boy on the football team).

Synchronicities are in the eye of the beholder, but there is something the Swifties are seeing in these connections. Taylor herself mentions the fact her favorite number (13) and Travis' football jersey number (87) adds up to one hundred. Suffice it to say there is some meaning she sees here. It is easy for Romantics to get swept up in a synchronicity such as this and automatically imbue it with the meaning of meeting their soulmate. While it cannot be argued that something necessarily profound has just occurred, the ultimate meaning of synchronicities such as these cannot be known at the moment. This is why I say Romantics can both get lost and be found when it comes to their relationship with synchronicity. By staying open to a variety of meanings, a Romantic can have faith and trust that a process larger than themselves is at play. The details of exactly what that unfoldment looks like can remain a mystery, waiting to be lived out and discovered.

A close cousin to synchronicity is the role of "fate" and "destiny" in the psyche of a Romantic. Believing there is a fated partner, that "everything happens for a reason," and looking to meet one's destiny in the eyes of the soulmate are a few of the ways this can show itself. These types of synchronistic encounters a Romantic has with their hoped-for soulmate are much more meaningful than meets the eye. Regardless of the relationship's outcome, I call these people who elicit these feelings of fate and destiny *helpmates*, because without their presence and the experience of the encounter, Romantics would not be able to learn, grow, and discover some of their unconscious parts. This is how a Romantic begins to take more agency and ownership of their own fate. Jungian psychology makes a clear case for Romantics to clarify what drives their desire for a soulmate, how and why discrepancies between the inner and outer occur, and what role the actual partner may have in their life (beyond their own individual fantasies of how this person will serve them).

One point worth raising surrounding the concepts of synchronicity, fate, and destiny in the role of the Romantic's life is how each of these things can bring a sense of being connected to the numinous. Main (2007) discusses this, as well as synchronicity's way of transforming the consciousness of the experiencer:

> In a typical synchronicity, one sees manifesting in the external world the parallel of some inner idea or image with which one is identified. Because of the paralleling, this identification transfers somewhat to the external expression, with the result that one comes to experience oneself as being partly externalized in the world. That which one formerly took to be separate from oneself, objective, turns out to be the same as that which one took to be oneself, one's subjectivity. Thus, from a state in which one is centered inwardly in one's psychic processes one is shifted into a state in which one's sense of identity extends beyond the psyche into the physical world. In this way one's identity is decentered—the observer becoming objectified while the observed is rendered subjective. The resultant holistic state of perception, however briefly it lasts, marks a profound transformation that can have far-reaching implications. (p. 49)

If a Romantic believes synchronicities are little nods from the universe that they are on the right path to finding their soulmate (i.e. "follow the trail of breadcrumbs"), then it is easy to see how encouraging and inspiring synchronistic encounters or experiences can be for them.

One phenomenon which accounts for synchronicity, fate, and destiny, all rolled into one is *precognitive dreams*. The idea of meeting a mate in the dream world before meeting them in the flesh is just the type of thing a Romantic would not only subscribe to, but also quite possibly experience! However, like all synchronicities, it is important to hold these kinds of experiences loosely, so as not to act from too one-sided a place. I will now illustrate a personal example of what I mean. Several years ago, I had a precognitive dream about meeting someone. Though I could not see his face, I registered his voice and energy in the dream. We discussed when we would like to meet in the dream and settled on ten days into the future. Upon waking, I did not necessarily circle the date on my calendar, but I was conscious of it to some extent. On day ten, I met him. I first heard his voice before I saw him and knew it was the figure from my dream. My body reacted in quite a strange manner, in that I became extremely anxious and began quivering. My head, on the other hand, was telling me, "It's him! This is your person!" We eventually spoke to one another and did spend time together a few times. I will spare the details of what happened next, but suffice it to say it was quite a traumatic experience all around for me. It took a while to process and unpack why I would have such a profound precognitive experience, only for it to turn out as badly it did. All too often, concepts such as synchronicity, fate, and destiny are presented from the one-sidedness of positivity. Perhaps all dreams are "positive" from a growth standpoint, even if the ego-identity might not judge it to be the case.

Jung (1939/1969c) discusses the Janus-face nature of the unconscious. On one side its contents take us back to prehistoric, preconscious instincts, while the other side can anticipate the future from a similarly instinctual level (p. 279). When it comes to precognitive dreams, it is important to hold this "both/and" perspective in that they can be "backward-looking images or forward-looking anticipations" (p. 279). There is difficulty in interpreting dreams, especially if looking at only at a singular one, and especially if the events have not yet played out in conscious, waking life. Therefore, interpreting these dreams may be more fruitful upon reflection at a later point down the line. However, if a Romantic meets someone who the dream says they are about to meet, they cannot help but project all of the desires for who this person is onto them, especially given the seemingly "divine" green-light for this person entering one's life. A Romantic's job is to be aware of where their heartfelt desires and hopes live, and to still attempt to treat each synchronicity as the mystery that it is. In other words, we cannot know the meaning of things until we do. And even then, it can still change through time.

Heartbreak

The quest to find one's personal beloved is often a path full of trial, error, and hopefully personal growth and development. Sometimes the path can seem bleak, and many Romantics can lose faith in their journey. Needless to say, at least one broken heart is often the price paid for Romantics who set out to find a soulmate, though I would imagine numerous heartbreaks to be more likely the case. Heartbreak shows up for a variety of reasons: repetition of early relational patterns, unrequited love, outgrowing the relationship/partner, betrayal, death of a partner, or perpetually coming up empty-handed after a lifetime's worth of investing oneself into the search for a soulmate. Despite the pain it brings , a broken heart can be a wonderful teacher and a catalyst to go deeper into self-understanding and self-compassion. Mauger (2008) discusses three ways to heal from within when suffering from a broken heart, and they are as follows, a) identify your inner archetypes, b) identify your patterns, and c) identify your stories. By identifying with your own archetypes through *active imagination* or other forms of engagement, more flesh can be put on the bones of who/what part of the psyche is internally trying to get the Romantic's attention. Identifying the patterns one finds in relationships allows for greater clarification of one's early bonding and attachment experiences which might be repeating themselves in romantic relationships. Identifying one's stories helps give insight into the unique vision of totality and wholeness, one's own mythic quest, continually expressed through a Romantic's love story with their various partners. All of these steps lead to self-enrichment and self-knowledge, which we are then able to apply on the path to love.

Socrates famously said, "The unexamined life is not worth living" (Plato, 1961/399 B.C.E., p. 23). If a Romantic has taken heart in their quest to find soulmate love and worked toward individuation along the way, then they have plenty of fruit to bear from their excursion into the unconscious. Using the experience of heartbreak to discover more about oneself is an invaluable way of making lemonade out of the sour lemons of love gone awry. The act of surrendering one's hopes and the courage to face times when love does not go according to one's plans may bring a Romantic closer to their own soul. Heartbreak, however, can also lead to a crisis of faith. Johnson (1983) states, "We may come to see that psychological faith and spiritual faith intersect at the deepest level…." (p. 174). To embark on any quest is an act of faith. The search for a soulmate is one which requires conviction, heart, humility, and an inner urge to keep going. To advance on the path of individuation and participate in the mystery of life, a person comes to know themselves as being connected to something larger than themselves. The experience and feeling of this can also dissipate some of the longing or inner urge to find a partner, as the "partner" may transition into being life itself. Here is yet another way the *Self* and the *syzygy* can be experienced in human form, even if only temporarily. It is as if the personal heart merges into the collective heart, which can provide an outpouring of love, acceptance, and belonging. Though this experience may sound quite beautiful, I do not mean to diminish the pain and disillusionment which often catalyze these types of experiences. As Mauger (2008) writes,

> From a spiritual perspective, learning to love is part of the challenge of human life. We are offered the gift of love, and the challenge to open our hearts. Accepting and enjoying human love is part of our spiritual growth. Enduring the joys and conflicts of the heart will ultimately propel us to encounter our divine natures, and to unite the opposites within us. Experiencing profound love and heartbreak is also the conduit to learning to love unconditionally and to experience compassion. (p. 204)

Conclusion

Being a Romantic is hard work, as it requires the fortitude necessary to overcome the inevitable setbacks, disappointments, and heartbreak on the journey to actualizing mature and meaningful love. Further, it calls for regular self-confrontation, curiosity, and an unwavering commitment to discover who one is on their mission to find the right partner for themselves. The quest to find a soulmate is wonderful, fertile ground to allow for the process of individuation to take root. In what other manner does a person bring their entire heart and soul to face the great unknown—*another person*—and hope for the best? Many of the trials and tribulations of seeking soulful partnership allow for the growth and development of the personality, and heartbreak is a way of breaking a person wide open to explore deeper parts of themselves, perhaps previously unknown to themselves.

Given the ever-shifting picture of relationships in today's society, it appears people are looking for something more, something different, and something they may not fully understand. Romantics are in a unique position, given they are clear about their aim: to find a soulmate. The belief in this type of partnership already sets them apart from others who see relationships as something more recreational, mundane, transactional, or having less potential for personal growth or spiritual fulfillment. The challenge is to ensure enough psychological stamina, maturity, and grace for the journey, as it is a vulnerable endeavor to undertake. By using their quest to find a soulmate to inform their own individuation, Romantics stay oriented to a goal beyond their attachment to a human soulmate relationship. Instead, they enter the archetypal realm and grow their consciousness of the *Self*, *anima/animus*, and the *syzygy*, each of which take on distinct forms and present themselves in a variety of ways.

Romantics are seeking transcendence in their relationships, and in some ways, encountering archetypes is a way of reaching beyond the personal realm of existence. Romantics want to taste the divine through their partnership with another human, and each of these archetypes invariably holds the potential to be numinous from the Romantic's perspective. An underlying question which remains is how much of one's individuation needs to occur before a Romantic is psychologically equipped for soulmate love? This chapter argues that the path to such a love *is* individuation, regardless of whether there is a human soulmate waiting behind the curtain as a prize won for all of the hardship, heartache, and muck dealt with along the way, Romantics are well-served to advance forward on their path. Romantic relationships are not easy, but Jungian psychology helps put a meaningful frame on how to better understand the journey as both an inner and outer phenomenon. As the great poet Rumi (1995) says, "Lovers don't finally meet somewhere. They are in each other all along."

Competing Interests The author has no conflicts of interest to declare that are relevant to the content of this chapter.

References

Ballard, J. (2021, February 10). Do Americans believe in the idea of soulmates? *YouGov*. https://today.yougov.com/society/articles/34094-soulmates-poll-survey-data?redirect_from=%2Ftopics%2Frelationships%2Farticles-reports%2F2021%2F02%2F10%2Fsoulmates-poll-survey-data

Barroso, A., Parker, K., & Bennett, J. (2020, May 27). As millennials near 40, they're approaching family life differently than previous generations. *Pew Research Center*. https://www.pewresearch.org/social-trends/2020/05/27/

as-millennials-near-40-theyre-approaching-family-life-differently-than-previous-generations/

Greene, L. (1977). *Relating: An astrological guide to living with others on a small planet*. Samuel Weiser, Inc.

Hannah, B. (2011). *The animus: The spirit of inner truth in women: Volume 1*. Chiron Publications.

Hendrix, H. (1988). *Getting the love you want: A guide for couples*. Henry Holt and Company, Inc.

Hollis, J. (1998). *The Eden project: In search of the magical other*. Inner City Books.

Illouz, E. (1997). *Consuming the romantic utopia: Love and the cultural contradictions of capitalism*. University of California Press.

Johnson, R. (1983). *We: Understanding the psychology of romantic love*. HarperCollins.

Jung, C. G. (1966). The psychology of the transference (R. F. C. Hull, Trans.). In H. Read et al. (Eds.), *The collected works of C. G. Jung: Vol. 16. Practice of psychotherapy* (2nd ed., pp. 163–323). Princeton University Press. (Original work published 1946).

Jung, C. G. (1969a). Archetypes of the collective unconscious (R. F. C Hull, Trans.). In H. Read et al. (Eds.), *The collected works of C.G. Jung: Vol. 9 (part 1). The archetypes and the collective unconscious* (2nd ed., pp. 3–72). Princeton University Press. (Original work published 1934).

Jung, C. G. (1969b). Concerning the archetypes, with special reference to the anima concept (R. F. C Hull, Trans.). In H. Read et al. (Eds.), *The collected works of C.G. Jung: Vol. 9 (part 1). The archetypes and the collective unconscious* (2nd ed., pp. 54–72). Princeton University Press. (Original work published 1936).

Jung, C. G. (1969c). Conscious, unconscious, and individuation (R. F. C. Hull, Trans.). In H. Read et al. (Eds.), *The collected works of C.G. Jung: Vol. 9 (part 1). The archetypes and the collective unconscious* (2nd ed., pp. 275–289). Princeton University Press. (Original work published 1939).

Jung, C. G. (1974a). Aion: Phenomenology of the self. In J. Campbell (Ed.), *The portable Jung* (pp. 139–162). Viking Press. (Original work published 1951).

Jung, C. G. (1974b). Marriage as a psychological relationship. In J. Campbell (Ed.), *The portable Jung* (pp. 163–177). Viking Press. (Original work published 1925).

Jung, C. G. (1974c). On synchronicity. In J. Campbell (Ed.), *The portable Jung* (pp. 505–518). Viking Press. (Original work published 1952).

Jung, C. G. (2009). *The red book: Liber novus* (M. Kyburz, Trans.). W. W. Norton & Co.

Knee, C. R. (1998). Implicit theories of relationships: Assessment and prediction of romantic relationship initiation, coping, and longevity. *Journal of*

Personality and Social Psychology, 74(2), 360–370. https://doi.org/10.1037/0022-3514.74.2.360

Lu, K., & Yeoman, A. (2023). Jungian psycho-social studies: Akira, Greta Thunberg and archetypal thematic analysis (ATA). *International Journal of Jungian Studies, 16*(1), 77–112. https://doi.org/10.1163/19409060-bja10034

Main, R. (2004). *The rupture of time: Synchronicity and Jung's critique of modern western culture*. Brunner-Routledge.

Main, R. (2007). *Revelations of chance: Synchronicity as spiritual experience*. State University of New York Press.

Mauger, B. (2008). *Love in a time of broken heart: Healing from within*. .

Moore, T. (1994). *Soulmates: Honoring the mysteries of love and relationship*. HarperCollins Publishers, Inc.

Peck, M. S. (1978). *The road less traveled*. Simon & Schuster, Inc.

Plato. (1961). Apology. In E. Hamilton & H. Cairns (Eds.), *The collected dialogues of Plato including the letters* (pp. 3–26). Princeton University Press. (Original work published 399 B.C.E.).

Plato. (2003). *The symposium* (G. Gill, Trans.). Penguin. (Original work published 380 B.C.E.).

Rumi, J. A. D. (1995). *The essential Rumi* (C. Barks, Trans.). Penguin.

Samuels, A. (1985). *Jung and the post-Jungians*. Routledge.

Schierse-Leonard, L. (1986). *On the way to the wedding*. Shambala Publications, Inc.

Thomas, K. W. (2016). *Conscious uncoupling: 5 steps to living happily even after*. Harmony.

Twenge, J. M. (2023). *Generations: The real differences between gen z, millennials, gen x, boomers, and silence–and what they mean for America's future*. Simon & Schuster, Inc.

U.S Census Bureau. (2022, November 17). Census bureau releases new estimates on America's families and living arrangements. U.S. Department of Congress. *United States Census Bureau*. https://www.census.gov/newsroom/press-releases/2022/americas-families-and-living-arrangements.html#:~:text=Marriage%3A,20.5%2C%20respectively%2C%20in%201947

Whitmont, E. (1978). *The symbolic quest: Basic concepts of analytical psychology*. Princeton University Press.

CHAPTER 8

Anima and Animus in Jung's Time and Ours

Benjamin J. Swogger

In his 1925 seminar on analytical psychology, Jung related a moment that occurred while working on the second of his *Black Books*:

> I said to myself, "What is this I am doing, it certainly is not science, what is it?" Then a voice said to me, "That is art." This made the strangest sort of an impression on me, because it was not in any sense my conviction that what I was writing was art. Then I came to this, "Perhaps my unconscious is forming a personality that is not me, but which is insisting on coming through to expression." I don't know why exactly, but I knew to a certainty that the voice that had said my writing was art had come from a woman.[1] (Jung, 1989/2012, p. 45)

[1] In his retelling for *Memories, Dreams, Reflections*, Jung added: "I recognized it as the voice of a patient, a talented psychopath who had a strong transference to me. She had become a living figure within my mind" (Jung, 1961/1989b, p. 185; see also Shamdasani, 2026). Kerr (1993, pp. 505–507) had made the case that the woman in question was Sabina Spielrein, but two years later, on the basis of new evidence, Shamdasani (1995, pp. 128–129) offered the now generally accepted view that this was, in fact, Maria Moltzer.

B. J. Swogger (✉)
University of West Georgia, School of Social Sciences, Carrollton, GA, USA
e-mail: bs00067@my.westga.edu

J. J. Dillon (ed.), *Complex and Archetype*,
https://doi.org/10.1007/978-3-032-02609-5_8

The following lecture, he recounted:

> I was much interested in the fact that a woman should interfere with me from within. My conclusion was that it must be the soul in the primitive sense, and I began to speculate on the reasons that the name "anima" was given to the soul. (p. 49)

He continued:

> After this I began to work on the problem already ancient in the world, "Has woman a soul?" I decided she could not possibly have an anima, because then there would be no check on the woman from within. Then I came to the idea that woman must have an animus, but it was not till much later that I was able to develop this further because the animus is much harder to catch at work. (p. 50)

Thus were born the notions of anima and animus in analytical psychology—notions that were destined to become controversial. The aim of this chapter is to present the historical context of these controversies. It begins by examining the basis upon which modern critiques are staked, namely, Jung's use of typology in identifying anima and animus and his beliefs about the prevalence of thinking and feeling types by gender. It then summarizes three early attempts to investigate these concepts which became emblematic of the structure of subsequent critiques and highlights the work of James Hillman, whose reformulation remains in many ways the most important and influential. It concludes by returning to Jung's original theorizing to show that gendered assumptions, while present, were not, in fact, essential aspects of the first articulations of these notions. Given Jung's most fundamental definition of anima and animus as *functions of relationship* between consciousness and the unconscious, it questions whether the typological associations of *feeling* with *anima* and *thinking* with *animus* might be replaced by more accurately equating *intuition* with both. Ultimately it argues that efforts to modernize these two notions require not a radical revisioning but a return to their roots in Jung's own thought.

Anima and Animus as Inferior Function

Throughout the 1925 seminar, the theme of anima and animus preponderated. In addition to divulging the moment he first heard the voice of his anima—an episode included neither in the *Black Books* nor *Red Book*—Jung also disclosed that Miss Frank Miller, about whom he had written for *Transformations and Symbols of the Libido* (Jung, 1911–1912/1991; see also Shamdasani, 1990) and the biblical Salome, who populated certain of his visions from his *Black Books* and *Red Book*, had each been for him an "anima figure." Toward the end of the seminar, Jung assigned three books to be analyzed: two on the anima and one on the animus.[2] At the time, there would have been little mention of anima and animus in Jung's writings, as his major works on the topic had not yet been published. A concise essay titled "Shadow, Animus, and Anima" appeared in German only in 1948 and in English in 1950 prior to its incorporation as chapters two and three of *Aion* in 1951; the essay "Concerning the Archetypes, with Special Reference to the Anima Concept" first appeared only in 1936; and although Jung's first formulations of anima and animus appear to have been added to the German manuscript of his 1916 lecture "The Structure of the Unconscious" (see below; see also Jung, 1916/1966c, p. 295, n. 21 and p. 269, n. 1), these were included neither in the French translation of 1916 nor the English of 1917. It was not until the major revision of 1928 that anima and animus occupied their now-familiar central position in "The Relation Between the Ego and the Unconscious," which formed the second of *Two Essays on Analytical Psychology* (Jung, 1928). Thus, in 1925 the primary reference for anima and animus would have been the definition given for "soul" in *Psychological Types* in 1921 (German) and 1923 (English).

That *Psychological Types* would have been an important precursor in this regard seems fitting since, at the time of the seminar, the spirit of that work was still very much alive. Despite Jung's narration in the seminar and elsewhere (e.g., Jung 1961/1989b, p. 207) that the type problem was born out of his attempt to reconcile differences between his own ideas with those of Freud and Adler, it clearly also had origins in the association

[2] Jung had originally proposed three books on the anima: H. Rider Haggard's *She*, Pierre Benoît's *L'Atlantide* [Atlantis], and Gustav Meyrink's *Das grüne Gesicht* [The Green Face]. The seminar notes record that upon the suggestion of the class that one of these be an animus novel, Jung substituted Meyrink's work for Marie Hay's *The Evil Vineyard*. For an analysis of all four novels, see Fike (2020).

procedure.[3] In "The Associations of Normal Subjects" published with Franz Riklin throughout 1904, two primary "types" were identified, which, when divided into subtypes, yielded six in total. The "objective" type responded to the stimulus word by adding something objective, based either on an associated verbal connection or something essential to the word's meaning. The "egocentric attitude," on the other hand, particularly the "predicate type,"[4] reacted "from a personal point of view"—that is, with "an unusually strong personal participation, which leads to a constant evaluation of the object, usually with reference to *herself* [emphasis added]" (Jung & Riklin, 1904/1973, pp. 161–162). This translation liberty of Jung and Riklin's otherwise neutral wording of "one's own person" [*die eigene Person*] was, it turned out, not entirely without merit.

Upon analyzing sex differences in word association under normal conditions, Jung and Riklin were at first "struck by the slightness of the difference between the two sexes" (p. 163). After, however, comparing results under distracted conditions, this no longer held. Under the condition of external distraction,[5] the number of predicate responses decreased to a lesser degree in woman than men. In other words, even under distracted conditions, the tendency of women to supply predicate responses to the stimulus words remained. Jung and Riklin hypothesized that predicate responses likely owed to "the primary, sensory vividness of the stimulus images" (p. 168). "It is therefore understandable," they added, "that with the vividness of the inner images, not only does the number of internal predicates increase but also the number of subjective value judgments generally—that is, of egocentric reactions" (p. 178). Although theoretically they concluded that they had "no reason to assume that the inner images are in general fundamentally more vivid in women than in men"

[3] In his 1948 address on the occasion of the founding of the C. G. Jung Institute in Zurich, Jung confirmed this connection, reflecting that his work on the association tests "led directly to the discovery of the *feeling-toned complex*, and indirectly to a new question, namely, the problem of *attitude*, which exerts a decisive influence upon the association reaction. ... From these researches there emerged a *psychological typology*, which distinguished two-attitude-types, the extravert and the introvert, and four function-types corresponding to the four orienting functions of consciousness" (Jung, 1948/1976a, p. 471).

[4] Five years later, in his Clark University lectures of 1909, Jung referred to this as the "evaluating predicate-type" (Jung 1909/1973b, p. 439).

[5] As against internal distraction, which was achieved by instructing subjects to concentrate on the visual images that arose upon hearing the stimulus words, external distraction was achieved by instructing subjects to make pencil marks to the beat of a metronome. On the role of distraction in the association experiments, see Swogger and Dillon (2023).

(p. 178), empirically they assessed that "there are relatively very many predicate types among the women" (p. 168).

By 1921, it was clear that the "objective type" and the "evaluating predicate-type" formed the rudiments of what became the thinking and feeling functions that Jung had introduced in *Psychological Types*. There, he was less equivocal than he had been years earlier with Riklin. "As feeling is undeniably a more obvious characteristic of feminine psychology than thinking," he averred, "the most pronounced feeling types are to be found among women" (Jung, 1921/1971, p. 356). In the "Definitions" chapter, Jung explained that "the anima…is, by and large, *complementary* to the character of the persona."[6] That is, "the anima usually contains all those common human qualities which the conscious attitude lacks." For example, "if the persona is intellectual, the anima will quite certainly be sentimental" (p. 468). Vis-à-vis masculine and feminine psychology, therefore, Jung stated:

> Whereas logic and objectivity are usually predominant features of a man's outer attitude, or are at least regarded as ideals, in the case of a woman it is feeling. But in the soul it is the other way round: inwardly it is the man who feels, and the woman who reflects. (p. 469)

Thus was made the connection between *anima* and *feeling* and *animus* and *thinking* on the basis of presumed gender differences. Four years later, in the 1925 seminar, Jung demonstrated the utility of these associations for interpretive work.

In his candid reflection on the role of his book *Transformations and Symbols of the Libido* in his life, Jung told his audience that his analysis of the fantasies of a young American woman represented nothing other than the analysis of his *own* unconscious processes. Recalling the book's opening chapter on "two kinds of thinking," the "fantastical" or "impure" thinking demonstrated by Miss Miller was precisely that which was underdeveloped in Jung—in the language of *Types*, it was his *inferior function*. "I took Miss Miller's fantasies as such an autonomous form of thinking," Jung shared, "but I did not realize that she stood for that form of thinking in myself. … In other words, she became an anima figure, a carrier of an

[6] As noted by the editors of the *Collected Works* (Jung 1921/1971, p. 467, n. 80) "anima" has been given here for Jung's use of *Seele* in the German original. The Baynes translation has "soul" (Jung, 1923, p. 594).

inferior function of which I was very little conscious" (Jung, 1989/2012, p. 28). Similarly, Jung gave account of a biblically laden vision that derived from his *Red Book* experiences years earlier. "I could see two people," he recounted, "an old man with a white beard and a young girl who was very beautiful. ... The old man said he was Elijah and I was quite shocked, but she was even more upsetting because she was Salome" (p. 69). Elijah Jung took to be his developed thinking function, Salome his unconscious feeling. A third element, a black snake, Jung took to be sensation. Referencing Salome's blindness, he indicated: "As I am an introverted intellectual my anima contains feeling [that is] quite blind. In my case the anima contains not only Salome, but some of the serpent, which is sensation as well" (p. 100; original brackets). In more general terms, Jung suggested that "Elijah is the personification of the cognitive element, Salome of the erotic. ... One could speak of these two figures as personifications of Logos and Eros very specifically shaped" (p. 97).[7]

The effect of the preceding developments was such that, by 1925, the precedent was set that masculine consciousness, typically identified with the thinking function, was the carrier of Logos, while the unconscious anima, the undifferentiated feeling function, carried Eros. Likewise, feminine consciousness, identified with the feeling function, was the carrier of Eros, while the unconscious animus, the undeveloped thinking function, carried Logos. This interpretive principle was most evident years later in another of Jung's seminars in English. From October 1930 to March 1934, Jung delivered lectures for the so-called *Visions* seminar in which he analyzed the fantasies of an American woman, Christiana Morgan.[8] He introduced her as follows:

> Our patient is a woman of about thirty years of age. She is highly educated, very intelligent, a typical intellectual, with an almost mathematical mind. She is a natural scientist by education and exceedingly rational. She has a great deal of intuition, which really ought to function but is repressed because it yields irrational results, and that is very disagreeable to the rational mind. ... People with such one-sided development of their thinking function have on the other side an inferior feeling function, because feeling

[7] Shamdasani points out that in *Liber Novus* Jung interpreted Elijah and Salome as forethinking and pleasure, respectively. In commentaries estimated to have been added sometime in the 1920s (and therefore in close proximity to this seminar), he interpreted them as Logos and Eros, as here (see Jung, 1989/2012, p. 97, n. 8).

[8] On Morgan, see Douglas (1993).

is opposite to thinking. The feeling is then archaic and has all the advantages and disadvantages of an archaic function. (Jung, 1997, p. 6)

By Jung's own definition, therefore, as a thinking-intuitive type guided by rationality, Morgan's relatedness and feeling function, as "archaic" and unconscious, would be carried by her animus. Yet throughout the seminar, Jung repeatedly interpreted Morgan's animus figures as her inferior opinionating, since, as he told his audience: "her own mind, or the Logos function, [as] in a woman's case is always an autonomous content of the collective unconscious; as relatedness in man, the eros function, is a content of the collective unconscious to begin with" (p. 570). It was precisely this disregard for the letter of his own theory that would be primary target for critics.

Three Contemporary Works

In her introduction to the *Visions* seminar, Claire Douglas (1997) drew attention to the "painful" discrepancy in Jung's treatment of Morgan's psychological material. "If Jung had kept in mind Morgan the intuitive thinker who was developing her feeling through the visions," she declared, "he would not have lumped her into a category of traditional, extraverted, feeling woman. The man who had written *Psychological Types* clearly knew better." Instead, by insisting that Morgan's animus figures served Logos rather than Eros, Jung, Douglas suggested, seemed "to be playing to an audience with collective expectations rather than hewing to the rigor of his own unique approach to psychological reality" (p. xxvi). Such issues were treated in Douglas' book *Woman in the Mirror* (1990) published seven years earlier. Upon its release, she joined the ranks of those who called into question the assumptions underlying Jung's theory of the contrasexual archetypes. The quest to more deeply explore the anima and animus had, however, begun much earlier.

In Jung's time, it was his wife, Emma, who first took on the task of explicating the animus in a fashion not only *similar* to that for which Jung did the anima, but one that *prefigured* it. In his 1946 book *The Psychology of the Transference* (Jung, 1946/1966a; see also Wallace, 2024), Jung ended his introductory chapter with a concise description of what he called "erotic phenomenology," a depiction of "the heterosexual Eros or anima-figure in four stages" (Jung, 1946/1966a, p. 174). It correlated, presumably, to a man's psychological development. The first stage was personified by Hawwah, or Eve, and was symbolized by earth and characterized by a biological relationship in which woman was equated with the mother and represented "something to be fertilized." The second stage was personified by Helen of Troy, and while still characterized by the sexual component of Eros, it was raised to "an aesthetic and romantic level where woman has already acquired some value as an individual." The third stage was personified by the Virgin Mary and thus represented a spiritualization akin to "religious devotion." The fourth stage was personified by Sophia, or *Sapienta*, a wisdom transcendent to even that which was most holy. While in the third stage, Jung clarified, "Hawwah has been replaced by spiritual motherhood," in the fourth there is "a spiritualization of Helen and consequently of Eros as such" (p. 174).[9]

Twelve years prior to this, in 1934,[10] Emma Jung had published an essay on the animus in which she identified four stages of animus development corresponding to a woman's psychic maturity. "Just as there are men of outstanding physical power, men of deeds, men of words, and men of wisdom," she stated, "so too does the animus image differ in accordance with the woman's particular stage of development or her natural gifts" (Jung, 1957, p. 3). The first stage, typified by animus figures of physical prowess, was seen primarily in young women, "primitive" women, or "the primitive in every woman" and was often personified by sportsmen, cowboys, or bullfighters. The second stage represented a subtle development in which the animus figure became a "man who accomplishes deeds," insofar as this meant that "he directs his power toward something of great significance." Given the mutuality of power and action, shifts in the animus figure from the first to second stages were usually difficult to catch but could be discerned by the type of woman giving him form, as the second stage was reserved "for more exacting women." The third stage, involving "words" or "meaning," corresponded to men of great intellectual capacity and was accordingly personified as such. The fourth and final stage involved wisdom and was therefore often depicted as a figure of great spiritual significance. "Such a man," Emma wrote, "exemplifies the animus in the narrower sense, understood as being a spiritual guide..."

[9] Jung's "erotic phenomenology" was popularized by its inclusion in Marie-Louise von Franz's chapter for *Man and His Symbols* (von Franz, 1964, p. 185) in which it appeared nearly verbatim to the passage in *The Psychology of the Transference*.

[10] An earlier version of this essay was read to the Zurich Psychological Club in 1931, which was, coincidentally, during the time of Jung's *Visions* seminar.

(p. 4). Insofar as Jung's and Emma's four-stage developmental schemas both began with instinctually and culminated in wisdom, they bore a remarkable, if unsurprising, resemblance.

In 1934, the same year as the publication of Emma Jung's essay on the animus, Toni Wolff likewise delivered a lecture to the Zurich psychological club and took up the notion of feminine typology that Jung had hinted at years earlier. In his 1925 seminar, Jung told his audience that he thought of women "as belonging in general to two types, the mother and the hetaira." He offered no detail other than his addendum that "the hetaira type acts as the mother for the other [i.e., unconscious] side of men's thinking" (Jung, 1989/2012, p. 34). Two years later he developed this further in his 1927 essay "Mind and Earth" (Jung, 1931/1970).[11] There, he suggested that once the *participation mystique* with one's parents began to dissolve, the parental imagos were supplanted in importance by the anima or animus, which then drove the individual toward new, non-incestuous love objects. But, Jung cautioned, "the more a man or women is unconsciously influenced by the parental imago, the more surely will the figure of the loved one be chosen as either a positive or a negative substitute for the parents" (p. 38). This presumably referred to the "mother" type of woman, one who then replaced the man's unconscious relationship to his actual mother. On the other hand, Jung contrasted, when the archetype of the anima outweighed in importance the parental imago, the love choice was of an entirely different sort. "The most striking feature about the anima-type," Jung offered, "is that the maternal element is entirely lacking. She is the companion and friend in her favourable aspect, in her unfavourable aspect she is the courtesan" (p. 39). This was the hetaira, the second of Jung's two types.

It was upon this foundation that Toni Wolff worked out her four "structural forms" of the feminine psyche. For while the "erotic phenomenology" that Jung would work out years later depicted the development of a man's anima—in other words, his *own* relationship to the unconscious and to the feminine here he offered what amounted to a *typology of woman*. And while Wolff acknowledged that her four forms also

[11] Although these two types only appeared in Jung's writing in sketchy form in 1927, he began his comments to the 1925 seminar audience by saying: "*As you know* [emphasis added] I think of women as belonging in general to two types…" (Jung, 1989/2012, p. 34), indicating that these ideas may have been more a part of the oral tradition of analytical psychology than the written one.

corresponded to the male anima, it was the typological aspect with which she primarily dealt.[12]

Two of Wolff's forms corresponded to Jung's: the *mother* and the *hetaira*. To these she added the *Amazon* and *medial* woman The mother was, naturally, nurturing and protective and was most fulfilled when involved in a relationship in which she could express these qualities. She tended to what was un- or underdeveloped in another, cared for it, and created the space and security for its growth. In its negative aspect, the mother was prone to "anxious nursing" and could even interfere with the development of the cared-for with overzealousness. The hetaira, as companion, was a *femmes inspiratrices*, and as such was "instinctively related to the personal psychology of the male" (Wolff, 1956, p. 7). She awakened in him values and aptitudes that lay dormant, leading him through to a fuller realization of his personality upon which her own development depended. On the shadow side, the hetaira was in danger of overlooking the practical aspects of reality, of inciting too much creativity in a man, and in this way becoming "a temptress...[a] Circe instead of Calypso" (p. 8). The amazon, as a woman in relationship not to human objects but to cultural values, was self-contained and independent of the male because her development did not depend on her relationship to one. She did not *adopt* the male's values since these were already her *own* values. She was driven by objective achievement and, on the positive side, was viewed by men as a comrade; on the negative side, she could appear as the sister of the male, driven by "masculine protest" to be his equal only never to be recognized as such. Lastly, the medial woman, Wolff pointed out, was not to be taken as the "common medium," as this represented merely "its lowest, i.e. most unconscious level" (p. 11). Rather, the medial woman existed *in between* worlds yet was in neither one of them fully. She was attuned to her immediate psychic environment but also the demands of the time. Most of all, she was immersed in the collective unconscious and driven to express it. In this way, she easily became the carrier of the anima for men but just as easily lost herself in it, since handling contents of the collective

[12]Wolff addressed the difference between "form" and "type" in an endnote, writing: "Instead of 'structural form' one might just as well use the term 'structural types' since the meaning is that of imprinting or 'typification', i.e. an abstraction of individual qualities into a formal denominator of common characteristics. But in view of the fact that the concept of types in Analytical Psychology...has by now its classic application, it may prevent conceptual confusion, if the term structural forms is used throughout" (Wolff, 1956, p. 16).

unconscious required a strong ego and adaptation to reality. To the extent that the medial woman had neither, her whole personality was overtaken.[13]

Toni Wolff, like Emma Jung, had taken an aspect of Jung's thinking on anima and animus and greatly expanded it, bringing female psychology more firmly under its purview. A third contribution, appearing at roughly the same time, came in the form of M. Esther Harding's *Woman's Mysteries: Ancient and Modern* published in 1935.[14] Its subtitle added for the 1955 edition, *A Psychological Interpretation of the Feminine Principle as Portrayed in Myth, Story, and Dreams* (Harding, 1935/1955), spoke to its emphasis not just on anima and animus, or even feminine psychology, but the feminine *principle*, what Rowland (2002) later called "something metaphysical" (p. 54). Harding's analysis was, in effect, an analysis of *Eros itself.*

Thus, with these three early works, three different ways of approaching gender studies in analytical psychology were championed, and nearly all subsequent work on the topic fits into one of these three categories. There are those who, like Emma Jung, address the topic of anima and animus directly; those who, like Toni Wolff, investigate the female psyche, or what it means to be a woman; and those who, like Esther Harding, target the feminine principle, or femininity as such. Samuels (1985, pp. 168–186) has surveyed much of this literature, and both Roesler (2016/2022, pp. 26–30) and Williams (2019, pp. 163–169) offer more recent summaries, but the most comprehensive treatment of modern critiques can be found in Douglas (1990) and Rowland (2002), the latter of which is, in many ways, still the central text on Jung and feminism. In it, James Hillman emerges as perhaps the most important and influential of modern reformers, a point which Rowland confirmed in 2011 by referring to Hillman as "the most significant and far-reaching developer of Jung's legacy" regarding gender (Rowland, 2011, p. 175). Given that Hillman

[13] For more on Toni Wolff's four "structural forms," see Molton and Sikes (2011).

[14] For the German translation *Frauen-Mysterien* published in 1949, Jung contributed a foreword in which he, as elsewhere, expressed beliefs in line with those that would later come under criticism for perpetuating prevailing social conditions. He wrote: "When, for instance, a woman develops too masculine an attitude—something that may very easily happen owing to the social emancipation of women today—the unconscious compensates this one-sidedness by a symptomatic accentuation of certain feminine traits. … But if more profound disturbances should occur, as when a women [*sic*] alienates herself from her husband through her insistence on always being in the right, then archetypal figures appear on the scene" (Jung, 1949/1976b, p. 520).

based his revisioning of anima/animus theory on a careful reading of Jung's own texts, his work warrants further consideration.

A Personified Notion

Originally published in two installments in *Spring* in 1973 and 1974, Hillman's two-part essay on the anima—slightly revised and repackaged as a book in 1985 (Hillman, 1985)—investigated not the *experience* of anima, as he acknowledged had been Jung's primary contribution, but the *notion* of anima—a *personified* notion. His formula was simple. Hillman collected and presented Jung's miscellaneous writings on anima and animus—some 500 in all—and offered commentary commensurate with his project of his "revisioning" analytical psychology. The first and perhaps most important point Hillman made, considering that the title of his essay privileged the anima, was that it was not a work for or about men. Rather, Hillman challenged the contrasexual orthodoxy of anima and animus, arguing that their assignment along biological lines resulted simply from Jung's allegiance to the "yoke of opposites" (p. 55). Depriving women of anima was no less consequential, Hillman suggested, than the theory of "penis deprivation" had been for psychoanalysis:

> [Woman] is no more blessed with a congenially saved soul than man who must pass his life in worry over its fate. She is no more exonerated from the tasks of anima cultivation than man; for her to neglect soul for the sake of spirit is no less psychologically reprehensible than it is in man who is ever being told by analytical psychology that he must sacrifice intellect, persona, and extraversion for the sake of feeling, inwardness, i.e., anima. (p. 61)

For Hillman, anima and animus, as soul and spirit, when not personified as *images*, were *archetypes-in-themselves*[15] and "as such cannot be attributed to or located within the psyche of either sex" (p. 53). Anima and animus were, therefore, available to all.

Anima, moreover, could be equated neither with Eros nor the feeling function. *Anima* and *psyche*, Hillman pointed out, had more to do

[15] Here, Hillman drew upon Jung's distinction made as early as 1946 between the *archetypal image* and the *archetype-in-itself*: "The archetypal representations (images and ideas) mediated to us by the unconscious should not be confused with the archetype-in-itself [*Archetypus an sich*] … [which] is not capable of being made conscious" (Jung, 1954/1969c, p. 213; translation modified).

linguistically and phenomenologically with air and breath than fire and desire. To conflate soul and Eros was an entirely Venusian perspective—Eros *only* as Aphrodite's son—one that lost sight of the Socratic/Platonic Eros (from where Jung took the expression[16]) which was definitively masculine. Likewise, just as eros was its own archetypal principle not to be delimited to anima or animus, feeling was a function of consciousness not to be confused with the function of the anima. For while Hillman recognized Jung's earliest and most fundamental definition of anima as a *function of relationship*—as Hillman put it, a relationship "between personal and collective, between actualities and beyond, between the individual conscious horizon and the primordial realm of the imaginal"—he observed that "anima as function of relationship is far indeed from relatedness [itself]" (p. 39).

But for all the time spent severing anima from what he perceived to be problematical notions, Hillman also crafted what anima *was*. Anima, as a function of relationship to interiority, was characterized by inwardness:

> Anima is inward (hence "closed" and called "virginal" in religious and poetic metaphors of the soul), devoted, yet labile, generous and generative, yet reserved (shy, shameful, retreating, pure, veiled – these latter qualities presented by the virgin nymphs and Goddesses such as Maria or Artemis). To this interiority belongs a movement of deepening downward (caves, deeps, graves) which in the phenomenology of Kore-Persephone connects her with the realm of the underworld. (p. 23)

Accordingly, for Hillman, "anima stays close to [the] field of the natural unconscious mind" (p. 25). That is, "anima is the reflective partner; she it is who provides the moment of reflection in the midst of what is naturally given. She is the *psychic factor in nature* [emphasis added], an idea formulated in the last century as 'animism'" (p. 23). Hillman thus connected anima to Jung's notion of the "reflective instinct"[17] and, by the end of the

[16] In a 1947 letter (in English) to Erminie Huntress Lantero, Jung wrote: "Of course, I did not invent the term Eros. I learnt it from Plato. But I never would have applied this term if I hadn't observed facts that gave me a hint of how to use this Platonic notion" (Jung, 1973a, p. 465).

[17] In a lecture delivered (in English) at Harvard in 1936, Jung identified five groups of instincts: hunger, sexuality, activity, reflection, and creativity. Regarding the penultimate one, Jung stated: "Through the reflective instinct [originally: "reflection-urge"], the stimulus is more or less wholly transformed into a psychic content, that is, it becomes an experience: *a*

first part of his essay, arrived at the conclusion that psyche itself derives from such anima reflection. Quoting Jung's selection from "A Psychological Approach to the Dogma of the Trinity" that "through reflection, 'life' and its 'soul' are abstracted from Nature and endowed with a separate existence" (Jung, 1948/1969a, p. 158), Hillman proclaimed:

> The archetype of both life and soul as distinct from 'only Nature' (procreative, biological Mother Nature) is anima, so that she would be that archetype which both performs the abstraction through reflection and personifies the life and soul in a reflected form. *Anima is nature now conscious of itself through reflection* [emphasis added]. (Hillman, 1985, p. 87)

As such, anima became what Jung called the "projection-making factor"[18]—not the projection *itself* but the process that *forms* it. Anima was, therefore, at once the process by which nature works and, when personified, that which revealed it.

Thus, in Part I of his essay, Hillman accomplished his task of arriving at a conceptual notion of anima that could be deduced from Jung's own. Although he parsed out animus as spirit as against anima's soul, he ended with a notion of anima remarkably congruent to those of Jung's earliest articulations of both. In typical Hillman fashion, however, just as quickly as he arrived at his conclusions he wriggled his way out of them. In Part II, he rejected two key corollaries following from the understanding of anima as a function of relationship between consciousness and the unconscious: (a) that the anima, as function, could in some sense be integrated into the personality; and (b) that, when personified, the anima served as *mediatrix* or *psychopomp*, a harbinger of psychological growth that helped one along one's way. Hillman's dismissal was part and parcel of his broader stance against the "myth" of individuation—a myth, he claimed, which *personalized* by centering on the ego rather than the plurality of the imaginal. By his own admission, Hillman was not engaged in historical research in his *Anima* book and was therefore more interested in *de*construction than construction. Nevertheless, by the end of Part I, he offered a historically accurate account of Jung's early thinking on anima and

natural process is transformed into a conscious content [emphasis added]" (Jung, 1937/1969d, p. 117).

[18] "What, then, is this projection-making factor? The East calls it the 'Spinning Woman'—Maya, who creates illusions by her dancing" (Jung, 1951/1968, p. 11). "The projection-making factor is the anima, or rather the unconscious as represented by the anima" (p. 13).

animus as notions that might have fared better had they continued to develop along these initial lines—lines which included less gendered assumptions, more emphasis on intuition than feeling and thinking, and greater affinity with such linguistic parallels as *animal* and *animate* than ad hoc associations of eros and logos. In what follows, a closer look at Jung's original theorizing serves to evaluate the strength of this claim.

Anima and Animus as Functions of the Psyche

When the missing German urtext that had evidently been the basis for both the French and English translations of Jung's 1916 lecture "The Structure of the Unconscious" was posthumously found, it contained a number of revisions and additions which, the editors of the *Collected Works* report, were "in a later hand of the author's" (Jung, 1916/1966c, p. 269, n. 1). Among them was a rudimentary depiction of anima and animus. Given that this was less developed than Jung's treatment of "soul" and "soul-image" in *Psychological Types*, it would therefore appear that the addendum to the 1916 manuscript represents Jung's very first articulations of these notions. In it, Jung defined the anima in relation to the *persona*, which in the original text he equated with "mask" and defined as that piece of the collective psyche annexed as one's individuality. In the addendum, he clarified that the persona "occupies a place midway between the real world and individuality [i.e., the ego or 'I']" (p. 298). The *other* side of the ego, that is, "the place between the individual and the collective unconscious, corresponding to the persona's position between the individual and external reality," Jung wrote, "appears to be empty." He continued:

> Experience has taught me, however, that here too a kind of persona exists, but a persona of a compensatory nature which (in a man) could be called the *anima*. The anima would thus be a compromise formation between the individual and the unconscious world, that is, the world of images, or "primordial images." (p. 299)

In other words, anima was "the function of relationship to the collective unconscious" (p. 299).

Here, at the inception of these seminal notions, despite Jung's recognition that, in dreams, the anima "appears as a feminine being in a man, and as a man (*animus*) in a woman," and in projection, "is regularly to be found…in the woman we are in love with" (p. 299), primacy was given to the anima's role as mediator between the individual and the unconscious, as the gendered aspects were left out of the second, revised summary in which the anima was defined as follows:

> The anima is an unconscious subject-imago analogous to the persona. Just as the persona is the image of himself which the subject presents to the world, and which is seen by the world, so the anima is the image of the subject in his relation to the collective unconscious, or an expression of the unconscious collective contents unconsciously constellated by him. One could also say: the anima is the face of the subject as seen by the collective unconscious. (p. 304)

By the time these notions found their way into *Psychological Types*, Jung's thinking was mired in opposites[19]—a characterization to which the entire structure of the book attests. In addition to dichotomies of nominalism versus realism, naïve versus sentimental poetry, the Apollonian versus the Dionysian, and no less than eight pairs of opposites in William James' distinction between tender-minded versus tough-minded types, there was also antagonism in the form of the figures Origen and Tertullian, Luther and Zwingli, Prometheus and Epimetheus—not to mention the opposites inherent to Jung's typology: extraversion and introversion, thinking and feeling, sensation and intuition, rational and irrational. It should, therefore, come as little surprise that when it came to the definition of "soul" and "soul-image," Jung emphasized not just the opposition

[19] Part of Jung's affinity for opposites, especially as they related to the soul, seemingly had to do with his experiencing his own soul as a child and a maiden in *Liber Primus*. In the second, interpretive layer of his entry for 14 November 1913 (see Shamdasani, 2009, p. 203), which would have occurred around the time of his first interaction with his anima as reported in 1925 (see above), he recorded: "…the spirit of the depths teaches me that I am a servant, in fact the servant of a child. This dictum was repugnant to me and I hated it. But I had to recognize and accept that my soul is a child and that my God in my soul is a child. / *If you are boys, your God is a woman. / If you are women, your God is a boy. / If you are men, your God is a maiden. / The God is where you are not*" (Jung, 2009, p. 234). See also Jung's use of opposites vis-à-vis sexuality in the privately circulated *Septem Sermones ad Mortuos* [Seven Sermons to the Dead] where he iterated: "The sexuality of man is more of the earth, the sexuality of woman is more of the spirit. / The spirituality of man is more of heaven, it goeth to the greater. / The spirituality of woman is more of the earth, it goeth to the smaller. / Lying and devilish is the spirituality of the man which goeth to the smaller. / Lying and devilish is the spirituality of the woman which goeth to the greater. / Each must go to its own place" (Jung, 1916/1989a, p. 387).

between consciousness and the unconscious but so too male and female. As a compensatory structure to the persona, the anima necessarily contained those elements that the persona lacked; an intellectual persona yielded a sentimental anima. But this also applied, Jung affirmed, to the "sexual character." That is, "a very feminine woman has a masculine soul, and a very masculine man has a feminine soul" (Jung, 1921/1971, pp. 468–469). The soul, moreover, was *more* masculine or *more* feminine to the same degree that the persona was exaggerated in the opposite direction, and this gave rise to those of Jung's oft-criticized assessments that, for instance, it was "just those very virile men…[whose] unconscious has a womanish weakness and impressionability" (p. 469).

Nevertheless, Jung also showed that one could account for such "weakness and impressionability" without any reference to one's being "womanish." Just as one was related to the *external* world via the persona, one was related to the *internal* world via the soul. It was this inner relation that was responsible for "those vague, dim stirrings, feelings, thoughts, and sensations which…well up like a disturbing, inhibiting, or at times helpful, influence from the dark inner depths." As a result:

> All those allegedly accidental inhibitions, fancies, moods, vague feelings, and scraps of fantasy that hinder concentration and disturb the peace of mind even of the most normal man, and that are rationalized away as being due to bodily causes and suchlike, usually have their origin, not in the reasons consciously ascribed to them, but in the perceptions of unconscious processes. (p. 466)

The gendered assumptions often attending to Jung's attributions of "anima moods" and "animus opinionating" were, therefore, hermeneutical additions, interpretive layers, added ex post facto but inessential to their basic meaning.[20]

Furthermore, it was clear from Jung's entry for "soul-image," that when a real person in one's life represented one's soul, it signified a case of the psychological mechanism of projection, as in those instances of "an impassioned, almost magical, relationship…between the sexes" (p. 471).

[20] In the Baynes translation of Jung's 1928 essay "The Relation Between the Ego and the Unconscious," Jung wrote that "the very sensitive feeling life" of "very masculine men" was "often incorrectly described as 'womanish' [*weiblich*]" (Jung, 1928, p. 203). This serves as further proof that Jung could slip in and out of using gender stereotypes to describe the role of anima and animus without fundamentally altering their meaning.

The choice of image, however, and all the associated masculinity or femininity of its carrier, was not to be confused with the soul *itself*, as Jung made clear in his warning that "that the *imago* should not be assumed to be identical with the object; it is better to regard it as an image of the *subjective relation* [emphasis added] to the object" (p. 473). In the case of the soul, the object in question vis-à-vis the image (the first use of "object") was both the individual onto whom it was projected and the unconscious itself. But the object in question vis-à-vis one's subjective relation (the second use of "object") was only the unconscious. Put simply, the soul-image, or anima figure, was not to be confused with the soul per se; this figure was a *symbol* of one's soul, which is to say, a symbol of one's relation to the collective unconscious. The theme of anima and animus as a *function of relationship* would feature in Jung's next major piece of writing on the topic.

By the time of the major revision of "The Structure of the Unconscious" into "The Relations Between the Ego and the Unconscious," the addendum to the original German manuscript had been greatly expanded and included as Part II of essay which included a lengthy and detailed chapter on anima and animus. There, Jung attributed three sources for the feminine nature of the soul: woman's presentation to man as biological and psychological "other," man's repressed femininity, and the archetype, or "inherited collective image of woman" that existed in man's unconscious (Jung, 1928/1966b, p. 190).[21] This archetype, moreover, with all his associated historicity and immortality, was especially constellated to the degree that there existed an "overvaluation of the material object without" (p. 192)—a condition, Jung suggested, which resulted from the "thoroughly extraverted attitude of the Western mind" (p. 191). As a result:

> It would be entirely logical, if by deepening that neglected, introverted side of our spiritual culture [*Geisteskultur*], there were to take place in us a transformation more akin to the Eastern frame of mind [*Geistesart*], where the quality of immortality would transfer itself from the ambiguous figure of the soul (anima) to the Self. (pp. 191–192)

[21] Unless otherwise noted (see, e.g., the preceding note) quotations to this essay are taken from the *Collected Works* (Jung, 1928/1966b). The Baynes volume (Jung, 1928) has been consulted, and where significant or interesting discrepancies exist between translations, the original German is given in brackets.

This then led to his assessment that "in the Eastern view the concept of the anima, as we have stated it here, is entirely lacking" (p. 192).

That by "Eastern" Jung meant "Chinese" was apparent in three ways. First, he opened the essay by alluding to the moralization and institutionalization of the "universal incidence of the ancestor cult" (p. 188) in China. Second, just a few paragraphs after his comment on the lack of the anima in the East, he quoted Lao Tzu. Most importantly, in his discussion of the necessity of adapting oneself to both outer and inner worlds, he lamented:

> Unfortunately, our Western mind, lacking all culture in this respect, has never yet devised a concept, nor even a name, for the *union of opposites through the middle path*, that most fundamental item of inward experience, which could respectably be set against the Chinese concept of Tao.[22] It is at once the most individual fact and the most universal, the most legitimate fulfilment of the meaning of the individual's life.[23] (p. 205)

The implication, therefore, was that the Eastern emphasis on interiority obviated the personification of the anima since there was a more direct line to the Self. This was indicated, Jung intimated the following year in his commentary to *The Secret of the Golden Flower* (Jung, 1938/1967a), by the prevalence of mandalas in the East. The West, by way of contrast, with its characteristic extraversion, necessitated a confrontation with the anima on one's way to realization of the Self. The process began by recognizing

[22] Jung reiterated this point in greater detail in his 1929 commentary on *The Secret of the Golden Flower*, in which, despite equating anima with the Chinese character *po* and eros, and animus with *hun* and logos, he again defined the anima as a "bridge" and a "function of relationship to the unconscious" (Jung, 1938/1967a, p. 42). In his preface to the 1935 edition of "The Relations Between the Ego and the Unconscious," Jung advised that "the reader will find a development of the last chapter, [with reference to the concept of the self], in my commentary to *The Secret of the Golden Flower*" (Jung, 1928/1966b, p. 124; original brackets). That this was so seems fitting since, as Shamdasani (2009) notes, both "The Relations Between the Ego and the Unconscious" and its precursor "The Structure of the Unconscious" represented efforts to map the individuation process as Jung had experienced it in his *Red Book* visions, and it was the *Golden Flower* text that brought these visions to a close. As Jung wrote in his epilogue to the *Liber Novus*: "The beginning of the end [of my work on the Red Book] came in 1928 when [Richard] Wilhelm sent me the text of the 'Golden Flower'" (Jung, 2009, p. 360).

[23] For the last two words, Baynes and Baynes (Jung, 1928, p. 225) have "living creature" [*lebendigen Wesens*], an important distinction given that Jung explicitly extended the principle of Tao to the animal kingdom and equated it with instinct (see below).

the anima's objectivity and autonomy as a distinct psychic entity. The individual than dialogued with this figure—as part of a process Jung called the *transcendent function*—and, he claimed, "to the degree that the patient takes an active part, the personified figure of anima or animus will disappear" (Jung, 1928/1966b, p. 224). In its place arose the "mana-personality" or "magician"—in women, the "Great Mother"—a figure more befitting of a personification of the Self. As a result, one achieved "the conquest of the anima as an autonomous complex and her transformation into a function of relationship between conscious and the unconscious—"a psychological function," Jung added, "of an *intuitive nature* [emphasis added]" (p. 227). At the end of his chapter on animus and animus, he summarized:

> These two crepuscular figures from the dark hinterland of the psyche… inhabit the twilight sphere, and we can just make out that the autonomous complex of anima and animus is essentially a psychological function that has usurped, or rather retained, a "personality" only because this function is itself autonomous and undeveloped. But already we can see how it is possible to break up the personification, since by making them conscious *we convert them into bridges to the unconscious* [emphasis added]. It is because we are not using them purposefully as functions that they remain personified complexes. So long as they are in this state they must be accepted as relatively independent personalities. They cannot be integrated into consciousness while their contents remain unknown. The purpose of the dialectical process is to bring these contents into the light; and only when this task has been completed, and the conscious mind has become sufficiently familiar with the unconscious processes reflected in the anima, *will the anima be felt simply as a function* [emphasis added]." (p. 210)[24]

Here, as throughout, Jung alternated in inconsistent fashion between employing anima and animus together and anima alone. But the subtext of the essay revealed that anima and animus played the same role. Despite defining animus similarly to anima as "the deposit, as it were, of all women's ancestral experiences of man" (p. 209), Jung insisted that animus

[24] In *Memories, Dreams, Reflections*, Jung indicated that he himself had achieved such a state, relating: "Today I no longer need these conversations with the anima… Today I am directly conscious of the anima's ideas because I have learned to accept the contents of the unconscious and to understand them. I know how I must behave toward the inner images. I can read their meaning directly from my dreams, and therefore no longer need a mediator to communicate them" (Jung, 1961/1989b, p. 188; cf. Shamdasani, 2026).

differed in two important ways. First, he asserted, "as the anima produces *moods*, the animus produces *opinions*" (p. 206). As demonstrated above, however, this was a vestige of the word-association tests, amplified in *Psychological Types*, that the male psyche correlated with thinking and the female feeling, with their respective opposites in the unconscious. It was, therefore, a second-order interpretation—a step removed from what was essential. Second, he indicated that while a man's anima was often a singular figure—in "the alluring form of a Circe or a Calypso"—a woman's animus was a plurality—"a bevy of Flying Dutchman." This he attributed to differing social demands:

> The man's world is the nation, the state, business concerns, etc. his family is simply a means to an end, one of the foundations of the state, and his wife is not necessarily *the* woman for him (at any rate not as the woman means it when she says "my man"). The general means more to him than the personal; his world consists of a multitude of co-ordinated factors, whereas her world, outside her husband, terminates in a sort of cosmic mist. [Owing to the principle of compensation] a passionate exclusiveness therefore attaches to the man's anima, and an indefinite variety to the woman's animus. (p. 210)

This too, of course, was an imposition of a stereotype. In all other respects, presumably, animus differed not from anima. "The animus does not belong to the function of conscious relationship," Jung wrote, "his function is rather to facilitate relations with the unconscious" (pp. 208–209).

That the animus as a function of relationship between consciousness and the unconscious operated in accordance with the way Jung had defined the anima was most evident three years later in Jung's *Visions* seminar. In his lecture on 4 February 1931, Jung picked up the thread of one of Morgan's fantasies in which a youth dressed in leopard skin, which he identified as Morgan's animus, is confronted by an old man with outstretched arms staring at the ground. At that spot flowers spring up, and the youth falls and buries his face in them. Suddenly, he finds himself in the lap of "the ancient mother" but leaps from her knees into the water below where he swims like a dolphin. Arriving at the end of the pond, he stands up to reveal that his hair has turned golden. Morgan's vision, as Jung reported it, continued:

> We ran together hand in hand until we came to a great chasm which we knew not how to cross. He called to the animals, but when they came he did

> not want them and they grazed about us. Then, setting foot on either side of the chasm, the youth told me to walk over him to the other side. This I did. (Jung, 1997, p. 199)

Once across:

> I took him by the hand but he could not come. He struggled to maintain his balance and then fell into the water at the bottom of the chasm. … Then I was afraid, I was alone in the dark woods. I lay down beside a stream and the animals came and licked my face. I rose and walked to the edge of the water. A woman rose up from the water wearing a high peaked cap. She laughed as I stepped into a golden boat pulled by a white sea horse. As I went I saw rainbows arching everywhere over the sky. (pp. 201–202)

In the lecture of the following week, Jung offered his interpretation. He began by acknowledging that the animus, like the anima, was the "bridge" or "communication" between consciousness and the unconscious. In the case of Morgan's fantasy, this was literally depicted. When animus occupied the space between an individual and the external world, it interfered with relationships and twisted one's words. But when it functioned as a bridge to the unconscious helping one across, as in Morgan's case, it was in the "right place." Jung explained:

> And here the animus is in the right place, he functions as a bridge; so he is on the side of the collective unconscious and not on the side of the obvious so-called material world. But there is always a certain danger that the animus falls backward, so to speak, disappears into the collective unconscious, and then for a while the connection with the unconscious world would be cut off. It is like a drawbridge, which has its moorings in the unconscious; when it is drawn up, the gate to the collective unconscious is shut. … By a certain attitude one can provoke that function to appear; but if it returns to itself, pulls up the bridge, that locks the gate. (p. 208)

In other words, the animus ceases being personified and returns to its role as *function*. That this was not a negative development was evident by the rest of Morgan's vision. Animals approached to lick her face, indicating that Morgan was finally in touch with her instincts. That Morgan's animus figure disappeared was therefore proof that she was becoming capable of instinctual behavior, which was, Jung indicated, the goal: "The ideal condition would be *that people could act out of pure instinct without the animus* [emphasis added]" (p. 211). To the extent that this was so, it meant that one was in "what the Chinese call Tao," which "means he is together with his instincts; his instincts are completely expressed in the things that happen, he is together with his animals" (p. 212). The lick on the face from the animals was, in this way, a sign of approval. But there was more. The woman rising from the water wearing a high-peaked cap Jung amplified by the symbol of the *pileus* deriving from the cult of Mithra.[25] This indicated sun symbolism, as did the golden boat and the rainbows, all of which stood for the Self. Hence, Jung's assessment:

> You saw that she succeeded in getting her animus into the right place and in making it function in the right way—as a bridge—and she crossed the bridge to the other side, thus establishing a connection with the collective unconscious. And in the moment when that happens, when the goal has been reached, one could say, so that the animus can plunge back into the collective unconscious, then the drawbridge is pulled up and the gate shut, and she is left alone with the animals in the darkness, all of which is perfectly all right. (pp. 213–214)

Thus, Morgan's fantasy nearly perfectly paralleled the formula Jung had given in "The Relations Between the Ego and the Unconscious" insofar as the dissolution of the personification of the anima into a function paved the way for the birth of the Self. The implication was unequivocal. That is, despite Jung's conflation of Morgan's well-developed thinking function with her animus elsewhere in the seminar, this selection revealed that the animus was, most fundamentally, the same as the anima: *a function of relationship* to the psyche.

Coda

To be sure, the sexual component of the contrasexual archetypes was, for Jung, a critical one, as were the gender-typological connotations accompanying it. If anything, the further one gets from Jung's introduction of anima and animus, the more these connotations become accentuated (see,

[25] Two decades earlier, in *Transformations and Symbols of the Libido* (Jung, 1911–1912/1991), Jung pointed to the pileus, or Phrygian cap, as a common feature of sun heroes including, from Greek mythology, the Dioscuri Castor and Pollux; from Mithraism, Mithra and the Dadophori (torch-bearers) Cautes and Cautopates; and from the Phrygian mysteries, Attis and Men.

e.g., Jung, 1951/1968, pp. 11–22). The above analysis is not to take away from those for whom orthodox application of these notions remains helpful. It is, however, to show that these gendered aspects are *interpretive levels*, or *layers*, as it were—ones that Hillman's excavation had deemed inessential.

The difference, of course, is that for Jung, as against Hillman, the role of anima and animus as functions of the psyche was intimately connected to the process of individuation, which is to say that anima and animus served teleological ends. Despite Jung's reserved tone in 1928 that "it would…be wrong to suppose that…the unconscious is working to a deliberate and concerted plan and is striving to realize definite ends" (Jung, 1928/1966b, p. 184), his original lecture of 1916 included the notion of "life-lines," one that was not carried over into subsequent revisions. He defined these as "lines of advance that are symbolically indicated" by one's fantasies (Jung, 1916/1966c, p. 293). That he viewed these as teleological was evinced by his foreword to the second edition of *Collected Papers on Analytical Psychology* where the lecture appeared for the first time in English as "The Concept of the Unconscious." In his Foreword, Jung wrote:

> If we wish to work in a really psychological way, we shall want to know the *meaning* of psychological phenomena. After learning the kinds of steel the various parts of a locomotive are made of, and from what ironworks and mines they come, we do not really know anything about the locomotive's *function*, that is to say, its meaning. But "function" as conceived by modern science is by no means solely a causal concept; it is especially a final or "teleological" one. (Jung, 1917/1920, p. xi; cf. Jung 1917/1967b, p. 296)

Viewed in this light, Jung's defining anima and animus as "functions" takes on even greater significance.

In all other respects, Hillman's "revisioning" of the anima coincided remarkably well with Jung's first articulations of both of these notions. As has been shown, Jung's early characterizations of anima and animus as functions of relationship between consciousness and the unconscious were primary to such second-order interpretations as eros and logos and feeling and thinking—each a bona fide psychic process in its own right. Hillman's emphasis on nature and animism was also strongly expressed by Jung. In fact, Jung's situating anima and animus alongside animal instincts and Tao suggests that if these notions should be equated with any of Jung's four functions of consciousness, they would be most accurately represented by *intuition*, the function that works via the unconscious, and a convincing argument might be made that this ought to be so. For example, in *Psychological Types*, Jung (1921/1971) offered the succinct definition of intuition as "the function of unconscious perception" (p. 366). In his commentary to *The Secret of the Golden Flower*, he suggested that the "ancient, cultural life of China [i.e., the birth of Taoism]...grew logically and organically from the deepest instincts" (Jung, 1938/1967a, p. 8). And in his 1919 essay "Instinct and the Unconscious" (Jung, 1948/1969b), the concept of instinct was related to those "*a priori*, inborn forms of 'intuition'" (p. 133) that Jung called *archetypes*. In this way, one's intuiting, via the unconscious, the middle way of Tao works via the same mechanism as an animal's unconsciously intuiting its instinctual behavior. That is, both processes are facilitated by the anima/animus, or the function of relation to the unconscious. Only when one deviates from this teleological path does the function become personified.

Nevertheless, insofar as a version of Hillman's position is taken to be emblematic of the current ethos regarding the status of anima and animus among those seeking to revise this aspect of analytical psychology, the similarity between his and Jung's early depictions suggests that the way forward with these notions is indeed one that is "radical"—not in the sense of Hillman's "revisioning" but in the sense of *returning to the root*, that is, of Jung's original theorizing. Doing so reveals anima and animus as fundamentally non-gendered, intuitive functions of the unconscious, which, as such, remain capable of aiding in the interpretation of a range of psychological, clinical, and literary material in the context of changing social conditions.

Competing Interests The author has no conflicts of interest to declare that are relevant to the content of this chapter.

References

Douglas, C. (1990). *The woman in the mirror: Analytical psychology and the feminine.* Sigo Press.

Douglas, C. (1993). *Translate this darkness: The life of Christiana Morgan, the veiled woman in Jung's circle.* Princeton University Press.

Douglas, C. (1997). Introduction. In C. G. Jung, *Visions: Notes of the seminar given in 1930–1934. Vol. 1* (C. Douglas, Ed., pp. ix–xxxiii). Princeton University Press.

Fike, M. A. (2020). *Four novels in Jung's 1925 seminar: Literary discussion and analytical psychology*. Routledge.

Harding, M. E. (1955). *Woman's mysteries: Ancient and modern. A psychological interpretation of the feminine principle as portrayed in myth, story, and dreams.* Pantheon. (Original work published 1935).

Hillman, J. (1985). *Anima: An anatomy of a personified notion.* Spring Publications.

Jung, C. G. (1920). In C. E. Long (Ed.), *Collected papers on analytical psychology* (2nd ed.). Baillière, Tindall and Cox. (Original work published 1917).

Jung, C. G. (1923). *Psychological types, or the psychology of individuation* (H. G. Baynes, Trans.). Pantheon Books.

Jung, C. G. (1928). *Two essays on analytical psychology* (H. G. Baynes & C. F. Baynes, Trans.). Baillière, Tindall and Cox.

Jung, C. G. (1966a). The psychology of the transference (R. F. C. Hull, Trans.). In H. Read et al. (Eds.), *The collected works of C. G. Jung: Vol. 16. Practice of psychotherapy* (2nd ed., pp. 163–323). Princeton University Press. (Original work published 1946).

Jung, C. G. (1966b). The relations between the ego and the unconscious (R. F. C. Hull, Trans.). In H. Read et al. (Eds.), *The collected works of C. G. Jung: Vol. 7. Two essays on analytical psychology* (2nd ed., pp. 121–241). Princeton University Press. (Original work published 1928).

Jung, C. G. (1966c). The structure of the unconscious (R. F. C. Hull, Trans.). In H. Read et al. (Eds.), *The collected works of C. G. Jung: Vol. 7. Two essays on analytical psychology* (2nd ed., pp. 269–273). Princeton University Press. (Original work published 1916).

Jung, C. G. (1967a). Commentary on "The secret of the golden flower" (R. F. C. Hull, Trans.). In H. Read et al. (Eds.), *The collected works of C. G. Jung: Vol. 13. Alchemical studies* (pp. 1–56). Princeton University Press. (Original work published 1938).

Jung, C. G. (1967b). Prefaces to "Collected papers on analytical psychology" (R. F. C. Hull, Trans.). In H. Read et al. (Eds.), *The collected works of C. G. Jung: Vol. 4. Freud and psychoanalysis* (pp. 290–297). Princeton University Press. (Original work published 1917).

Jung, C. G. (1968). *The collected works of C. G. Jung: Vol. 9 pt. 2. Aion: Researches into the phenomenology of the self* (R. F. C. Hull, Trans. & H. Read et al., Eds.). Princeton University Press. (Original work published 1951).

Jung, C. G. (1969a). A psychological approach to the dogma of the Trinity (R. F. C. Hull, Trans.). In H. Read et al. (Eds.), *The collected works of C. G. Jung: Vol. 11. Psychology and religion* (2nd ed., pp. 107–200). Princeton University Press. (Original work published 1948).

Jung, C. G. (1969b). Instinct and the unconscious (R. F. C. Hull, Trans.). In H. Read et al. (Eds.), *The collected works of C. G. Jung: Vol. 8. Structure and dynamics of the psyche* (2nd ed., pp. 129–138). Princeton University Press. (Original work published 1948).

Jung, C. G. (1969c). On the nature of the psyche (R. F. C. Hull, Trans.). In H. Read et al. (Eds.), *The collected works of C. G. Jung: Vol. 8. Structure and dynamics of the psyche* (2nd ed., pp. 159–234). Princeton University Press. (Original work published 1954).

Jung, C. G. (1969d). Psychological factors determining human behavior (R. F. C. Hull, Trans.). In H. Read et al. (Eds.), *The collected works of C. G. Jung: Vol. 8. Structure and dynamics of the psyche* (2nd ed., pp. 114–125). Princeton University Press. (Original work published 1937).

Jung, C. G. (1970). Mind and earth (R. F. C. Hull, Trans.). In H. Read et al. (Eds.), *The collected works of C. G. Jung: Vol. 10. Civilization in transition* (2nd ed., pp. 29–49). Princeton University Press. (Original work published 1931).

Jung, C. G. (1971). *The collected works of C. G. Jung: Vol. 6. Psychological types* (R. F. C. Hull, Trans. & H. Read et al., Eds.). Princeton University Press. (Original work published 1921).

Jung, C. G. (1973a). *Letters: Vol. 1. 1906–1950* (R. F. C. Hull, Trans. & G. Adler & A. Jaffé, Eds.). Princeton University Press.

Jung, C. G. (1973b). The association method (D. Riviere & L. Stein, Trans.). In H. Read et al. (Eds.), *The collected works of C. G. Jung: Vol. 2. Experimental researches* (pp. 439–465). Princeton University Press. (Original work published 1909).

Jung, C. G. (1976a). Address on the occasion of the founding of the C. G. Jung institute Zurich, 24 April 1948 (R. F. C. Hull, Trans.). In H. Read et al. (Eds.), *The collected works of C. G. Jung: Vol. 18. The symbolic life* (pp. 471–476). Princeton University Press. (Original work published 1948).

Jung, C. G. (1976b). Foreword to Harding: "Woman's mysteries" (R. F. C. Hull, Trans.). In H. Read et al. (Eds.), *The collected works of C. G. Jung: Vol. 18. The symbolic life* (pp. 518–520). Princeton University Press. (Original work published 1949).

Jung, C. G. (1989a). Appendix V: Septem sermons ad mortuos (1919). In C. G. Jung (Ed.), *Memories, dreams, reflections* (pp. 378–390). Vintage Books. (Original work published 1916).

Jung, C. G. (1989b). *Memories, dreams, reflections* (R. Winston & C. Winston, Trans. & A. Jaffé, Ed.). Vintage Books. (Original work published 1961).

Jung, C. G. (1991). *The collected works of C. G. Jung: Supplementary vol. B. Psychology of the unconscious: A study of the transformations and symbolisms of the libido. A contribution to the history of the evolution of thought* (B. Hinkle, Trans. & W. McGuire, Ed.). Princeton University Press. (Original work published 1911–1912).

Jung, C. G. (1997). In C. Douglas (Ed.), *Visions: Notes of the seminar given in 1930–1934. Vol. 1 & 2.* Princeton University Press.
Jung, C. G. (2009). *The red book liber novus* (M. Kyburz, J. Peck, & S. Shamdasani, Trans. & S. Shamdasani, Ed.). W. W. Norton.
Jung, C. G. (2012). In S. Shamdasani & W. McGuire (Eds.), *Introduction to Jungian psychology: Notes of the seminar on analytical psychology given in 1925.* Princeton University Press. (Original work published 1989).
Jung, C. G., & Riklin, F. (1973). The associations of normal subjects (D. Riviere & L. Stein, Trans.). In H. Read et al. (Eds.), *The collected works of C. G. Jung: Vol. 2. Experimental researches* (pp. 3–196). Princeton University Press. (Original work published 1904).
Jung, E. (1957). On the nature of the animus (C. F. Baynes, Trans.). In E. Jung (Ed.), *Animus and anima: Two essays* (pp. 1–43). Spring Publications.
Kerr, J. (1993). *A most dangerous method: The story of Jung, Freud, and Sabina Spielrein.* Alfred A. Knopf.
Molton, M. D., & Sikes, L. A. (2011). *Four eternal women: Toni Wolff revisited – A study in opposites.* Fisher King Press.
Roesler, C. (2022). *C. G. Jung's archetype concept: Theory, research, and applications* (A. Ulyet & C. Roesler, Trans.). Routledge. (Original work published 2016).
Rowland, S. (2002). *Jung: A feminist revision.* Polity Press.
Rowland, S. (2011). Anima, gender, feminism. In K. Bulkeley & C. Weldon (Eds.), *Teaching Jung* (pp. 169–182). Oxford University Press.
Samuels, A. (1985). *Jung and the post-Jungians.* Routledge.
Shamdasani, S. (1990). A woman called Frank. *Spring, 50*, 26–56.
Shamdasani, S. (1995). Memories, dreams, omissions. *Spring, 57*, 115–137.
Shamdasani, S. (2009). Liber novus: The "red book" of C. G. Jung. In C. G. Jung (Ed.), *The red book liber Novus* (pp. 193–221). W. W. Norton.
Shamdasani, S. (Ed.). (2026). *Jung's life and work: Interviews for* Memories, Dreams, Reflections *with Aniela Jaffé* (H. McCartney & J. Peck, Trans.). Princeton University Press.
Swogger, B. J., & Dillon, J. J. (2023). Historical foundations of affectivity and learning research: C. G. Jung's word-association experiments. In P. Fossa & C. Cortés-Rivera (Eds.), *Affectivity and learning: Bridging the gap between neurosciences, cultural and cognitive psychology* (pp. 587–603). Springer.
von Franz, M.-L. (1964). The process of individuation. In C. G. Jung & M.-L. von Franz (Eds.), *Man and his symbols* (pp. 158–229). Aldus Books.
Wallace, W. (2024). Jung's erotic phenomenology: I. A new translation. *Journal of Analytical Psychology, 69*(1), 27–50.
Williams, R. (2019). *C. G. Jung: The basics.* Routledge.
Wolff, T. (1956). *Structural forms of the feminine psyche* (P. Watzlawik, Trans.). C. G. Jung Institute Zurich.

CHAPTER 9

The Child Within and the Child Without: Parenting, the Childfree, and Individuation

Andrea M. Stover and James J. Dillon

Modern times offer people possibilities and amenities unfathomable to previous generations. Perhaps one of the most powerful freedoms now available to modern people is the freedom to choose whether or not to become a parent. According to the latest *U.S. Census Bureau* data, between 1990 and 2019, the fertility age decreased by 43% for women aged 20–24 and increased by 67% for women aged 35–39. Fertility rates overall in the United States decreased from 1990 to 2019, and annual births declined in the United States from around 4.1 million to 3.7 million (Morse, 2022). There is a shifting landscape of parenting in America, as fewer babies are born, and many of the babies who are born belong to older parents.

An increasing number of people in the modern West choose to remain *voluntarily childless*, *childless-by-choice*, and *childfree* (all terms used in the literature to denote the same phenomenon). Identifying the number of those who decide to be childfree is not easy, in part due to the important distinction between those who are *childless* and those who are *childfree*.

A. M. Stover (✉)
Licensed Marriage & Family Therapist, Kansas City, MO, USA

J. J. Dillon
School of Social Sciences, University of West Georgia, Carrollton, GA, USA

J. J. Dillon (ed.), *Complex and Archetype*,
https://doi.org/10.1007/978-3-032-02609-5_9

The childless either do not have a child but intend to, or they want children but are unable to have them due to fertility or other reasons. The childfree, on the other hand, are intentionally without children. Neal and Neal (2022) speculate that the percentage of childfree adults is much higher than originally thought, reaching upwards of one-fifth of the adult population in the United States.

Perhaps there is nothing more influential to one's own sense of identity than their relationship with their own parents. Though it is far from necessary to have children of one's own to work through one's childhood inheritance, the question arises about how a person who is childfree might be able to work through the complexes associated with having a child. Without real children to project this potent psychological material onto, alternative "children" might serve as a way to continue to grow and develop one's consciousness. As with all relationships to complexes, there is a more positive or ideal outcome, as well as a more negative or shadow side. The aim of this chapter is to emphasize the potential for growth and development through the parental situation of childfree individuals while avoiding less optimal developmental outcomes. We begin with a discussion of the ways real children can activate complexes in their parents, before turning to the nature of choice, and the reasons research gives as to why people choose not to become parents. We conclude with an exploration of how the parental complexes manifest in the childfree population and illustrate positive and negative ways of working them through to achieve greater wholeness.

The Role of the Child in Adult Individuation

Jung defines *individuation* as coming to establish a "productive marriage" between an independent, personal ego and a collective unconscious (1928/1971). It is a process guided by the *archetype of the Self* which facilitates the healthy organization of the entire psychic system. Individuation involves many things such as dissolving the persona, contending with the shadow, and establishing a transpersonal control point, but one of the most important steps involves withdrawing projected complex material and bringing it into a productive relationship with consciousness. As has been noted in previous chapters, complexes are "feeling toned associations" of memories, thoughts, desires, and perceptions which are activated by life events, relationships, and developmental stages. In this section, we discuss the complexes which tend to be constellated by parenting children and how addressing these child-related complexes might facilitate individuation. If complexes are feeling toned associations, most parents would agree that children surely arouse strong emotions! But which complexes do children tend to constellate? Theoretically, children can activate any of the complexes which reside in the adult psyche (e.g., inferiority, power, Oedipus, Salome, etc.). Focusing on all the possibilities is quite beyond the scope of this chapter, so we focus instead on the complexes commonly elicited by the parenting situation. These include the complexes which rest upon the *archetype of the child*, *mother*, and *father*.

Child Complexes

The first class of complexes commonly constellated by children are those which rest upon the *archetype of the child*, an archetype which Jung says "...represents the strongest, the most ineluctable urge in every being, namely the urge to realize itself" (1940/1969c, p. 170). These *child complexes* each relate in some way to the current state of psychological maturity of the parent, that is, to where the parent is on the journey of individuation. As one eases into the role of mother or father, one's relationship and experience with growth, wholeness, the past, newness, innocence, youth, and the future inevitably come into play. Our positive and negative experiences with these issues build the particular chain of ideas, associations, and feelings of a unique child complex which rests upon and is animated by an archetypal foundation. Though there are numerous possibilities, we can highlight three major child complex types: the *puer/puella*, *divine child*, and *Prometheus complex.*

With the *puer/puella complex*, one becomes fixated on the aspects of the archetype having to do with the past, youth, and innocence. One fights the passage of time, refuses to grow up, and to squarely face the difficulties of life. Jung suggests that the *puer* looks to another to solve all his problems. Becoming a parent could pose the temptation for such an individual to use the child to parent themselves. Jung says the *puella*, on the other hand, obsessively focuses on their youthful appearance, which hides a depressed, lifeless interior. Having one's own child may serve as a constant reminder to such a person of the cruel passage of time, arousing a Wicked Queen's rivalrous hatred of their child's youth and beauty ("Mirror, Mirror on the wall..."). Perhaps such an individual is so focused on their own youth, they may ignore the youth and real needs of the child, or instead identify with the child in an attempt to be a sibling or peer rather than a parent. With the *divine child complex*, one pins all one's hopes for the future on one's actual child. Though the archetype of the child represents divinity, this divinity is an *inner reality*, not an external person. In the grip of the divine child complex, one ignores all possibility for inner newness, redemption, growth, hope, and rebirth, and pins it instead on one's child.

Similarly, with the *Prometheus complex*, which concerns ideals for the future and a pitched mania for progress, one looks to the child as a means of continuing the steady march of history away from the dark past toward a future enlightenment. In the grip of this complex, one uses the child to build a world purportedly better than the world of one's parents or ancestors. The parent constantly shapes and educates the child toward this desired ideal through a process Jung calls *furor paedogogicus* (1940/1969c, p. 175). What this complex ignores is that the child is not just "the future" but also serves as a reminder to the parent of the still existing state of the past and the need for the *parent* to grow. In addition, the child has its own inclinations and is not simply raw material to be shaped for a future paradise. The child can educate the adult as much, or even more than the adult can educate the child.

Developing a complex related to the child can, if we are sensitive to it, point the way to the next steps in one's own process of individuation (see Jung, 1940/1969c, p. 175). The process of working with complex material would follow this general pattern: (a) consciousness of strong feeling tones and behavioral disruption, (b) understanding the unconscious processes behind this disturbance brought on by complexes, (c) ceasing to treat this material as foreign and dissolving projections, (d) bringing complex/archetypal material into productive relationship with consciousness, and (e) integrating one's complexes under a single, transpersonal directive organized by the archetype of the Self.

Mother Complexes

The second class of complexes commonly constellated by children are those which rest upon the core of the *archetype of the mother*. Jung refers to these as *mother complexes*. The mother archetype involves images of fertility, fruitfulness, holding, containment, protection, rebirth, magic, spiritual ecstasy, and images of the goal of our longing for redemption (Jung, 1938/1969a, p. 81). On the negative side, "the mother archetype may connote anything secret, hidden, dark; the abyss, the world of the dead, anything that devours, seduces, and poisons, that is terrifying and inescapable like fate" (Jung, 1938/1969a, p. 82). As one eases into the role of mother with a real child, one's relationship with one's own biographical mother, other maternal figures in life (e.g., grandmothers, stepmothers, teachers, coaches), significant maternal figures from literature and culture (e.g., Elizabeth Bennett, Laura Ingalls, Princess Leia, the Virgin Mary), and the archetypal Mother herself inevitably come into play. Our positive and negative experiences with these mothers build the particular chain of ideas, associations, and feelings of a unique mother complex which rests upon and is animated by an archetypal foundation. Jung outlines four types of mother complex: *hypertrophy of the maternal*, *overdeveloped eros*, *identity with the mother*, and *resistance to the Mother*.

Jung claims the mother complex is never as clear in the son as it is in the daughter since the son possesses an *anima* which tends to interfere with the Mother archetype, as well as a male body which makes it more difficult for him to identify with the mother. We leave these important gender distinctions to the side for the moment and briefly explore each kind of mother complex in general terms. *Hypertrophy complexes* involve intensification and exaggeration of all feminine instincts, particularly the maternal instinct. Jung writes, "her life is lived in and through others, in more or less complete identification with all the objects of her care" (Jung, 1938/1969a, p. 88). Without children, the person with such a complex has no existence whatsoever. *Eros complexes* involve an eradication of the maternal instincts and a jealous fixation on outdoing the mother by seducing the father. Jung writes, "A woman of this type loves romantic and sensational episodes for their own sake, and is interested in married men, less for themselves than for the fact that they are married and so give her an opportunity to wreck a marriage..." (Jung, 1938/1969a, p. 89). In a man, this would be a *Don Juan complex* (Jung, 1938/1969a, p. 85). An individual with such a complex would find parenting a child an excessive burden to their desires and would struggle with the temptation to neglect or abandon their child.

Identity complexes involve a complete projection of the personality onto the mother and a repression of both the maternal and the erotic instincts. The person with such a complex serves as an empty appendage of the mother. When an individual with such a complex becomes a parent, they will struggle with being emotionally available to the child, as well as with the assertion and direction parenting often requires. *Resistance complexes* involve a rejection of the mother and all she stands for. Jung notes the motto of this type is, "Anything, so long as it is not like Mother!" (Jung, 1938/1969a, p. 90). Such an individual would find being a parent akin to a process of becoming all that they hate. They may struggle to provide the child with the support which would come through the adoption of the traditional parental role. As with the child complexes, developing a complex related to the mother holds great potential to advance growth and individuation.

Father Complexes

The third class of complexes which are commonly constellated by children are those which rest upon the core of the *archetype of the father*. Jung refers to these as *father complexes*. The father archetype involves images of authority, law, protection, wisdom, guidance, obedience, judgment, royalty, divinity, salvation, moral commandments, prohibitions, sin, guilt, consciousness, and spirit (Jung, 1909/1989). Jung writes, it is typically symbolized as "…an active, winged, swift-moving being as well as that which vivifies, stimulates, incites, fires, and inspires…" (Jung, 1945/1969b, p. 210). On the negative side, the father archetype connotes images of a harsh, punitive, capricious, unforgiving, "terrible Father," a monster to be overcome, a giant who guards a treasure (see Shalit, 2002, p. 100). As one eases into the role of father with a real child, their relationship with their own biographical father, other paternal figures in life (e.g., grandfathers, stepfathers, teachers, coaches), significant paternal figures from literature and culture (e.g., Obi-Wan Kenobi, Mufasa, Ned Stark), and the archetypal Father himself (as Zeus, Dyaus Pita, Allah, Yahweh, etc.) inevitably come into play. Our positive and negative experiences with these fathers form the particular chain of ideas, associations, and feelings of a unique father complex which rests upon and is animated by the archetypal foundation. While Jung's writings on father complexes are not nearly as developed as his work on mother complexes, we can discern three main types of father complex in his work: *hypertrophy of the paternal*, *identity with the father*, and *resistance to the Father*.

As with the mother complexes, Jung notes that since the daughter possesses an *animus* which can sometimes interfere with the Father archetype, father complexes can manifest differently in sons compared to daughters. We leave these important gender distinctions to the side for now and simply focus on the general features of the father complex. With *hypertrophy of the paternal*, there is an exaggeration of all masculine instincts, particularly the paternal instinct, which involves features related to intellect, spirit, authority, control, or aggression/assertion. Jung writes, "The father ... is the representative of the spirit, whose function it is to oppose pure instinctuality" (Jung, 1956/1967, p. 261). This complex involves a concomitant repression of Eros, feeling, instinctuality, and embodiment. Jung (1909/1989) notes that with some instances of this complex we can speak of a near-complete identification with the father archetype, "...for instance with the *patris potestas* [*pater familias*] or with the queen ant" (p. 315). An individual with such a complex may be overly harsh and struggle to emotionally connect with their children.

Identity complexes involve a complete projection of the personality onto the father, along with a repression of both the paternal and martial instincts. As in the case of the mother complex, such a person functions as an empty appendage of the father, becomes "his father's son" (Dieckmann, 2014), perhaps taking over the family business. Jung writes that in men, such a father complex, "...very often produces a certain credulity with regard to authority and a distinct willingness to bow down before all spiritual dogmas and values" (Jung, 1945/1969b, p. 214). When an individual with such a complex becomes a parent, they will struggle with being interpersonally present to the child, as well as with the guidance and self-assertion parenting often requires. *Resistance complexes* involve a rejection of the Father and all he represents (see Shalit, 2002, p. 92). Such an individual would find being a parent akin to a prison, feeling like they are slowly being someone they have tried their whole life not to be. They may also struggle to provide the child with the support which would come through the adoption of the traditional parental role. Wrestling with the father complex, while painful, holds great promise to help advance growth and individuation. Perhaps the single most important factor determining whether efforts to wrestle with complexes are successful or not depends upon ego development and the capacity to make choices with integrity. We turn to this issue in the next section.

Choice as a Byproduct of Ego Development vs. Unconscious Complex Possession

Though the word *choice* may seem simple enough to grasp, the enactment of choice is a complex phenomenon. From a psychological perspective, choice requires agency. Agency is where intention and decisive action meet. Moore (2017) notes that agency:

> ...[it] considers how decisions and actions are enabled and constrained by various factors external to an individual's cognition. Agency informs pathways to motherhood because agency accounts for how and why individuals make choices that are always contextualized and constrained. (p. 1146)

Given that self-development is a lifelong endeavor, the various choices one makes throughout life might come from different places within themselves, as well as from external factors which shape their life path. For the purposes of this chapter, it is also important to name the possibility of making a "choice" from an unconscious place within oneself (i.e., from the grips of a complex, archetypal possession, a one-sided reaction to psychological material not yet recognized as belonging to oneself, or the collapse of the personal ego to other forces outside of oneself). Choices such as these are unconsciously reactionary, as opposed to making a choice from a more holistic, intact ego. As one advances in their journey of individuation, choice becomes more personal and available. Without both facing and developing oneself as a psychological adult, the choice of whether or not to become a parent could remain an unconscious reaction to one's own complexes and/or social influences.

Developmentally speaking, childhood and adolescence are times of acting "as if" and living a "provisional life" in a non-pathological way. The imagination stirs and the individual dreams up what type of person, life, and lifestyle they want to be in the future. Though Jung (1955) considers individuation to begin around age 37, early life is considered to be the breeding grounds for ego development. There are those individuals who from an early age have a strong sense of ego and clearly state they do not wish to have children when they are older and later remain childfree. *Early articulators* are people who decide to be childfree in their teens and early 20s. A recent study found the majority of childfree adults to be early articulators (Neal & Neal, 2022), though more research is required to understand the scope and application of this for the childfree population at large.

Postponers, on the other hand, are people who put the decision of parenthood off to try to meet other goals in their life and end up making the decision either on their own or as part of a couple (Neal & Neal, 2022). It is unknown what percentage of people who postpone their decision end up not having a child, but the point is that a delay in parenthood can result in the decision to be childfree. One complexity in researching childfree individuals is the fluidity of the journey and decision, as it can evolve over the course of one's life (Neal & Neal, 2022; Smith et al., 2020). For example, a person might declare they want to become a parent from a young age, only to grow ambivalent as their life begins to take more shape, and they ultimately decide they want to be childfree. This makes sense, given identity emerges and develops through time, and decisions can change based on having more information, both about oneself, as well as one's life structure and unique circumstances.

One important scenario relevant to ego development and the choice of whether or not to become a parent pertains to those who postpone but never officially decide one way or the other. People who are psychologically caught up in the *puer/puella* complex tend to live in their own version of "Neverland" and avoid making commitments in which they would be bound or tethered by limitation. According to von Franz, et al., (1981), an individual identifies with the *puer aeternus* archetype is an individual who remains caught in adolescent psychology, often remaining too dependent on their mother or in the grips of a mother complex (p. 7). Instead of grappling with the decision to have a child or not, the *puer/puella* masterfully avoids any type of confrontation with the matter. We now shift our focus to those who are clear in their decision not to have children of their own and provide an overview of their reasons.

Reasons for Choosing to be Childfree

It is impossible to provide an exhaustive list of the reasons why people choose to be childfree, as the reasons can be highly personal and vary between individuals. However, research on people who are childfree reveals several commonly cited reasons for that decision. Moore (2017) cites research on the impact of one's own negative parenting models, the desire to live an adult-oriented lifestyle, one's perception of their personality and lack of parenting skills, one's career aspirations, generalized negative feelings about children, and worry about population growth (p. 1145). Other reasons include going "green" and helping the planet by decreasing the carbon footprints, the non-monetary costs of one's time and energy, and financial freedom (Hymas, 2014). Growing research is being conducted on an often-understudied population: men who choose to be childless. Research shows men are increasingly going in a different direction than fatherhood (Bozick, 2023), though their reasons are vague and unclear. In a study of Australian men who choose to remain childless, their rationales include "financial concerns, fears about the state of the world, their own family history, and the vicarious experiences of others" (Smith, et al., 2020, p. 333). Men who perceive their own father to be absent or distant are also less likely to be interested in being a father themselves (Lunneborg, 2000; Smith, et al. 2020, p. 339).

Another common reason people choose not to have children stems from being in a relationship with a partner who does not want to become a parent. Research is sparse on how couples arrive at this decision, but Lee and Zvonkovic (2014) discuss how heterosexual married couples who are voluntarily childless reach this decision didactically. They identify three phases of this process: *agreement*, *acceptance*, and *closing of the door*. They also identify three different types of couples who reach the agreement phase which are based on each spouse's degree of conviction: *mutual early articulator couples*, *mutual postponer couples*, and *nonmutual couples*. The two factors they identify as making childlessness an ongoing reality are *the importance of the relationship* and *the strength of conviction* for each partner. In other words, some couples reach agreement and remain childless even when one partner might wish to have a child due to one partner's strength of conviction in not becoming a parent, while the other partner values the relationship with their spouse more than becoming a parent. Revisitation and reaffirmation are also a common theme for couples (Lee & Zvonkovic, 2014). This emphasizes the fluidity of the decision and how it is an active process engaged over time.

One final reason to remain childfree relates to one's own childhood trauma. Matthews and Desjardins (2020) studied 15 participants with histories of childhood abuse and neglect to see how this experience impacted their decision to have children or not. The study shows three different outcomes: the (7 women) *meant-to-be-mothers* who decided to become mothers who would not pass on dysfunction but rather have a good family life; the (4 women) *not-meant-to-be mothers* who chose to remain childless in order to avoid passing on dysfunction; and the (2 men, 2 women) *maybe or maybe not a mother or father* due to fear of uncertainty in being able to stop the transmission of dysfunction. From a Jungian perspective, these three outcomes show different ways of working with parental complexes. The *not-meant-to-be-mothers*, for example, could be choosing to exercise their own parental agency and protect the unborn child from future harm, thereby perhaps giving themselves a sense of completion and closure to a cycle of pain and suffering. We will soon discuss more outcomes and options in working through the complexes for the childfree, but we first address a social challenge common to those who choose the childfree path.

Stigma and Complexes

Before addressing how to work with complexes themselves, it is important to draw attention to the social stigma many people face when choosing to be childfree and how this activates complexes. The United States is a pronatalist nation, which puts forth the notion that parenthood is normative, even a moral imperative (Thompson, 1974). Studies allude to the less favorable perception of those who are non-parents compared to those who are parents, particularly in terms of being seen as less fulfilled, selfish, and more poorly adjusted psychologically (Ashburn-Nardo, 2017; Jamison et al., 1979). Further, voluntarily childless individuals often suffer from backlash due to a perceived violation of social norms and are recipients of moral outrage—including anger, disgust, and disapproval—by those who often view parenthood as a moral imperative (Ashburn-Nardo, 2017). Though the stigma is decreasing, the choice to not have children still comes with heightened stakes from a psychological standpoint. As a result, being childfree can become more than simply a choice a person makes; rather, it can become part of the self-identity construct (Moore, 2014). Further, arriving at this decision requires a certain amount of intact selfhood, self-knowledge, and personal agency in order to live life in accordance with one's authentic self-expression and values, regardless of how society-at-large and one's own family might perceive the childfree individual.

Social pressures to become a parent differ between men and women (Lee & Zvonkovic, 2014), with women being perceived more negatively, though some research suggests the stigmatization between childfree men and women is more equal (Ashburn-Nardo, 2017, p. 399). Grill (2019) argues that classical Freudian psychoanalysis of a woman questioning whether to become a mother tends to get relegated to analyzing the woman's relationship with her mother, rather than viewing her questioning as a valid stance in its own right with a wide variety of reasons. Though the desire for a woman to become a mother or not is presented as a binary—either she wants to be one or she does not want to be one (in which case, it is seen as a problem)—there is not much room allowed for exploration of the tension between the two and reasons for such (Grill, 2019, p. 61). The expectations girls and women face to become a mother are both implicit and explicit, and come from a variety of sources. They feel pressure from their family-of-origin, peers, partners, and society as a whole (Grill, 2019, p. 65). It can be challenging for women to let go of the idea that being a parent/mother is something she *should* want (Grill, 2019, p. 67).

By becoming society's projection carrier of the "bad mother" or "bad father" in one's refusal to fit into the socially scripted narrative of how a life should be lived, it is easy to see how one's own *child*, *mother*, and *father complexes* could be actively engaged and worked through as a result. In the most ideal sense, confronting one's Self in relation to these complexes would help to find and further solidify one's own desire to be childfree. If one were to be caught up in a negative *puer/puella complex* in refusing to grow up, society's confrontation could bring about an awakening to one's adult self and allow for a conscious choice to be made. In a *father complex*, one might be caught in overidentifying with being unconventional, not fitting the mold, and bucking all traditional norms. Smith et al. (2020) found childfree men who identified as being different, sometimes with a sense of wanting to challenge societal norms. By choosing to be childfree, one would, therefore, have to challenge "the father" in order to live life according to one's own values and sense of what is right for themselves. These examples are a brief attempt to point to how the complexes are stirred by simply declaring oneself voluntarily childless in our society. We now begin a discussion of how the childfree might find alternative "children" to work with which they are able to work on their child and parental complexes.

Working Through the Complexes When One Is Childfree

The goal in Jungian work is not to become complex-free *per se*, but to withdraw one's projections and develop a different relationship with the archetypal realm, thereby changing the way the complex manifests in one's life. Being in the grips of unconscious projections or archetypal possession is a common experience for all people. What do the child, mother, and father complexes look like for those who are childfree? How do they constellate, and how might they be worked through? Our contention is that there needs to be some type of alternative way of "mothering" or "fathering" a "child" in order to work through these complexes in a *symbolic* way. We present a few examples of these alternatives and show the resulting positive and negative manifestations of working through the complexes. Focusing on all the possibilities is an impossibility, but these few examples will help to give a sense of the various ways the child, mother, and father complexes may be worked through for childfree individuals.

Alternative "Children"

Alternative children are a way of discussing how the parental complexes constellate around something in which the *child archetype* is able to be projected upon. A child represents new life through the power of creation from the divine union of sperm (masculine) and egg (feminine). This new life takes time to be developed and is quite vulnerable, innocent, and malleable. A child can also represent the legacy adults leave behind as part of their own lived experience. Erikson (1959/1980) sees this being a natural need and a developmental crisis born from the stage of *generativity vs. stagnation*. Children are also often the projection carriers of the unlived lives of their parents. Children serve as reminders to their parents that life is finite by watching them grow through time, and if a parent is conscious, they can work through this material in order to advance the individuation process. There are several examples of alternative "children" which would serve as a way to allow the childfree to work through their child and parental complexes. Some of the alternatives we do not have space to explore in detail in this chapter are being a teacher, playing an active role as an aunt/uncle, working on an important creative project to oneself, becoming a leader of an organization or within the community, and gardening/farming. We explore two specific and common examples in more detail to illustrate how the complexes might reveal themselves and be worked through via an alternative to having a real child.

Pets. The first alternative "child" we will explore is one's pet/s. It is estimated that in 2023, 66% (nearly 85 million) of American households are pet owners (Megna & Tilford, 2023). Kunerth (2020) compares the number of households with pets (85 million) to the households with children (35 million) and states we are a nation of pet owners, "paw parents" to "fur babies," instead of parents to human children. Pets can serve many purposes in a person's life such as emotional support, companionship, and friendship ("man's best friend"). For childfree individuals, pets can serve as a surrogate child and constellate the *child*, *mother*, and *father complexes*. Pet owners often refer to themselves as "Mommy" or "Daddy" to their pets and their pet as their "baby." This offers insight into how the complexes manifest in these relationships. By projecting the "child" onto the pet, people access their inner complexes and express these parts of themselves through this dynamic.

The unique relationship with the pet rests upon the fact that they are *not human*, and therefore, are not going to relate back in the same way as another human would. On some level, this resembles childhood, a time when children often have a relationship with inanimate objects and/or subjects that are not human. One's own experience of being "the child" can be brought forward through one's relationship with their pet. Perhaps someone did not feel loved by their own parent/s when they were younger, and they felt abandoned, neglected, or unsafe in some way. Maybe they felt lonely and did not feel they had anyone to play with as a child. Having a pet be excited to see them when they reenter the home and seek to connect with them can be medicinal for their own inner child and help improve the quality of the internalized relationship between the parental and child complexes. This is one healthy way the complexes could be worked out with pets.

One manifestation of a positive Father complex at work with pets is providing the structure, guidance, and discipline which often accompanies training a pet, particularly dogs. Teaching dogs obedience and providing corrective behavioral interventions when they miss the mark are a few ways to lean into the father side of pet ownership. Fathering the pet also can show up by helping the pet become a functioning member of society at large (i.e., to not go bananas when out on a walk around others), thereby opening the world to them beyond the containment of "the mother" (i.e., the home). The Father complex could turn negative if it turns to being overly aggressive or domineering of the animals. For example, the *hypertrophy of the paternal* manifestation of this complex could look like the person only being able to relate as a disciplinarian, rather than with empathy or compassion.

In regard to pet relationships, one common phenomenon is the "rescue" pet, adopting a pet from a shelter who is homeless and whose life is in danger of being put down. This could serve to represent *the divine child complex* and the Mother complex. Here we have a life which is up against all odds, only to find rebirth and redemption through the care of the "mother." By projecting the divine child onto the animal, a person is able to care for, shelter, protect, feed, and nurture life, such that it is renewed and able to come back to life through the relationship with its owner. Depending on one's own relationship with their mother, this could serve to be either a recapitulation of the same pattern (only with a pet as opposed to a real child), or it could serve to redo what did not feel as though it was rightfully done to the child one once was. One unhealthy manifestation of being in the grip of the complexes pertains to *identity complexes*, whereby one over-identifies *as* the mother/father, forsaking all other parts of the personality. An example of how a pet constellates this complex is becoming a crusader for all rescue animals and unconsciously overidentifying as the rescuer of all pets, thereby losing touch with one's own self and the personal meaning put on the importance of finding a sense of individual purpose. This brings to mind an image of the proverbial "cat lady" with a hundred cats and no time to do anything other than sit with them!

Another shadow manifestation of the complexes constellated by pets serving as "children" is anthropomorphizing the animals. According to Mota-Rojas et al. (2021), there is a high risk of causing distress to an animal, and even causing adverse effects, when humans anthropomorphize their pets. The child and parent complexes might help to shine a light on how this occurs, as there is such a thing as "loving" a pet too much by overcompensating and giving it "the best" to perhaps make up for what one felt like they did not get in their own childhood, as in the case of *Prometheus complexes.* In today's time, there is pet insurance, doggie daycares, dog spas, and various clothing and accessories available for one's pets. It seems there is more to pet ownership than ever before. The *puer/puella complex* could show itself by having the pet get regular pampering, including special haircuts, having their nails painted, buying clothing and special accessories, all as if the pet's appearance defines their worth and sense of value.

Overall, pets can serve as one way of having an alternative "child" and working toward increasing one's individuation by engaging with the material stirred in response to the pet. It depends on the level of consciousness of the person as to how successfully this will be played out through time. As Kunerth (2020) notes, it is important to recognize that pets are not children. Two key differences between them are: a) parents of humans expect their child to outlive them, while pet owners expect to outlive their pet; and b) parents of humans try to successfully help their children grow into being independent, whereas a pet will always be a dependent. The psychological differences between these two things do not allow for a one-to-one comparison to be made between raising pets and raising children, but there is enough of a similarity between pets and children to help bring forth analogous psychological material for those who are childfree.

Advocacy. The next alternative "child" we discuss is advocacy and activism. Though there are many forms advocacy can take, we focus specifically on those who take an active approach to *saving the planet*. Environmental consequences of child-rearing is a growing concern and is one of the reasons people choose to remain childfree (Zeveloff, 2010). The GINK movement (Green Implications, No Kids) is growing in size, as more people see the effects of the carbon footprint each human life leaves on the planet (Hymas, 2014). Some may remain childfree and feel they are helping the planet out by doing so, while others choose to not have children due to concerns that "poor environmental quality may threaten the well-being of potential offspring" (Arnocky et al., 2012, p. 280).

Schneider-Mayerson (2022) notes the perceived "opportunity cost of parenting" as a reason why people who are conscious of climate change choose to remain childfree. Research participants in the study felt the time and energy parenting would require would interfere with their involvement in environmental campaigns and organizations (p. 164). Further, some research participants expressed they were glad about their choice, as they had more time to dedicate to political activities and activism. Schneider-Mayerson (2022) cites "fertility as a socio-political tool" which means that participants used their choice to be childfree as a "socio-political way of weaponizing fertility" to bring greater awareness to environmental issues facing today and future generations (p. 165). We now discuss how the complexes could be worked through within this advocacy framework.

In discussing the child, mother, and father complexes, we would be remiss not to mention the obvious moniker often used to describe our planet: *Mother Earth*. This connotes an immediate sense of being a child who belongs to/comes from the Earth. If we assume one takes on their own child complex by parentifying the Earth through projection, we are able to see how advocating for Mother Earth gives someone the opportunity to relate with both their child and mother complexes in a different manner. For example, a *resistance complex* involving one's mother indicates it is imperative to the individual not to become their own mother. It is possible someone might project the "Good Mother" onto Earth, whereas their own personal mother was the "Dark Mother." Mother Earth becomes everything their own mother was not to them: the embodiment of the all-loving maternal figure who provides an abundance of sustenance, nourishment, safety, shelter, and containment. The person might be identifying with the *divine child complex* by feeling they have all they could ever need, so long as they have this connection to their life-giving Mother Earth. They could also be possessed by the *Prometheus complex*, fighting against the personal "Dark Mother" and all of the devouring children roaming around on Mother Earth. In this case, the darkness is projected onto all who do not seem to care about or are even harmful to Mother Earth, as well as onto those with real children. They are the ones perceived to have the power to destroy. Therefore, advocacy could take an angle of dissuading others from having children, for the sake of the Great Mother.

The negative outcome of attempting to work these child and mother complexes out this way would be a person who maintains a position of polarity and sees all those who choose to have children as being "bad" while those who choose to not have children are "good." In this case, there is not really any work that has been done with the negative child or mother complex; rather, it remains as it always has been, just with a reconfiguration of who is going to play which role within the dynamic. This complex could be worked through in a constructive way if the person is able to withdraw their one-sidedness with the "all good" vs. "all bad" war being waged on behalf of the Mother. Instead, they might find Mother Earth to be a healing presence in their life and are able to "reparent" themselves through the projection of the "Good Mother," while still maintaining grounded awareness of the complexities of real parents and real children's experiences. Mother Earth is an aid in their own healing and wholeness, but she does not become the "all good" to compensate for the "all bad" they project onto their personal mother, nor does the child remain the cause of the mother's ails and suffering.

As an example of how a father complex could be worked through in this regard, we explore the *resistance complex* related to the father. In this case, it is possible one rejects all that a father is based on their own negative experiences with their personal father and turns to advocacy to work this out. For example, perhaps the person felt their own father to be weak and lacking in martial power. They wished to see something more action-based, more of a force to be reckoned with, but were instead denied it. Perhaps they felt their father could have done a lot more to support their mother, resulting in their own inner desire to be different from him. Perhaps he was absent in some form or another. As an adult, they now choose to exercise their own inner father complex by becoming the exact opposite of their biological father: someone who fights, someone who protects, someone who goes to bat with the law for the conservation and benefit of the Mother (Earth), someone who shows up. This could be a healthy way of working through this complex, so long as the polarities get broken down and result in a third force, or a new way. As with the *resistance complex* with the mother example listed above, no real progress will be made if the complex remains unexamined and continues to operate merely as an overcompensation for what was not experienced by the personal father.

There is great potential to work through one's child and parental complexes through advocacy work for the planet. By projecting the innocence (child) and identifying the vulnerability (child) of the planet, a person is able to parent the Earth and work toward leaving a legacy for all future children to come. The decision to remain voluntarily childless for the sake of humanity and a passion for "saving the planet" could be a heroic sacrifice of one's own individuality for the sake of all people across all time. Therefore, a greater meaning could be ascribed to remaining childfree when doing this kind of psychological work.

Conclusion

Parenting is an important part of individuation, if for no other reason than to put people in touch with their complexes. However, this does not mean all people must have actual children in order to access this material. The decision to have or not have children is a deeply personal one, and many people who are childfree view their choice as a mature exercise of sound logic. It could be said that by making this decision, they are exercising their "inner parent" as they consider personally meaningful implications for their potential unborn child and decide to protect them by choosing to not bring them into the world. Regardless of whether people have real children of their own, it is important they find a way to access the complexes connected with their childhood. In doing so, they have the opportunity to work through them, integrate them, grow, develop, and become more whole as a result.

One challenge associated with the choice around parenting involves the "biological clock" and the finite amount of time one is potentially granted fertility in their life. The window of time in which this decision needs to be made most often coincides with what Jung (1955) terms the *morning of life* (i.e., the first half of life). Whichever choice they make, it is possible the afternoon of their life will lead them to reflect upon whether they should have made a different decision, and what impact their actual decision made upon their life's legacy. Another challenging facet to consider is the psychological maturity and self-knowledge required to make a sound and informed decision for oneself on this important matter. Though many research participants report feeling they made the choice to remain child-free from a mature and logically sound place, this certainly is not the case for everyone. It is easy to see how being in the grips of a complex itself might lead to indefinite indecision, regression, or rebellion against perceived familial or societal norms of having a child. Future research should explore the various ways complexes could be identified and worked through in these types of instances, as well as how development of consciousness is stymied or encouraged. Overall, the complexes associated with parenting hold a key potential for the personality to realize itself more fully over the lifespan.

Competing Interests The authors have no conflicts of interest to declare that are relevant to the content of this chapter.

References

Arnocky, S., Dupuis, D., & Stroink, M. (2012). Environmental concern and fertility intentions among Canadian university students. *Population & Environment, 34*(2), 279–292. https://doi.org/10.1007/s11111-011-0164-y

Ashburn-Nardo, L. (2017). Parenthood as a moral imperative? Moral outrage and the stigmatization of voluntarily childfree women and men. *Sex Roles, 76*, 393–401. https://doi.org/10.1007/s11199-016-0606-1

Bozick, R. (2023). An increasing disinterest in fatherhood among childless men in the United States: A brief report. *Journal of Marriage and Family, 85*(1), 293–304. https://doi.org/10.1111/jomf.12874

Dieckmann, H. (2014). *Complexes: Diagnosis and therapy in analytical psychology.* Chiron Publications. https://www.amazon.com/Complexes-Diagnosis-Therapy-Analytical-Psychology-ebook/dp/B00OYAGD2G/ref=sr_1_1?crid=

CJPERN3AF8H2&keywords=complexes%3A+diagnosis&qid=1690461953&s=digital-text&sprefix=complexes+diagnosis%2Cdigital-text%2C89&sr=1-1

Erikson, E. H. (1980). *Identity and the life cycle.* WW Norton & Company. (Original work published 1959).

Grill, H. (2019). What women want: A discussion of "childless." *Psychoanalytic Dialogues, 29*(1), 59–68. doi:https://doi.org/10.1080/10481885.2018.1560867

Hymas, L. (2014). Making a green choice: Childfree living. *Mother Earth News, 262*, 79–83.

Jamison, P. H., Franzini, L. R., & Kaplan, R. M. (1979). Some assumed characteristics of voluntarily childfree women and men. *Psychology of Women Quarterly, 4*, 266–273. https://doi.org/10.1111/j.1471-6402.1979.tb00714.x

Jung, C. G. (1955). *Modern man in search of a soul.* Mariner.

Jung, C. G. (1967). Symbols of the mother and of rebirth (R. F. C. Hull, Trans.). In H. Read, M. Fordham, G. Adler, & W. McGuire (Eds.), *The collected Works of C.G. Jung: Vol. 5. Symbols of transformation* (2nd ed., pp. 297–337). Princeton University Press. (Original work published 1956).

Jung, C. G. (1969a). Psychological aspects of the mother archetype (R. F. C. Hull, Trans.). In H. Read et al. (Eds.), *The collected Works of C.G. Jung: Vol. 9 (part 1). The archetypes and the collective unconscious* (2nd ed., pp. 75–110). Princeton University Press. (Original work published 1938).

Jung, C. G. (1969b). The phenomenology of the spirit in fairytales (R. F. C. Hull, Trans.). In H. Read et al. (Eds.), *The collected Works of C.G. Jung: Vol. 9 (part 1). The archetypes and the collective unconscious* (2nd ed., pp. 207–254). Princeton University Press. (Original work published 1945).

Jung, C. G. (1969c). The psychology of the child archetype (R. F. C. Hull, Trans.). In H. Read et al. (Eds.), *The collected Works of C.G. Jung: Vol. 9 (part 1): The archetypes and the collective unconscious* (2nd ed., pp. 151–203). Princeton University Press. (Original work published 1940).

Jung, C. G. (1971). Relations between the ego and the unconscious. In J. Campbell (Ed.), *The portable Jung* (pp. 70–138). Penguin. (Original work published 1928).

Jung, C. G. (1989). The significance of the father in the destiny of the individual (G. Adler, & R. F. C. Hull, Trans.). In G. Adler & R. F. C. Hull (Eds.), *The collected works of C.G. Jung: Vol. 4. Freud and psychoanalysis* (pp. 302–323). Princeton University Press. (Original work published 1909).

Kunerth, J. (2020, August 19). Pets are not people. *UCF Today.* https://www.ucf.edu/news/pets-are-not-people-even-if-we-pretend-they-are/

Lee, K.-H., & Zvonkovic, A. M. (2014). Journeys to remain childless: A grounded theory examination of decision-making processes among voluntarily childless couples. *Journal of Social and Personal Relationships, 31*(4), 535–553. https://doi.org/10.1177/0265407514522891

Lunneborg, P. W. (2000). *The chosen lives of childfree men*. Bergin and Garvey.

Matthews, E. J., & Desjardins, M. (2020). The meaning of risk in reproductive decisions after childhood abuse and neglect. *Journal of Family Violence, 35*(8), 793–802. https://doi.org/10.1007/s10896-019-00062-2

Megna, M., & Tilford, A. (2023, June 21). Pet ownership statistics in 2023. *Forbes Advisor*. https://www.forbes.com/advisor/pet-insurance/pet-ownership-statistics/#sources_section

Moore, J. (2014). Reconsidering childfreedom: A feminist exploration of discursive identity construction in childfree livejournal communities. *Women's Studies in Communication, 37*(2), 159–180. https://doi.org/10.1080/07491409.2014.909375

Moore, J. (2017). Facets of agency in stories of transforming from childless by choice to mother. *Journal of Marriage & Family, 79*(4), 1144–1159. https://doi.org/10.1111/jomf.12402

Morse, A. (2022, April 6). Stable fertility rates 1990-2019 mask distinct variations by age. *United States Census Bureau*. https://www.census.gov/library/stories/2022/04/fertility-rates-declined-for-younger-women-increased-for-older-women.html#:~:text=Fertility%20Trends%3A%201990%2D2019&text=In%201990%2C%20there%20were%20about,to%202019%20(Figure%201)Books

Mota-Rojas, D., Mariti, C., Zdeinert, A., Riggio, G., Mora-Medina, P., Del Mar Reyes, A., Gazzano, A., Domínguez-Oliva, A., Lezama-García, K., José-Pérez, N., & Hernández-Ávalos, I. (2021). Anthropomorphism and its adverse effects on the distress and welfare of companion animals. *Animals (Basel), 11*(11), 3263. https://www.ncbi.nlm.nih.gov/pmc/articles/PMC8614365/

Neal, Z. P., & Neal, J. W. (2022). Prevalence, age of decision, and interpersonal warmth judgements of childfree adults. *Scientific Reports, 12*(1), 1–7. https://doi.org/10.1038/s41598-022-15728-z

Schneider-Mayerson, M. (2022). The environmental politics of reproductive choices in the age of climate change. *Environmental Politics, 31*(1), 152–172.

Shalit, E. (2002). *The complex: Path of transformation from archetype to ego*. Inner City.

Smith, I., Knight, T., Fletcher, R., & Macdonald, J. A. (2020). When men choose to be childless: An interpretive phenomenological analysis. *Journal of Social & Personal Relationships., 37*(1), 325–344. https://doi.org/10.1177/0265407519864444

Thompson, V. D. (1974). Family size: Implicit policies and assumed psychological outcomes. *Journal of Social Issues, 30*, 93–124.

von Franz, M. L., Mlekuž, M., Kušar, M., Zupančič, B. M., & Podbevšek, K. (1981). *Puer aeternus*. Sigo Press.

Zeveloff, N. (2010, April 6). Gink is the new dink: Going childless for mother nature. *Ecosalon*. https://ecosalon.com/gink-is-new-dink/

CHAPTER 10

Encountering the Archetypes Through Sacred Practices

Mark S. Rich

There is a deep human desire to search for a meaning in life which is greater than ourselves. This impulse has been developed throughout the centuries into a nearly endless number of religions, movements, activities, and paths of inquiry which search for a "higher power." For the purposes of this chapter, I refer to these concrete expressions as *sacred practices*. This desire for self-transcendence ultimately springs from archetypal imagery in the collective unconscious. This material can constellate in the personal unconscious, and if attended to in a particular way by our conscious awareness, it can be experienced as an archetype (rather than a complex) and expressed outwardly in the world of lived experience. This happens only when we move in the direction of individuation and "joining the psychological opposites." If this material is ignored or repressed, on the other hand, it can be the cause of neurosis and even psychosis. This chapter will show how people involved in sacred practice can pay attention to this material and be rewarded with the feeling of wholeness that is a positive indicator on the journey of individuation.

M. S. Rich (✉)
Independent Scholar, Bowdon, GA, USA

J. J. Dillon (ed.), *Complex and Archetype*,
https://doi.org/10.1007/978-3-032-02609-5_10

The Archetype Expressed Through the Ordinary and the Common

The most obvious and likely place to encounter the expression of archetypes is to look at the common, the routine, and the ordinary situations of life. Jung (1973) once said that "Individuation is just ordinary life and what you are made conscious of" (p. 442). Archetypal images and material from the unconscious can present themselves in the realm of lived experience as significant, inspirational, even oversized and larger than life. Many of these experiences are unbidden and unannounced. Later in the chapter, I will explore these experiences which are the result of planning and intention. For now, I consider the unbidden. An example from the *Holy Bible* can serve to illustrate this idea of the archetype experienced in the ordinary. In the *Book of Exodus*, Moses is busy tending sheep in the hills when something catches his eye. He notices a bush which appears to be on fire, and he turns aside to investigate. The bush is burning, yet the fire does not consume it. Moses hears the voice of God asking him to come closer. In the middle of an otherwise ordinary day, Moses sees and hears the extraordinary; a bush burning with fire yet unconsumed, and the voice of God asking him to approach. As Moses comes closer, God makes a startling and unexpected declaration. He tells Moses to remove his shoes, for the place on which he is standing is holy ground (Delegates and Syndics, 1972, p. 56). We will return to this illustration later in the chapter, but for now, it shows how the archetypal image of the sacred can show up in an outsized and dramatic fashion in what is otherwise a profoundly ordinary moment. The difference is that on this particular day, Moses noticed the unusual, the unordinary, and he turned aside to take a closer look. Maslow (1970) gives a good summary of this kind of encounter when he says, "…the sacred is *in* the ordinary, it is to be found in one's daily life, in one's neighbors, friends, and family, in one's back yard…" (p. x).

For Jung (1958/1969f), the thrust, direction, and ultimate goal of life is to move along the journey of individuation. A fundamental part of this process is to integrate unconscious material into our everyday lived experience, where we exist moment to moment. If we take it up with an attitude of awareness, it can move us along the road of individuation. There is nothing "special" or "extraordinary" about today or any of the other moments in the day. It remains up to us to give our everyday ordinariness the attention and intention that can allow the archetypal to be seen when it is expressed by our unconscious. This intentionality is a catalyst of integration and union, a moderator between our interiority and the external mundaneness of daily life. A group of trees is just trees. A path in the woods is simply a path of worn soil and dirt, but if we move with intention along that path into those trees, the ordinariness of the circumstance can be a profound and sacred moment in time and place. Even the liminal space between the open ground and the trees of the forest can itself become part of the sacrality of the otherwise ordinary moment.

The novelist Kurt Vonnegut (2005) tells a story about buying an envelope. Purchasing an envelope would not be what many would consider anything more than a routine, mundane, and painfully common chore. But for Vonnegut, it was a magical experience. As he was leaving to buy the envelope, his wife reminded him that he could just order a box of envelopes and have them delivered. This was of no interest to him because he was on a magical journey. Leaving their apartment, he made his way several blocks to the newsstand to buy the envelope, along the way meeting and talking to any number of people about any number of things. At the newsstand, he had other conversations and interactions with different people who were also out running errands or going about their daily activities.

Once he got the envelope, he went next door to the post office to mail it to his typist with an enclosed manuscript. All of this would be common and ordinary, but Vonnegut takes it up as a sacred mission to interact with and be alive in the world (Vonnegut, 2005, pp. 58–62). The key to having or not having this sense of the sacred in life is one's attention to those ordinary moments of everyday living. We might think of it as approaching the ordinary with a sense of the magical. As Emerson (1929) notes, "The invariable mark of wisdom, is to see the miraculous in the common" (p. 23). Similarly, Rich (2018) argues, "…there must be a return to the magic in the living of life, and a reverence for the sacred commonality that is the wonder of being alive in the world" (p. 11).

Throughout his *Collected Works*, Jung describes the psyche as encompassing not only the particular individual but the entirety of the universe. The soul is what gives us that sense of elation or specialness during those times when our inner self responds or is moved by some outward image or event. Jung (1950/1969c) writes, "…if some great idea takes hold of us from outside, we must understand that it takes hold of us, only because something in us responds to it and goes out to meet it" (p. 120). This "going out to meet it" consists of approaching our circumstances with intention and awareness. The limitations of our human nature are the main impediments which cause us to remain superficially distracted and miss those moments when the extraordinary presents itself to us in our daily lives. As Belden Lane confesses, "I seldom make myself fully present to those occasions when the ordinary whispers of the holy" (Lane, 2002, p. 67).

An analogy can help describe these missed opportunities of ordinary living. Imagine a calm body of water, a lake or pond. Then imagine taking a flat rock and skipping it rapidly along the surface of the water, allowing it to come in contact with the water. Only as the rock slows down does it enter into the depths. Much of our daily life in Western society consists of a rapid skimming along on the surface at a break-neck speed, with too little time to slow our momentum long enough to sink into the depths of life and experience those sacred moments in the ordinary. Kurt Vonnegut knew this and put it into practice. He walked to the newsstand and the post office, when it likely would have been faster and easier to drive.

A poignant illustration of how the ordinary can point to archetypal forces in our consciousness and activate that psychic material into a sacred moment can be found in a brief story told by the British poet and theologian Malcolm Guite (2020). It is the story of an old brier tobacco pipe. Malcolm Guite is a lifelong pipe smoker, and he tells the story of a childhood game he played in England using the seeds of the Horse Chestnut tree and how the shape, texture, and appearance of his brier pipes reminded him all these years later of the conkers (chestnuts) used in the childhood game of so long ago. He recalls getting the most enjoyment not from playing the actual game itself, rather,

> it was picking up the conkers themselves that gave me the greatest pleasure. I loved the swirls and patterns in their shiny brown sides, like the grain of highly polished wood … and to think, as I uncovered it, 'I am the first person ever to see this.' (p. 76)

The key to this process lies in making oneself fully present and available for the ordinary to take on an additional meaning.

The acclaimed author and Kentucky farmer Wendell Berry (2017) describes these ordinary moments of the sacred through his description of being in the woods on his farm. In the frantic and hectic environment of twenty-first-century life, it seems that if we are not frenetically consumed in work, we do not feel productive. But Berry describes one way in which he takes an ordinary moment and infuses it with sacrality,

> I have been walking in the woods and have lain down on the ground to rest. It is the middle of October ... the leaves are quietly sifting down ... and I lie easy, coming to rest within myself as I seem to do nowadays only when I am in the woods ... The event, among all its ramifying causes ... and its mysteries, begins to take on the magnitude of history. Portent begins to dwell in it. (p. 37)

bell hooks (2009) describes a similar experience from her rural, small-town childhood in Kentucky,

> one of the most immediate experiences that calls us is the slowing down of everything. In childhood my siblings and I often hated the languid slow pace of everyday life ... Now I want to be still, I want to live in that experience of knowing unity with the divine in stillness. (p. 65)

Perhaps in physical stillness a portal is opened into our personal unconscious. Coming toward stillness with the intention of looking within, we may discover not only the profound impact presented by our external environment but an equally prescient and valuable realization that in our stillness we may invite into consciousness that complex material that has made the journey from the archetypal depths of the collective unconscious and has made its residence in our personal consciousness. It is in the unifying of these opposites that one truly moves into the journey of individuation. For hooks (2009), a life lived in the pursuit of wholeness requires an examination of both the world of the exterior and the interior, "I am able to reclaim a sublime understanding that living in harmony with the earth renews the spirit" (p. 65).

These examples show the interactions and effects of archetypal material moving from the depths of the unconscious into our conscious experience. The intention of this chapter, however, is to illustrate the role of the archetype of the Self, which Jung identifies as the *Christ imago*, the God within us. Jung (1928/1966) writes, "I have called this centre the *self* ... It might equally well be called the 'God within us'" (p. 238). The archetypes are there in the unconscious, and if one is willing to embrace this material and "sit with it," the journey of individuation begins. However, if the material has constellated as a complex, is ignored, or repressed, it will make itself known on its own terms, often as neurotic or psychotic behavior. Jung (1940/1969e) writes,

> Archetypes were, and still are, living psychic forces that demand to be taken seriously … Always they were the bringers of protection and salvation, and their violation has as its consequence 'perils of the soul'… they are the unfailing causes of neurotic and even psychotic disorders. (pp. 156–157)

Jung's admonition to us is to embrace the archetypes as they manifest themselves to us, to incorporate the archetypal imagery into daily lived experience, and thereby make our way on the journey of individuation. Having examined the manifestations of archetypes in everyday life, I turn now to the equally ubiquitous phenomenon of experiencing the archetypes in place and space.

The Sacredness of Place and Space in the Expressions of the Archetypes

Each of us occupies space and dwells in a place. These ideas are so common and routine that we give little thought to the profound significance of space and place. In *The Four Quartets*, T. S. Eliot writes, "We shall not cease from exploration, and the end of all our exploring will be to arrive where we started and know the place for the first time" (Eliot, 1962, p. 145). This section shows that place and space are particularly important to sacred practice and to our inner experience of the archetypes. Edward Casey helps us define these terms when he explains, "…we should look for the efficacy of places within our intimate lives … the lives we live from within … into the interiority of the self… into a psychical depth that cannot be determined by any objective measurement…" (Casey, 1993, p. 311). Following Casey, *place* is specific and experiential, while *space* is general, unspecified, and anonymous.

Each of us exists in space, but we also occupy a single and very specific place at any particular moment. Sheldrake (2001) offers a more philosophical expression when he says that "Space is an abstract analytical concept whereas place is always tangible, physical, specific and rational … 'place is the house of being.' In other words, to be a person is literally 'to be there,' to be in a particular place" (p. 7). Brueggemann (1977) elaborates upon these differences even further,

> Place is space which has historical meanings, where some things have happened which are now remembered and which provide continuity and identity across generations. Place is space in which vows have been exchanged,

> promises have been made, and demands have been issued. Place is indeed a protest against the unpromising pursuit of space. It is a declaration that our humanness cannot be found in escape, detachment, absence of commitment and undefined freedom. (Brueggemann, 1977, p. 7)

An excellent description of the way the sacred is connected to place is found in the writings of bell hooks. In describing her return to her childhood home in Kentucky, hooks outlines the important connection between the world of inner life and that of external lived experience. She writes,

> Coming home to live in Kentucky was for me a journey back to a place where I felt I belonged … a place that I felt needed me … a place where I as a citizen could be in community with other folk seeking to revive and renew our local environment, seeking to have fidelity to a place. (hooks, 2009, p. 65)

Here hooks brings into frame the idea that as social creatures, we often find our better way forward in community. The sacredness of place can be experienced on the level of the individual, but it fully embodies itself in community, even if that means just a few people in places of worship, places of ceremony, places of ritual, or places of gathering. hooks describes her uneasiness with living in New York City, and her resolution to leave for home in terms that poignantly align with Jung's description of the process of individuation. She writes,

> I began an inward search for place. This seeking led to a psychic archeological dig where I plundered the depths of my being to see when and where did I feel a sense of belonging, when and where did I feel at home in the universe. That searching led me home to Kentucky. (hooks, 2009, p. 67)

Sacred place can be a grand cathedral, or Moses at the burning bush in the desert. It can be a designated location for a drum circle, or a common, even mundane spot, such as a random encounter with long-lost friends that leads to a powerful cathartic moment of joy or grief (or both). From the general to the specific, space becomes place, and any place can become profoundly sacred by assignment or specificity. That particular place then will likely always be known as such to the ones who have been together in those deeper moments of encounter with the archetypes. This can remain so, even if the place returns to its previously mundane and ordinary existence, for it will be known as such in the memories of those who felt the archetypal energy within it. It will live on in the psyche of those who were there in those moments of sacred encounter.

Constellated psychic material does not wait to show up until we can formulate a plan or strategy to deal with it. It operates outside of our usual rigidity of reason and logic. It appears in the most ordinary places, or the least likely moments. A poignant example of this "eruption" of archetypal material into our lived experience can be found in a story told by the poet and author Kim Addonizio. Kim's mother had been a patient in a psychiatric facility for some time. One day Kim went to visit her. Keeping notes in a journal as she often did, Kim wrote, "I noted that she was in Room 7, Bed 2, Ward 12A, as though fixing things in place-her words, her diagnosis, her exact location-could somehow change her circumstances" (Addonizio, 2016, p. 198). In this particular circumstance, Kim had to create her own "sacred" in and through space while trying to advocate for her mother. At lunch the following day, she found herself seated next to a man who had been a patient in the facility for a long time. The psychiatrist asked the man how he was feeling, and the man replied, "except for a little headache, I'm feeling pretty good." To which the Dr. replied, "let's wait and see how you do tomorrow." Kim's internal dialogue about this was, "*Today you're happy. Better wait a bit though, since tomorrow you may be miserable.*" She thought, "Why couldn't the doctor just say 'Merry Christmas?' It was Christmas now … clearly we were trapped in time and space. Neither Santa Claus nor Jesus was on his way anytime soon" (Addonizio, 2016, pp. 201–202). This shows how time is tied to place in the experience of those moments of the sacred. The poet moved through space in the world in time, coming to one specific place to be in the presence of her mother in what was a moment of sacrality with archetypal energy expressed through the group at the table, despite the doctor's negative energy. The sacred can show up unexpectedly, but it does not necessarily come as we want or expect it to; it comes to us as it is, with the colors, feelings, and intensity of that meeting place of inner life and outer experience. Both Kim and her mom found themselves in a moment of sacrality, where the Self, the *Imago Dei*, showed up for lunch in the cafeteria.

There is often a specific connection between place and time that is significant to our experience of archetypal imagery. Scott Russell Sanders (1993) provides an elegant description of the importance and significance of place and the power of staying put in time. He writes, "The likeliest path to the ultimate ground leads through my local ground. I mean the land itself… I cannot have a spiritual center without having a geographical one; I cannot live a grounded life without being grounded in a place" (p. 120). For Sanders, a local place, an actual piece of ground can be a conduit to the unconscious. He continues, "I am suspicious of any philosophy that would separate this-worldly from other-worldly commitment. There is only one world, and we participate in it here and now, in our flesh and our place" (p. 121).

In every endeavor in which the human creature acts upon or is influenced by archetypal material of the unconscious, a specific place is necessarily involved either intentionally or coincidentally. This is the reason why there are sacred places built all around the world and throughout history. The differences have to do with the particular beliefs and practices of those involved, the particular psychic material accessed, and the unique way the archetypes are taken up and embodied in the real world of lived experience. To underscore the significance of sacred place, how it is tied to time, and how it is a ubiquitous part of working with archetypal material from the unconscious, Sanders (1991) writes,

> It is a spiritual discipline to root the mind in a particular landscape, to know it not as a visitor … but as a resident, as one more local creature alongside the red-tailed hawks and sycamores and racoons … By renewing our vision of the land, we rediscover where it is we truly dwell … It is rare for any of us, by delicate choice, to sit still and weave ourselves into a place, so that we know the wildflowers and rocks and politicians … so that we feel a bond to everything in sight. (p. 94)

There are many similarities between the moments of the sacred experienced in the ordinary described in the first section and the sacred experienced in the specificity of place discussed in this section. Both can function as containers for holding the archetypal imagery which comes to us from the unconscious. My hope and intention is that the reader will take up contemplative work to examine the inner life and richness of the archetypes, to feel the energy of the complex in the personal unconscious and ultimately bring it forth into everyday lived experience. Additionally, we can be engaged in activities such as farming, religious rituals, or caring for a loved one, and completely miss the profound connection that can be made between the life of the interior and that of the exterior. The significance of approaching such activities with intentionality was not lost on

Joseph Campbell. In the book *The Power of Myth*, Bill Moyers asks him about his personal ideas on the importance of place and the sacred as it concerns our unconscious life, "What does it mean to have a sacred place?" Campbell replies,

> This is an absolute necessity for anybody today. You must have room for a certain hour or so a day, where you don't know what was in the newspapers that morning. You don't know who your friends are, you don't know what you owe anybody, you don't know what anybody owes you. This is a place where you can simply experience and bring forth what you are and what you might be. This is the place of creative incubation. At first you may find that nothing happens there. But if you have a sacred place and use it, something eventually will happen. (Campbell & Moyers, 1988, p. 92)

There are four common elements of any experience of sacred practice conducted with the intention of getting down into the depths of and working with the archetypes. The experience will be (a) *transcendent* by giving an awareness of life as more than mere existence; (b) *transformative* by changing our perception and significance of being; (c) *transitional* by assigning a particular change to a particular place; and (d) *timely* by giving perspective to the specific moment as being of special importance. In my own life, I have a specific spot, a particular area in the woods on our farm which I have set aside as a sacred place. I can walk around during the course of routine work and not experience that place as sacred, but if I am there with the intention of meeting with the unconscious, it becomes sacred for me. It becomes a moment of transformation with often significant effects on my being. Going down or sinking into my psychological depths is also transcendent in the sense that it takes me beyond the otherwise ordinary moment. The time in which this is happening provides a transition to the contents of the personal unconscious to assign themselves to place. But this is a place both in the psyche and in the external world where I cannot remain, for the timeliness of the experience compels me to eventually move back into my daily life.

Sacred places are liminal in the sense that they function as a threshold across which we move or step from the everyday world of routine activity into an extraordinary place. To anyone outwardly observing, the place before and the place after may look indistinguishable, but to the person involved in the expression of the sacred, the liminal space, the threshold across which we move, is of profound importance. A well-known program called Outward Bound has provided this experiential learning to countless young people over the past 50 years. In a wilderness environment, each participant picks a particular spot in which they will be alone and isolated for several days, having only a single daily check-in with one of the leaders. This is an opportunity for them to experience the transformative aspects of being, and they often describe the place in which they decide to spend the time as having a special or sacred quality. While from the outside it is no different than any other part in the wilderness, it is a special place for them, setting it apart from all the territory around it, and in which participants can experience the sacred for themselves. The place becomes transformative in that it brings the person into contact with archetypal material of which they were not even aware. This then leads to a transitional departure from the stress and troubles of their everyday lives that can provide context and perspective. Godfrey (1980) writes, "One of the characteristics of the Outward Bound experience is the way in which a diverse group of individuals from broadly varied backgrounds are immersed in a situation that *automatically* generates a high degree of intimacy and an unavoidable interdependency" (p. 24).

With regard to the transitional aspect of the experience of sacred place, liminal space can be "assigned" by the event or ceremony involved, or it can appear organically, such as when a group decides to hold a drum circle extemporaneously. The crossing of the liminal threshold from the ordinary to the extraordinary gives a significance to the setting beyond its merely physical space. This transition may occur during extemporaneous or impromptu occasions, or it may be, as Joseph Campbell explained, a previously set aside time and place within which to meet the sacred and the attendant archetypal imagery.

The final aspect of the experience of sacred place is timeliness. We can have these special experiences and meet material from the unconscious, but the intention should ultimately be to incorporate and unite the opposites within us. This requires movement. We cannot be in these moments of sacred practice and simply stay there, for this removes us from returning to living daily life, with all of its responsibilities, activities, and commitments. Just as with any endeavor in life, one must learn through study and experience, but this is only helpful if that learning, and experience is put into application in the actual living of daily life.

Encountering Archetypes Through Conventional Religious Practices

I began this chapter by looking at the specific, the individual person experiencing the archetype of the Self in the ordinariness of the common and the mundane. Moving to the second section, we saw that place also plays a key role in psychic work. This section explores a third form of sacred practice: conventional religious practice. As Jung (1940/1969e) describes, "...religion is a vital link with psychic processes independent of and beyond consciousness, in the dark hinterland of the psyche" (p. 154). Conventional religious practice is an enormous category, so for the purposes of this chapter, I confine my examination to Western Christianity, beginning with Protestantism in England and America from the Great Awakening of the late eighteenth century up through the consequential religious movements of the nineteenth century. Highlighting certain specific moments of history during the past 150 years, I will look at the profound ways these practices have affected their practitioners. I begin by looking at how archetypal material comes into lived experience through the conventional religious practices of the Great Awakening.

The Great Awakening began as a movement in the 1740s emphasizing faith over intellectual pursuit. It was a critical response to the Industrial Revolution and the mechanistic tenets of the Enlightenment. This reactionary milieu of the Great Awakening in England and western Europe made its way to colonial America, and the ensuing revivals and growth of religion there were an inevitable consequence. The Great Awakening was a powerful outlet for archetypal energy. It was inextricably tied to the political, industrial, and economic upheaval ushered in by the Industrial Revolution, and, by extension, America's fight for freedom from England. For space reasons, I confine myself to an examination of particular samples and slices of life and culture in this time to highlight the strong role that conventional religious practices played with the outward expression of archetypal material.

I begin with the events in the life of an uneducated itinerant preacher, Henry Alline of Nova Scotia. Through a series of visions and vivid impressions, both ecstatic and nightmarish, Alline struggled with the powerful imagery that had broken into his consciousness. The experience is best described in his own words from 1775, "At that instant of time ... redeeming love broke into my soul ... with such power, that my whole soul seemed to be melted down with love" (Kidd, 2007, p. 310). Alline described his conversion as a deeply emotional, almost sexual experience, "attracted by the love and beauty I saw in his divine perfections, my whole soul was ravished with the blessed redeemer" (ibid., p. 310). From this ecstatic experience, Alline went on to preach to hundreds of thousands of people in that area over the next several years. This kind of fervor serves to illustrate the idea of innate archetypal material coming through from the collective unconscious into the personal unconscious, which is then consciously attended to and given expression by Alline in his years of revivals. The "proof" of this (though empiricism cannot speak of the ineffable) is in the many thousands of people who came to hear Alline preach, to affirm and proclaim this archetypal imagery which resonated so strongly with them. If this were not the case, Alline would be preaching not to crowds of hundreds and thousands, but scarcely to anyone at all. This is especially true considering the times and the modes of transportation available, days of primitive and dangerous travel, taken either on foot, on horseback, or with a horse and buggy. Even a cursory perusal of the documentation of those decades shows that a large percentage of the population of this "new world" was "captured" by the archetype of the Self, the God-image. As Jung writes, "…the God-image does not coincide with the unconscious as such, but with a special content of it, namely the archetype of the self" (Jung, 1952/1969a, p. 469).

One hallmark of Alline's experience, and why he fits well in this look at conventional religious sacred practice, is that he "anticipated one of the distinctives of the Second Great Awakening in his rejection of Calvinistic theology" (Kidd, 2007, p. 311). Calvinism is the idea that all persons are "predestined" to either heaven or hell, and that there is really nothing one can do to change this outcome. The Puritans were Calvinists, and a hallmark of Puritan dogma "understood that God had unconditionally predestined some believers to election and others to eternal damnation" (Rubin, 1994, p. 35). But these revivals and awakenings belonged to a larger movement, a movement of the collective unconscious involving the archetype of the Self. "Christ … signifies psychologically the self; that is, he represents the projection of this most important and most central of archetypes" (Jung, 1955–56/1970b, p. 368). McLoughlin (1980) notes that these revivals and awakenings were not the result of external forces or conflicts, "but of critical disjunctions on our self-understanding … not periods of social neurosis. They are times of revitalization. They are therapeutic and cathartic, not pathological" (McLoughlin, 1980, p. 2). Alline proclaimed to each individual person to take up religion for oneself. He opened the possibility of having one's own personal relationship with all things spiritual, without the predetermined baggage of being either perpetually saved, or perpetually damned. This was a movement that, while starting in Europe and especially England, spread throughout the new American colonies. It was time when the expression of this archetypal material was almost palpable. Given that this transpired during the age of Enlightenment, many thought that the milieu would reflect a more rational and sober expression of religious belief and sacred practice, but this did not happen at all. The movement of the Great Awakening and its many thousands of participants provided energetic and seemingly unbounded affirmations of the expressions of the unconscious in that place and time. As we will see later in the chapter, this movement also had the unintended consequence of expanding the spiritual horizon of sacred practice not only out to the edges of conventional religious expression but indeed well beyond it.

Events were taking place on a grand scale in the United States which can be viewed as an expression of the God-image. After America won its independence, a doctrine known as *Manifest Destiny* took over the mass migration to the west in the early eighteenth century. Hankins (2004) writes that "close to 800,000 people from New England alone immigrated west between 1790 and 1820. As people moved westward, they left their churches and often their pastors behind" (p. 3). The result of this movement saw the traditional expressions of sacred practice decline, but at the level of the psyche, it opened an access point to more alternative ways of engaging the sacred. Hankins (2004) continues, "the 1820s touched off another phase of revival intensity … and from it sprung several new and unorthodox religious movements … and religious experimentation" (p. 17).

As masses of people moved westward in this migration, the archetypal material followed them, for it was in them and they were in it. Leaving their churches and pastors behind did nothing to change this. As Jung (1940/1969e) stated,

> we can never cut loose from our archetypal foundations unless we are prepared to pay the price of a neurosis … we are confronted, at every new stage in the differentiation of consciousness to which civilization attains, with the task of finding a new *interpretation* appropriate to this stage. (p. 157)

This is the time in history when we begin to see a transformation into alternative expressions of sacred practice in America such as the Transcendentalist movement of 1836, "…when George Ripley, a Unitarian minister … in Boston … called together his friends" (Hankins, 2004, p. 23). Among this group was Ralph Waldo Emerson, at that time also a unitarian minister, who would eventually become the de facto leader of this group of likeminded individuals. Henry David Thoreau would later join this movement, and it was marked by an enormous variety of people from all walks of life. This movement exemplifies the way in which the collective psyche behind traditional religious sacred practices was compelled to give expression to the archetype of the self through wider varieties of sacred practice.

Encountering Archetypes Through Alternative Sacred Practices

From these waves of unconscious energy, archetypal imagery began to push into the personal unconscious of individuals in very particular ways which gave inspiration to sacred practices which were quite different from the conventional form. "The spontaneous irruption of collective contents whose existence in the unconscious has long been known to psychology is part of the general tendency of mediumistic communications to filter the contents of the unconscious through to consciousness" (Jung, 1948/1969d, p. 317). Many notable individuals were at the forefront of these movements of esoteric beliefs and rituals. We begin our look at these alternative practices by examining movements that developed in both America and Europe: the Transcendentalist Movement, Spiritualism, and Occultism.

Unlike the Great Awakening which sought to "do away" with perceived sin, evil, and wickedness in life, the alternative practices that developed in its aftermath show how profoundly the archetype of the Self (*Imago Dei*) sought to manifest in daily lived experience in a way which was not one-sided, but joined the psychological opposites. Joining the opposites is a central tenet of Jung's psychology and is imperative to the psyche's healthy development. When pairs of opposites—good/evil, male/female, light/dark—are held in tension, it provides for the most desirable development of the psyche. "I have called the mediating or 'uniting' symbol which necessarily proceeds from a sufficiently great tension of the opposites the 'self' ... by 'self' we mean psychic wholeness" (Jung, 1958/1970a, p. 410).

The problem with achieving this wholeness is the one-sidedness often present in conventional religious sacred practice which seeks to repress, remove, or ignore one side of the tension at the expense of the other, or at the other extreme, to seek an undifferentiated union of both opposites into one. Jung considered these two options equally dysfunctional, "...the Christ symbol lacks wholeness in the modern psychological sense, since it does not include the dark side of things but specifically excludes it in the form of a Luciferian opponent" (Jung, 1959/1969b, p. 41). Speaking directly about the influence of the Great Awakening and its influence on these esoteric movements, McLoughlin (1978) notes that from "...its more mystical side of communion with God in nature came a new cultural milieu from which a truly national literature, art and architecture could develop, as well as the literary flowering of New England in the Transcendentalist movement" (p. 139). To illustrate this phenomenon, I turn to the Transcendentalist movement as a response to the one-sidedness of conventional religious sacred practice, seeking a reunion of man with nature.

Meeting with a small group in September 1836 in Boston, a Unitarian minister invited Ralph Waldo Emerson and others to discuss "the shortcomings of Unitarianism" (Hankins, 2004, p. 23). What resulted was something quite unexpected and profound: a movement that would be a precursor to many of the alternative forms of sacred practice throughout the nineteenth century and twentieth century. Emerson, whom I will consider the representative of the Transcendentalist movement, "...believed that the natural world was the actual manifestation of God; nature was part of the universal spirit ... individuals should not study nature as if it were an object but experience it as if it were a living spirit" (Hankins, 2004, p. 27). This willingness to embrace the person as a whole in sacred practice, not just what is considered the good "bright and shiny" parts, is one of the foundational ideas for the alternative and esoteric movements that developed at this time.

Although America and much of western Europe were solidly in the midst of the Industrial Revolution during these early decades of the nineteenth century, there were still strong undercurrents of the archetype of the Self moving through unexpected channels in surprising ways. These constellated energies, discounted and ignored by most conventional religious movements, found a voice in the world of literary and nature enthusiasts. Versluis (2005) writes, "...modern scientific rationalism and earlier Western esoteric traditions appeared incompatible with one another, and during the nineteenth century in America, scientific rationalism won what seemed a convincing victory in suppressing or marginalizing occult or more broadly, esoteric traditions" (p. 22). There was a tendency by most to simply "go about their business" and enjoy the fruits of the massive technological and industrial progress that made life easier for so many. But these significant changes to everyday life, while providing external enjoyment, material prosperity, convenience, and efficiency at work and at home were focused on the external world to the exclusion of the internal life and well-being of the soul. Versluis (2005) continues, "...a closer examination of this period suggests that even as Western esoteric traditions ... by and large vanished from Americans' public lives, these esoteric themes were taken up by major American authors" (p. 22). As a result, the constellated material of the *Imago Dei* made its way to the consciousness of the group that in society usually takes up the call of the unconscious: the writers, painters, poets, and sculptors.

Sacred practice and esoteric movements consequently continued, and as in the case of the transcendentalist movement, thrived during this time. However, it was not only the "usual suspects" of artistic bent that took up the clarion call of the unconscious. There were also movements during this time, both in Europe and in America, that came from some of the most unexpected places. For example, *spiritualism* is the attempt to contact the deceased by various means. This movement gained a large following in some places during the nineteenth and early twentieth centuries. A prototypical example of spiritualism during this time is the 1848 case of the Fox sisters which can be considered the beginning of the movement. Kate and Margaret, aged 12 and 13, "...began to interpret the strange knocks that had been heard in their small farmhouse for some nights" (Kucich, 2005, p. 34). The Fox sisters quickly became a catalyst for the general ideation of the masses of spiritual seekers of the new working-class culture in America.

One is reminded in this context of the strange visit between Jung and Freud in which they are having a protracted discussion about parapsychology and occult phenomena, and as Freud expressed his disfavor of the topic, "...there was such a loud report in the bookcase standing right next to us that we both started up in alarm ... I said to Freud, 'There, that is an example of a so-called catalytic exteriorization phenomenon'" (Jung, 1963, p. 155). This highlights the mysterious and ineffable quality that carried over into everyday life and was experienced by believers, non-believers, sceptics, practitioners, and leaders of many of these movements of the nineteenth and into the twentieth century. An important aside to the phenomenon that began with the Fox sisters include the very significant and lasting effects upon people from all social and ethnic backgrounds. "Every person had equal access to the Creator, and the prevalence of young, uneducated farm girls as mediums proved class, education and gender irrelevant in gaining access to the spirit world" (Kucich, 2005, p. 40).

From this humble and obscure beginning in Hydesville, New York, spiritualism moved quickly through ranks of social class and even came to influence intellectuals and academics in profound ways. "By 1854, more than one and a half million Americans were Spiritualists" (Green, 2022, p. 78). It is important to acknowledge one of those intellectuals upon whom spiritualism had a lasting impact, and who had an influence on Jung's work. F.W.H. Myers was a founding member of the Society for Psychical Research and staunch supporter of the ideas that developed out of spiritualism. Myers wrote, "…the first in the English-speaking work to describe systematically the phenomenon of subconsciousness or unconsciousness, to which he gave the name *subliminal* (beneath the threshold)" (Myers, 1903/1954, p. iii). One can see a clear connection between this idea and Jung's (1959/1969b) work on the collective unconscious and the archetype of the Self where he writes, "…the spontaneous symbols of the Self or of wholeness cannot in practice be distinguished from a God-image … an ever-present archetype of wholeness … it proves harmful and impossible to endure when an artificial unconsciousness-a repression-no longer reflects this life of the instincts" (p. 40).

This instinctual search for wholeness took on a particular significance during the American Civil War, in which both the Union and the Confederate armies lost many thousands on the battlefield. Traditional religious belief was held in high regard during this time. There is little doubt, for example, that many soldiers of both the north and the south carried the same Bible into battle. At the same time, there was something missing that seemed ineffable to those who survived: a continuous desire and longing for contact and closure with those who were killed. This had the unintended effect of strengthening some of the alternative sacred practices I have discussed in this section. As Pontiac (2023) notes, "The Civil War led to a searching for meaning that opened the way not only for Spiritualism, but for Theosophy and then for public Rosicrucian groups, in a continuing evolution and elaboration of the central themes of American Metaphysical Religion" (p. 262). This consciousness-seeking wholeness is a large part of the motivation in adherents' spreading spiritualism and its offshoots.

There was inevitable connection and overlap in many of the spiritualistic movements during the middle decades of the nineteenth century, which included Platonic clubs, utopian societies, pagan communes, and hermetic brotherhoods. There were at least two things that all of these religious movements, societies, and clubs had in common: (a) they all sought an alternative way to express the archetype of the Self, and (b) they all sought to do so outside the perceived confines of conventional religious practice. To illustrate this point, let us examine one case that was highly influential on many of the esoteric practices to come after. Alphonse Constant was an ex-seminarian who was previously bound for priesthood in the Catholic Church. He is better known by his pseudonym, Éliphas Lévi. His writings had a profound effect upon many esoteric movements that developed in the final decades of the nineteenth century, and into the twentieth and twenty-first centuries. In the interest of space, I will present just a few aspects of his story.

As a young man, Constant was studying for the Catholic priesthood. Born in 1810, he was raised a devout Catholic and maintained a profound sense of the religious throughout his life. But as he progressed through seminary toward his goal of ordination as a priest, his doubts and misgivings about the Church came to a crescendo two weeks before his ordination. His hesitation, existential crisis, and ultimate rejection of Catholic ministry can best be summed up in his own words, "I began to wonder if the priests really believed in God, and I shuddered- I whose religion was my only love- to see it fallen into such hands" (McIntosh, 1972, p. 76). After days of agonizing and soul searching, he ultimately decided, "I could not take my vows before the altar of a cold and egotistical cult without remorse" (McIntosh, 1972, p. 82).

After leaving the seminary at the age of 27, Constant searched for a place to belong after having devoted so much of his life to the Church. Having an affinity for Christian mysticism and Gnostic writings from an early age, a fortuitous meeting in 1852 with Hoene Wronski, a poor mathematician/philosopher, would forever change the trajectory of his life and work. Wronski had been a military career officer and Polish immigrant, but after taking time away to study philosophy, mathematics, and astronomy in Marseilles, he produced a large amount of literature on these subjects. When Constant met Wronski a year before Wronski's death, Wronski's writings worked like a magical charm on Constant and helped him reconcile the conflicts and confusion he had between the religion of his youth and his strong interest in Gnosticism and mystical practice. Wronski called his main work *messianisme*, which he defined as the union of philosophy and religion. This work had a profound impact on the esoteric milieu of the nineteenth and into the twentieth century, influencing the development of Theosophy, groups such as the Golden Dawn, Aleister Crowley and his esoteric religion of Thelema, and even Gerald Gardner, the retired British civil servant who in the 1930s developed what is known and still practiced by many today as Wicca.

Constant had such an influence on Crowley that, "Crowley … believed himself to be a reincarnation of Lévi … The date of Éliphas Lévi's death was about six months previous to that of Aleister Crowley's birth" (McIntosh, 1972, p. 226). The influence of Aleister Crowley on the development of nearly all Western esoteric and alternative sacred practices and movements in the twentieth century cannot be overstated. He was profoundly open to the world of the archetypes and the collective unconscious. Of particular influence on Crowley was an organization that was already established in England when Crowley was a young man in the 1890s: the Order of the Golden Dawn. Crowley was initiated into this order, which marked the beginning of his reworking of his religious background into an alternative practice that came to be known as Thelema, still an active movement in the second decade of the twenty-first century.

Another figure who drew on Éliphas Lévi's work was Helena Blavatsky. She developed a new Theosophy in the 1880s that exists into the twenty-first century. Not to be confused with the ancient religious movement based on Gnostic and Neoplatonist teaching, Blavatsky's Theosophy was a syncretic amalgamation of various movements of the 1800s which came to influence practices that followed. "Blavatsky presented occultism as a form of *magia naturalis*. It 'did not contradict the laws of nature, but rather used natural powers that science did not yet acknowledge…'" (Hanegraaff, 1998, p. 450). The mystical/philosophical/religious sacred practice of Theosophy is still practiced in several countries today.

With respect to Gardner and his religion of Wicca, "Gardner did not revive an old religion, but created a new one. His main sources of inspiration were occultist ritual magic in the tradition of Aleister Crowley and the *Hermetic Order of the Golden Dawn*" (Hanegraaff, 1998, p. 87). Gerald Gardner had to keep his new religion discreet as the open practice of witchcraft was illegal in Great Britain until 1951. It was then that Gardner published his writings, and Wicca was an immediate success and hugely popular with groups and individuals looking for an alternative sacred practice. Through numerous iterations, Wicca permeates nearly all of what is popularly known today as New Age/Neopagan practices.

This new religion almost singlehandedly led to the phenomenal growth of similar groups and practices throughout the 1960s and 70s, and persists today in the twenty-first century, aided greatly by the internet and the resulting ability of like-minded people to participate from all parts of the world. These examples of alternative sacred practice show that there is a pervasive and ubiquitous desire for the human creature to be involved in some meaningful practice that meets the complex of constellated archetypal imagery and gives expression to it in the external world of lived experience. Jung believed that we were at the beginning of a sea change in the twentieth century, a psychical movement that we cannot fully see because we are all in it. Looking to the future, one hopes for a time when the "joining of the opposites" in sacred practice is more the rule than the exception. For now, we can heed Jung's admonition, "...we could set out on the road to the union of the opposites and would then ... come to the place where the 'gods of destruction and the god of salvation are together" (Jung, 1955–56/1970b, p. 200).

My hope in this chapter is that the reader will ponder this veritable explosion of worldwide interest in sacred practice and further examine its practitioners as we move deeper into the twenty-first century. This archetypal energy has a strong affective pull which defies easy explanation. The energy of the unconscious stirs the emotions of writers, musicians, dramatists, and other artists. It also is a driving force of the dizzying scientific and technological breakthroughs of our current age. Throughout history, there have been visionaries such as Giordano Bruno, Marsilio Ficino, Thomas Aquinas, Hildegard von Bingen, and thousands of others who feel the energy of archetypal material and meet it in the personal consciousness of their psyche in a way which "joins the opposites." No doubt there are those today of unknown name and location whom we will see in later generations as people who heard the call of the archetypes, a call that is available to all of us who listen.

Competing Interests The author has no conflicts of interest to declare that are relevant to the content of this chapter.

References

Addonizio, K. (2016). *Bukowski in a sundress: Confessions from a writing life*. Penguin.

Berry, W. (2017). *The world-ending fire: The essential Wendell Berry*. Counterpoint Press.

Brueggemann, W. (1977). *The land*. Fortress Press.

Campbell, J., & Moyers, B. D. (1988). *The power of myth*. Doubleday.

Casey, E. (1993). *Getting back into place: Toward a renewed understanding of the place-world*. Indiana University Press.

Delegates and Syndics. (1972). *The new English Bible*. The University Press at Cambridge.

Eliot, T. S. (1962). *The complete poems and plays 1909–1950*. Harcourt, Brace, and World.

Emerson, R. W. (1929). *The complete writings of Ralph Waldo Emerson*. William Wise.

Godfrey, R. (1980). *Outward bound: Schools of the possible*. Anchor Press.

Green, D. (2022). *The religious revolution: The birth of modern spirituality, 1848–1898*. Farrar, Straus, and Giroux.

Guite, M. (2020). *Heaven in ordinary*. The Canterbury Press Norwich.

Hanegraaff, W. J. (1998). *New age religion and western culture*. State University of New York Press.

Hankins, B. (2004). *The second great awakening and the Transcendentalists*. Greenwood Press.

hooks, b. (2009). *Belonging: A culture of place*. Routledge.

Jung, C. G. (1963). *Memories, dreams, reflections*. Vintage Books.

Jung, C. G. (1966). The mana-personality (R. F. C. Hull, Trans.). In H. Read, M. Fordham, G. Adler, & W. McGuire (Eds.), *The collected works of C. G. Jung: Vol. 7. Two essays onanalytical psychology* (2nd ed., pp. 227–241). Princeton University Press. (Original work published 1928).

Jung, C. G. (1969a). Answer to Job (R. F. C. Hull, Trans.). In H. Read, M. Fordham, G. Adler, & W. McGuire (Eds.), *The collected works of C. G. Jung: Vol. 11. Psychology and religion* (2nd ed., pp. 355–470). Princeton University Press. (Original work published 1952).

Jung, C. G. (1969b). Christ, a symbol of the self (R. F. C. Hull, Trans.). In H. Read et al. (Eds.), *The collected Works of C.G. Jung: Vol, 9 (part 2). Aion: Researches into the phenomenology of the self* (2nd ed., pp. 36–71). Princeton University Press. (Original work published 1959).

Jung, C. G. (1969c). Concerning rebirth (R. F. C. Hull, Trans.). In H. Read et al. (Eds.), *The collected works of C. G. Jung: Vol. 9 (part 1). Archetypes and the collective unconscious* (2nd ed., pp. 113–147). Princeton University Press. (Original work published 1950).

Jung, C. G. (1969d). The psychological foundations of belief in spirits (R. F. C. Hull, Trans.). In H. Read et al. (Eds.), *The collected works of C. G. Jung: Vol. 8. Structure and dynamics of the psyche* (2nd ed., pp. 301–318). Princeton University Press. (Original work published 1948).

Jung, C. G. (1969e). The psychology of the child archetype (R. F. C Hull, Trans.). In H. Read et al. (Eds.), *The collected Works of C.G. Jung: Vol. 9 (part 1). The archetypes and the collective unconscious* (2nd ed., pp. 151–203). Princeton University Press. (Original work published 1940).

Jung, C. G. (1969f). The transcendent function (R. F. C. Hull, Trans.). In H. Read et al. (Eds.), *The collected works of C. G. Jung: Vol. 8. Structure and dynamics of the psyche* (2nd ed., pp. 67–91). Princeton University Press. (Original work published 1958).

Jung, C. G. (1970a). Flying saucers: A modern myth of things seen in the skies (R. F. C. Hull, Trans.). In H. Read, M. Fordham, G. Adler, & W. McGuire (Eds.), *The collected works of C. G. Jung: Vol. 10. Civilization in transition* (2nd ed., pp. 307–433). Princeton University Press. (Original work published 1958).

Jung, C. G. (1970b). *The collected works of C. G. Jung: Vol. 14. Mysterium coniunctionis* (R. F. C. Hull, Trans.). Princeton University Press. (Original work published 1955–56).

Jung, C. G. (1973). *C.G. Jung letters, volume 1* (R. F. C. Hull, Trans.). Princeton University Press.

Kidd, T. (2007). *The Great Awakening: The roots of evangelical Christianity in colonial America*. Yale University Press.

Kucich, J. (2005). Ghostly communion: Spiritualism, reform and Harriet Jacobs' incidents in the life of a slave girl. In C. Gutierrex (Ed.), *Occult in nineteenth-century America* (pp. 31–82). The Davies Group.

Lane, B. (2002). *Landscapes of the sacred: Geography and narrative in American spirituality*. Johns Hopkins.

Maslow, A. (1970). *Religions, values, and peak experiences*. Penguin.

McIntosh, C. (1972). *Eliphas Lévi and the French occult revival*. .

McLoughlin, W. (1980). *Revivals, awakenings, and reform*. University of Chicago Press.

Myers, F. (1954). *Human personality*. Longmans, Green, and Co. (Original work published 1903).

Pontiac, R. (2023). *American metaphysical religion*. Inner Traditions.

Rich, M. (2018). *The rediscovery of the sacred* (Publication No. 10829524). Master's thesis, University of West Georgia, ProQuest Dissertations and Theses Global.

Rubin, J. (1994). *Religious melancholy and the Protestant experience in America*. Oxford University Press.

Sanders, S. (1991). *Secrets of the universe: Essays on family, community, spirit and place*. Beacon Press.

Sanders, S. (1993). *Staying put: Making a home in a restless world*. Beacon Press.
Sheldrake, P. (2001). *Spaces for the sacred: Place, memory and identity*. Johns Hopkins.
Versluis, A. (2005). The 'occult' in nineteenth-century America. In C. Gutierrex (Ed.), *Occult in nineteenth-century America* (pp. 1–30). The Davies Group.
Vonnegut, K. (2005). *A man without a country*. Seven Stories Press.

CHAPTER 11

The Angry Gods of the Modern Academy: An Anatomy of Possession

James J. Dillon

On May 2, 2023, Adjunct Professor Shellyne Rodriguez steps from a busy New York City street and enters the Hunter College Academic Building on the way to teach her Art class. In the large central hallway, she notices a table with a small banner opposing abortion scattered with various information pamphlets. Behind the table sit a male and female student. In what was captured on cell phone video, Rodriguez approaches the table and yells at the male student, "You're not educating sh-t. This is f-cking propaganda. What are you going to do, like anti-trans next?" The male student calmly responds, "I mean, no, we're talking about abortion." Rodriguez then abruptly answers, "This is bullsh-t. This is violent. You're triggering my students." The student replies, "I'm sorry about that." Rodriguez retorts,

> No, you're not. You can't even have a f-cking baby. So, you don't even know what that is. You don't know what this is [pointing to their literature]. Get this sh-t outta here [violently pushes their materials off the table]. F-ck this sh-t!

J. J. Dillon (✉)
School of Social Sciences, University of West Georgia, Carrollton, GA, USA

J. J. Dillon (ed.), *Complex and Archetype*,
https://doi.org/10.1007/978-3-032-02609-5_11

Rodriguez then walks away as the students pick up their materials and try to place them back on the table. To view the entire scene, see Griffin (2023).

There are other contemporary examples of emotional and/or physical campus incidents like this, including verbal attacks by students on university professors and staff (e.g., Shibley, 2016), lawsuits (Patel, 2023), and firings (Flaherty, 2022; Stripling, 2023) over contentious statements or publications by university professors, as well as disinvitations (Alonso, 2023; Jackson, 2016), property damage (Bodley, 2017), and physical attacks on professors and students (Jaschik, 2017) in response to controversial speakers invited to campus. As disturbing as these events are, I am more interested in the unsensational, though far more common instances of a similar kind of behavior which does not capture the headlines. These include the use of the classroom (and laboratory) as a platform for political action or advocacy (Bromwich, 1992; Ellis, 2020), a general incivility in campus and classroom disagreement (Watkins, 2021), and the creation of a fearful emotional climate in which campus community members feel like they constantly walk on eggshells, just one fateful step away from saying the "wrong thing" and getting into real trouble (FIRE, 2023). In this chapter, Professor Rodriguez' outburst serves as a metaphor for the many smaller acts of coercion, emotional blackmail, and inappropriate disagreement which take place across campuses every day. I seek to provide a psychological explanation of this behavior and some constructive ways to address it.[1]

The Hidden Role of the Psychological Complex

Whatever else one may say about the state of the modern academy, there are surely some strong "feeling tones" on today's campuses. But exactly which kinds of topics tend to elicit powerful emotions? Constellating issues concern two general areas: (a) people being treated badly or unfairly (e.g., the overall plight of marginalized and excluded peoples, racial inequality, gender identity, sexual orientation, economic injustice), and (b) power (e.g., hierarchy, authority, and Western civilization more generally). I develop the argument in this chapter that a small set of complexes constellate around these two topic areas, come to dominate academic life

[1] I note here that this chapter was composed before attempts at university reform initiated by the Trump Administration in the United States beginning in late January of 2025.

in a near-obsessional way, and lead to the kinds of problematic campus behaviors described above.

Recall from Chap. 2 that a complex is a feeling-toned associational chain of perceptions, memories, thoughts, and desires clustered around a core of meaning and activated by life events, relationships, or developmental stages (see Shalit, 2002, p. 32). The central feature of the complex is the *feeling tone*, an absorbing emotional motif which behaves like a magnet, drawing all things to itself. If complexes are too "one-sided" and not brought into productive relationship with the ego, they will split off entirely and confront the ego as an "animated foreign body" (see Jung, 1928/1969c, p. 11; Jung, 1934/1969a, p. 96). While there are dozens of complexes, the *cardinal* complexes rest primarily upon the archetypes of *father*, *mother*, and *child*. The angry gods of the modern academy all emanate from these three archetypes.

It is also important to note in this context that complexes are either *positive* or *negative*. Dieckmann (2014) writes, "Diagnosis of a mother complex says very little unless we know whether it is positive or negative" (p. 1612). He says the same holds true with a father complex, "...where the archetypal figures of the father can tend more toward an Apollonian severity and rigidity or a Dionysian, intoxicating, and deductive experience" (p. 1612). With *positive* complexes, the person moves toward the archetype (*hypertrophy complexes*), typically identifying with its perceived generative-constructive aspects, as when one recognizes only the life-giving and liberatory aspects of the mother archetype, while repressing, ignoring, or projecting its perceived negative pole. With *negative* complexes, the person moves away from the archetype as a whole (*resistance complexes*), typically seeing it only in terms of its eliminative-reductive-destructive aspects, as when one casts the mother as only enveloping, capturing, smothering, and so repudiates her completely. In the next section, I discuss the principal complexes which dwell in the modern academy: the *negative father*, *positive mother*, and *Prometheus* (or *positive child*) complexes.

Negative Father Complexes in the Academy

The *father archetype* involves images of authority, law, protection, wisdom, guidance, obedience, judgment, royalty, divinity, salvation, moral commandments, prohibitions, sin, guilt, consciousness, and spirit (Jung, 1909/1989). The more attractive pole of the archetype is typically symbolized as "…an active, winged, swift-moving being as well as that which vivifies, stimulates, incites, fires, and inspires…" (Jung, 1948/1969f, p. 210). The negative pole of the archetype is associated with images of a harsh, punitive, capricious, unforgiving "terrible Father," a monster to be overcome, a giant who selfishly guards a treasure (Jung 1952/1967, p. 261). In a typical complex, one pole of the archetype is emphasized, while the other is repressed or projected. But with the negative complexes, there is a *complete rejection* of the father and all he represents (see Shalit, 2002, p. 92). The motto of this complex is, "Anything, so long as it is not like Father!"

Jung (1948/1969f) notes that in men, a "positive father-complex very often produces a certain credulity with regard to authority and a distinct willingness to bow down before all spiritual dogmas and values" (p. 214). Leaving the question of gender aside, the first aspect of the negative father complex completely reverses the positive father complex by introducing a recalcitrant, unconventional protest stance against norms of any kind, which are seen as being within father's purview (Dieckmann, 2014). In the academy, individuals in the grip of a negative father complex engage in persistent rebellion, deconstruction, iconoclasm, and moral transgression, constantly attacking the culture's most cherished beliefs along with its historical representatives (see Lind, 2023).

For a woman, Jung (1948/1969f) notes that the positive father-complex, "…induces the liveliest spiritual aspirations and interests" (p. 214). Again, leaving the question of gender aside, the second major aspect of the negative father complex reverses this situation by eschewing all spiritual aspirations, contemplation, and knowledge as a matter of principle. In the academy, this aspect of the negative father complex induces an overt skepticism, if not outright hostility to organized religion, a constant "problematizing" of the very notion of knowledge and abstract truth, and an emphasis upon action and social transformation rather than contemplation (Dieckmann, 2014, p. 182). Academics in the grip of this aspect of the negative father complex transform the very definition of the academy from a place to discern the good, true, and beautiful to a platform to engage present material and social reality.

Positive Mother Complexes in the Academy

The *mother archetype* concerns images of fertility, fruitfulness, holding, containment, protection, rebirth, magic, spiritual ecstasy, and the goal of our longing for redemption (Jung, 1938/1969e, p. 81). On the negative side, "the mother archetype may connote anything secret, hidden, dark; the abyss, the world of the dead, anything that devours, seduces, and poisons, that is terrifying and inescapable like fate" (Jung, 1938/1969e, p. 82). Positive mother complexes (or *hypertrophy complexes*) involve an intensification and idealization of the constructive elements of the maternal instinct, with any negative feelings toward the mother deeply repressed (Dieckmann, 2014, p. 1313). Jung writes that those with this kind of complex live life "...in and through others, in more or less complete identification with all the objects of her care" (Jung, 1938/1969e, p. 88). Without needy, vulnerable objects of concern, the person with a positive mother complex has no sense of existence whatsoever. With positive mother complexes, the constructive pole of the archetype is emphasized, for example, protection, nurturing, creativity, and generativity, while the adverse pole is repressed or projected, for example, constriction, inescapable fate, desire to return to the womb of the Great Mother, and devouring envelopment. In the academy, the positive mother complex translates into relentless advocacy for those identified as marginalized and weak, including fierce attempts to nurture the belonging, protection, empowerment, and liberation of society's "victims."

Prometheus Complexes in the Academy

Like the other archetypes, the archetype of the child has a twofold dynamic. On the one hand, it represents the future, "...the strongest, the most ineluctable urge in every being, namely the urge to realize itself" (Jung, 1940/1969g, p. 170). This aspect involves images of growth, wholeness, newness, innocence, and youth. On the other hand, the child archetype also represents the past, tradition, the unconscious, our "original state." The *Prometheus complex* (or *positive child complex*) stresses the future aspect of the child archetype and represses or projects its past dimension. It concerns itself with ideals of tomorrow, along with a pitched mania for progress.

In the academy, those in the grip of this complex feel a strict mandate to redeem the future from a past which is seen as fundamentally defective and unjust. They are constantly on guard for people, events, and forces which will "set us back." They use language reflecting a deep sense of urgency about addressing purportedly intolerable social or economic conditions, for example, "Justice demands we act now," or "There is no time to waste!" They say we "have no choice," "must," "ought," or "have to" to take some proffered ameliorative action. Those who do not adopt the same posture of moral emergency are labeled "part of the problem," or worse. Professors and university personnel with a Prometheus complex look to their students as a means to continue the steady march of history away from the dark ages of the past toward a future enlightenment. In the grip of this complex, they engage in a process Jung calls *furor paedogogicus*, in which they attempt to emancipate students from tradition in order to build a world (purportedly) better than the one their parents and ancestors grew up in (see Jung, 1940/1969g, p. 175). This sentiment is reflected in the words of former U.S. President Woodrow Wilson, then President of Princeton University, who said, "The purpose of a university should be to make a son as unlike his father as possible" (Wilson & Link, 1966, p. 19).

The Angry Gods of the Modern Academy

Complexes help us digest overwhelming psychological reality by presenting just one side of a paradoxical and bipolar archetype. If it is extreme enough, this one-sided disavowal of unconscious material can create conditions which are ripe for *possession*, a state wherein the ego *completely identifies* with a single pole of the archetype, while repressing the other pole so extensively that unconscious material becomes a "secondary personality" (Jung, 1913/1973, p. 601), which eventually assimilates the ego to itself. To illustrate this phenomenon of possession, Jung (1939/1969b) provides the example of a person who so completely identifies the ego personality with the positive aspects of the *persona* archetype that the repressed shadow material takes on a life of its own, constantly threatening to swallow up the ego (p. 122). We might refer to these more extreme complexes as *autonomous complexes*, distinguishing them from *simple complexes* which involve splits, but not outright possession.

When the psyche is "possessed" by unconscious material like this, four significant things occur. First, repressed material is acted out at the literal level rather than experienced at the symbolic level. As Shalit (2002) notes, the autonomous complex cannot hold a dialogue with its own archetypal core. Instead, "the actual father is rejected, slain, or conversely, adulated and sexualized; the [actual] mother is overly attached to, or abandoned in panic" (p. 63). Thus, the powerful forces of the archetype, particularly aggression and relatedness, become actually destructive and/or consuming, which adds an element of relational instability, perpetual drama, conflict, and even violence to the affected person's life.

Second, a possessed ego is a vulnerable and overtaken ego, continuously feeling not only "unsafe" but constantly victimized, assaulted, offended, violated, and defiled. It thus becomes emotionally volatile, touchy, defensive, feels helpless, inferior, and constantly enraged (Shalit, 2002, p. 66). Third, the possessed ego becomes inflated with so many unconscious contents that it eventually becomes unable to realize its own limitations. Such an ego is narcissistic and grandiose. Shalit (2002) writes,

> The inflated ego … does not discriminate between ego and Self, nor does it distinguish between polarities, such as good and evil. It assumes godlike proportions, approving of the Commandment to have "no other gods before me," where "me" means the ego. (p. 104)

An inflated ego feels supremely special, behaving as if laws and rules which govern the natural world, social discourse, and moral behavior do not apply to it.

Fourth, disowned unconscious material in the possessed ego takes the form of *actual personalities* who visit, speak, and haunt (see Jung, 1934/1969a, pp. 97–8; Jung, 1939/1969b, p. 132; Jung 1954/1969d, pp. 270–1; Shalit, 2002, p. 75). I call these beings *gods* to remain consistent both with the experience of their overwhelming power, and with the way this phenomenon has been understood throughout history (excepting the modern era). As discussed in Jung's (1936/1970) analysis of the "possession" of an entire country by the god Wotan, my claim is that today's universities are similarly possessed by the manic and willful gods within the Prometheus complex, the devouring chthonic Mother goddess within the positive mother complex, and the mercilessly exacting Father god within the negative father complex. These are the "angry gods of the modern academy." I turn now to how each god manifests on today's campuses.

The Shadow of the Father (Shiva)

When we reject *all* of the Father, as occurs with the negative father complex, it eventually leads to the formation of the autonomous personality Dieckmann (2014) calls the *negative senex*, the shadow of the entire father archetype. In his personified aspect, we might call him *Perses* or *Shiva* after the ancient gods of destruction and disorder. An individual with a negative father complex can only experience this disowned archetypal material in other people or external events. Thus, Shiva only comes to such a person from the outside. Think here of Professor Rodriguez, who violently pushes literature off the table saying at the same time, "This [external material] is violent." Repressed material is so undeveloped, it unfortunately only manifests in its most immature and primitive forms. Shiva shows himself in three specific ways.

The positive core of the father archetype contains the quintessential Spirit Being. If this Being is categorically rejected, as it is in the negative father complex, instead of drawing upon and experiencing a being of highest purity and radiant consciousness, we see only his shadow in the world. Instead of clarity, boundless knowledge, truth, justice, and nobility, we see confusion, skepticism, relativism. We experience tribal loyalties, base desires, we reduce everything high and noble to its lowest common denominator: to money, skin color, and the twitching of our sex glands. Instead of true spirituality, fire, vivification, and inspiration from above, we draw everything down to the ground, we burst with emotional frenzy and bloodlust over present political and economic realities.

Second, the positive pole of the father archetype houses a gentle, benevolent Protector. But if this being is categorically rejected as it is in the negative father complex, instead of relating to and knowing a caring Father god, we experience only his shadow who appears to us as a giant who selfishly guards treasure, as a monster to be overcome, for example, as whiteness, organized religion, language, morality, the state, hierarchy, Western civilization. Living in a world where one is perpetually under assault by monsters simultaneously gives rise to a deep need for "safe spaces" and rigid rules to keep the monsters at bay. What such a person cannot see is that the real monster does not primarily derive from the external world, but from the archetypal core of our own psyche.

Third, the positive pole of the father archetype houses a wise old man, an experienced teacher, a just judge. If we reject all aspects of the father, as we do with a negative father complex, we project his shadow outward, unconsciously enacting his most primitive form in our own behavior. Instead of manifesting inner wisdom and knowledge, we propagate fads, trends, and impenetrable jargon. We become false prophets who lead the youth astray. Instead of the just judge, we become unforgiving, overly stern grand inquisitors, tyrants with murderous aggression. Instead of the tolerant and mature personality, the calm observer, we become partisan, emotionally imbalanced, and recklessly biased.

The Devouring Mother (Demeter)

When we embrace only the positive aspects of the mother archetype, as occurs in the positive mother complex, it leads to the formation of an autonomous personality von Franz calls the *devouring mother* (von Franz & Boa, 1994). In her personified aspect, we might call her *Demeter*, after the ancient goddess of the harvest and fertility who becomes so singularly preoccupied with protecting her daughter from death, she ignores her sacred duties to the harvest, causing widespread famine, and, ironically, destroying the vital surrounding community any child would need to thrive. As with the father complex, a person with a positive mother complex can only experience disowned archetypal material in other people or external events. The idea that we could be leaving a trail of destruction to the surrounding community (or even harming our own children) while we are "caring" for them would never occur to such a complex-fixated person. Demeter manifests in the academy in two major ways.

First, the positive mother complex develops only the positive aspects of the mother archetype which have to do with holding, containment, and protection. The negative aspects of the same archetype concerning constriction and devouring are repressed. The individual can, therefore, only experience others as constricting or devouring *them*, and/or unconsciously constricts others, even devouring the very dependents within their care. In our scenario, note how Professor Rodriguez approaches the table and experiences herself and her students as being constricted from the outside, "You are triggering my students," she says. "This is violent." In "caring" for her students, she then curses and violently tosses material to the ground, which ironically makes the environment unsafe for everyone else. Like Demeter, the possessed ego ironically destroys the surrounding world in trying to save those within its care. If the child survives the repressed mother's wrath, there is no stable and nurturing world for them to return to.

Another variation of this same theme is more like the Cybele-Attis pairing, where the mother's care unconsciously unleashes the repressed constricting and devouring forces *upon the child*. When "care" and "protection" are possessed by Cybele, they become constricting and disabling for the recipient. In our campus context, consider the Marxist scholar Fredrik de

Boer's (2023) analysis that despite all the energy and attention given to marginalized groups in the aftermath of the George Floyd killing, all the corporate and university statements, policies, and protests, when one looks at the problems that marginalized communities actually face—economic insecurity, employment, home ownership, high school and college graduation, access to healthcare—things have not improved at all during this period of time, and on some measures have gotten *worse*. This happened, he argues, because the "care" and "protection" given to these vulnerable groups was not real, but a disabling, narcissistic care which tends to the needs of the *caregiver* rather than to the cared-for. This claim is borne out in de Boer's demonstration that the condition of corporate leaders and university personnel has *improved* across these same measures during this period of time. He argues the care given in the wake of George Floyed harmed its intended recipients not only by being narcissistic but by casting recipients as passive victims, mere representatives of larger structures, with no individuality or agency of their own.

The Inexorable Fates (Moirai)

When we embrace only the future-oriented aspects of the child archetype, as occurs in the Prometheus complex, it leads to the formation of the autonomous personality we might call the *inexorable fates*. In their personified aspect, they are the *Moirai*, after the three ancient goddesses who allot to each human being his/her specific path and destiny in life. As with the other complexes, the individual with a positive child complex can only experience disowned archetypal material in other people or external events. The Moirai can thus only come to such a person from the outside, manifesting in the most immature and primitive ways. The Moirai appear in two specific forms.

First, the positive child complex only develops the aspects of the child archetype having to do with unlimited possibility and transformation wrought by the will. Aspects of the same archetype having to do with our "original state," fate, the urge to be what we are, or "actualize our nature" are repressed. We instead project these qualities onto others and see them there. Opponents are thus experienced as rigid, doctrinal, or conservative. But who is it who asserts a rigid and unchanging doctrine, even insisting upon the use or banishment of particular words and phrases? Who demands intellectual uniformity, searches for, and often punishes heretics who deviate from the common doctrine? At the same time, the content of the common doctrine is itself often possessed by the Fates, stressing the determinative role of skin color, gender, sexual orientation, or socioeconomic class.

Second, the Prometheus complex develops only those aspects of the child archetype having to do with the future, and represses aspects of the same archetype which seek to adhere to the past or tradition. We instead project these qualities outward and can only experience them there. The ego possessed by the Morai thus becomes fixated and haunted by the past. The past plagues us, attacks us, oppresses us. It becomes difficult to think about anything else but the past, and so we seek to completely eradicate it by attacking foundational ideas from the past, historical figures and monuments, even the concept of nature itself, which is the primary vehicle of the past. Instead of placing ourselves in a position of critical dialogue *within a tradition*, we abstract ourselves and occupy an intellectual space where we reside nowhere. We mistake this abstracted domain for freedom and liberation, but the negative identity we have formed depends upon what is rejected (the past and tradition) much more than nearly any other kind of intellectual position. The Fates will have their say one way or the other.

Dynamics of Possession in the Academy

In this section, I discuss how the negative father, positive mother, and Prometheus complexes function in the academy in a *possessing* way rather than as benign, garden-variety complexes. Recall the first aspect of psychological possession is that repressed material is acted out at the literal level rather than experienced at the symbolic level. Displacement and fixated attention are the orders of the day, as the affected individual slays actual monsters, protects real vulnerable children, and forces the present away from a wicked past. In addition, the energy that is displaced in ego possession is not normal psychic energy, but *archetypal* energy. Titanic and religious force is thus transposed into inappropriate and mundane contexts, causing the affected individual's behavior to appear exaggerated and explosive. Shalit (2002) writes,

> An autonomous complex is like an infected wound, and when touched, triggered, activated, constellated, we are affected, as evidenced by an exaggerated emotional response; for instance, oversensitivity, feelings of sadness, outbursts of anger or embarrassment, etc. (p. 35)

Consider Professor Rodriguez' behavior in this regard. This was the foyer of an academic building on a typical Tuesday afternoon. Students at the table were presenting a reasonable case against abortion and wanted to talk about it with other university community members. Instead of hearing a counterargument from a professor, what came out was completely inappropriate for the context, that is, violent protection of children/students from harm, real slaying of oppressive male monsters, all in an effort to furiously shape a new and better future. Because of the autonomous complexes, Rodriguez simply cannot hold the intellectual space with other people. Relatedly, consider the many other examples from contemporary campus life of inordinate energy displaced onto otherwise mundane contexts. At one moment, a department discusses the pedestrian matter of scheduling classes for the next academic year, and in the next, the conversation becomes a pitched, colossal dispute about the oppressive nature of Western civilization itself.

Second, a possessed ego is a vulnerable and overtaken ego, constantly feeling not only "unsafe," but victimized, assaulted, offended, violated, and defiled even when there is no external threat to speak of (see Shalit, 2002, p. 66). Projected and split-off psychic material confronts the ego as a persecutory spirit, causing it to become emotionally volatile, touchy, defensive, feeling helpless, inferior, and constantly enraged. Consider, for example, how people often disagree in the contemporary academy. It is not that one party makes a claim the other simply disagrees with, but the claim is seen as an assault upon the possessed party's very existence. The weakened ego experiences words themselves as actual attacks, as "violent," to use Rodriguez' phrase. With such a view of the power of words and ideas, things can get heated rather quickly in intellectual spaces. The beleaguered ego also becomes increasingly obsessed with safety. Witness the lengths the contemporary academy has gone to create safe spaces, protect feelings, ensure belonging, and avoid "verbal violence" to aggrieved community members. Comfort comes to replace truth as the standard used to judge the worthiness of ideas.

Third, the possessed ego becomes inflated with so many unconscious contents that it cannot realize its own limitations. It is narcissistic and grandiose. Consider the many popular theories in the contemporary academy which are premised on the transcendence of physical, moral, or historical limitation, as when academics suggest that language, culture, or thought "constructs reality" (de Man, 1979), or that the ego or human groups are free to decide what is right and wrong (Lyotard, 1984), what gender it is (Butler, 2007), even to transcend death itself (Young, 2006). At the behavioral level, the inflated ego on campus feels entitled to dispense with the norms of civil discourse, university procedures, Roberts Rules of regular order, standards of logical inquiry, scientific investigation, even basic English grammar. *Everyone* must bend to the inflated ego's concerns, fears, and preoccupations. In the Hunter College scenario, consider how easily Professor Rodriguez sets aside the customary rules of rational discourse and polite behavior. She behaves the way she does not because she makes her interlocutor into an inhuman "object" whom she can then denigrate (or because she is actually attacked), but because *she separates herself* from the bonds which regulate human groups from as early as preschool, behaving instead like a special, exempted being.

Consequences of Ego Possession

This section assesses the negative consequences of ego possession upon the affected academics themselves, their colleagues, students, and the wider world. The main consequences include: (a) the creation of a stifling group-think mentality, and (b) serious injury to the academic community though repeated acts of incivility, bullying, and intimidation. First, when complexes are extremely one-sided, as they are in ego-possession, we come to rely on the *collective consciousness* to do our thinking for us, rather than employing our own considered reasoning. Following Jacobi (1959), collective consciousness is an archetype dealing with "representatives of the typical norms, customs, and views prevailing in a particular environment" (p. 110). Jung (1940/1969g) refers to it as the "mass man,"

> everything that has been overcome and left behind by so called 'progress' sinks deeper and deeper into the unconscious, from which there re-emerges in the end the primitive condition of *identity with the mass*. Instead of the expected progress, this condition now becomes reality. (p. 175, emphasis in original)

Since a possessed ego is in such a weakened developmental state, and since it has no inner resources to draw upon, it instead relies upon the external pattern of the collective consciousness for meaning and direction. Jacobi (1959) writes,

> From the relatively harmless 'it is done' or 'it is not done,' pedantries that afflict young and old alike, to the intoxicating demagogic theories of paradise on earth which rob whole nations of their reason, one might list an endless series of rules, customs, laws, systems, and theories whose purpose it is to fetter man's natural dispositions from childhood on … Thus many an intellectual succumbs to the slogans, the "isms," the collective commandments and prohibitions that come to him from outside, while he remains utterly uncomprehending toward the symbols that rise up from within him, for his mind has long since lost all relation to the other parts of his being. (p. 112)

The collective consciousness serves to anchor a one-sided ego firmly in its inner forgetting. For its part, the possessed ego is all-to-willing to oblige.

The content of the collective consciousness will change through time and between cultures, but the pattern of the archetype remains the same. The content of our current collective consciousness is what we might call the *orthodoxy of justice and fluidity*, which involves: (a) eschewing the metaphysical and elevating the material/social; (b) cultivating a robust liberation from tradition, nature, the body, from who others tell us we are, and from what others tell us to do; and (c) redeeming an order of being which is experienced as hopelessly defective and unjust. This is our intellectual default position, the water in which modern academics swim.

Of course, many of the assumptions of this orthodoxy are quite valid for certain questions and contexts, but it is logically impossible that they can apply to every question as a matter of axiomatic principle. Over time, overreliance upon collective consciousness leads to shallow, lazy thinking. Our intellectual faculties lie fallow and are not given the opportunity to exercise and develop (Shalit, 2002, p. 28). In addition, when we rely on the collective consciousness to do our thinking for us, it often leads to poor personnel and policy decisions. We end up hiring what Deresiewicz (2014) calls, "excellent sheep," those who have ascended the academic career ladder not by nuanced critical thinking and honest research but by kowtowing to the academic pieties of the day. Academic groupthink and ideological uniformity also damage trust in the university by a public who increasingly sees it not as a place where questions are squarely investigated and valid knowledge produced but as an activist community dedicated to advancing a monolithic political platform (see Belkin, 2023; Camera, 2023; Ellis, 2020).

The second major consequence of ego-possession is that when so many academic community members have touchy, fragile egos, it becomes nearly impossible to form the kind of collegial body that can engage in the robust give-and-take of inquiry required to advance the collective pursuit of truth and the common good. Instead of employing real thinking by clearly defining terms and premises, dispassionately sharing/discussing evidence, many members of the academy use the guise of thinking to do something else entirely, that is, pursue grandiose, ego-inflated projects which do not recognize natural, moral, or physical limits, enact repressed unconscious dynamics, and work toward an ever-elusive emotional security by hiring a plethora of like-minded colleagues and erecting a labyrinthine system of speech codes, rules, and sanctions. Instead of a community devoted to the shared pursuit of truth, the academy becomes more like a clique requiring a professed orthodoxy for entry and continued membership. Gatekeepers routinely use fallacious rhetorical tactics such as the smear (e.g., "Adolf Hitler said the same thing"), the *ad hominem* (e.g., "That's just what a privileged, middle-class white person would say"), and name-calling (e.g., "That's racist") to enforce academic orthodoxy and cast dissenters as beyond the pale of common group membership.

It is often forgotten that the academy is a real, living being. I refer to it as the *collegial body* (Dillon, 2022, pp. 69–70). This body, like other occupational bodies, is a group of people, organized within an institutional structure, who labor together to produce a common end or product. In the academy, this labor is inquiry and teaching, and the product is knowledge and learning. The living tissue of the collegial body sustains real injury through repeated acts of incivility, emotional blackmail, bullying, and distortion of the body's primary purpose. Let us return to Professor Rodriguez for a moment. What knowledge or learning has been advanced by her actions? What opportunities for dialogue, insight, mind-changing have been missed? What kinds of injury has she caused, not so much to those particular students, but to the healthy functioning of the entire intellectual community? Such damage is not taking place at Hunter College alone. A recent national survey of colleges and universities points to the negative effects of this kind of ongoing communal injury. Faculty report a widespread feeling of stress, fear, and self-censorship on university campuses *even among those who profess belief in university orthodoxies* (FIRE, 2023). Such an emotional climate cannot help the group fulfill its overall mission of producing knowledge and learning, and it stifles the growth of the community's individual members.

Internal and External Solutions to One-Sidedness

This final section presents some internal and external solutions designed to address the various problems I have outlined. *Internal solutions* concern those things that individual members of the academic community can (and should) do on their own. *External solutions* are about transforming institutional structures and creating new administrative initiatives. Both kinds of solutions are required for real change to occur. The internal prescriptions include: (a) renewing faith in the primacy of reason over action or power in one's personal and professional life, and (b) addressing negative father, positive mother, and child complexes by "doing the work" described in Chap. 2. The external prescriptions include: (a) administrative action toward increasing viewpoint diversity in faculty hiring, (b) restoration of the vision of the university as a place primarily devoted to the exploration of truth versus political action or advocacy, (c) a meaningful assessment regime which focuses on student learning, and (d) the formation of a national professional society which would articulate and monitor clear standards of professional knowledge and behavior for university professors.[2]

Internal Solutions

While intellect is our most distinctively human feature, it does not develop and flourish without serious intention and work. This discipline involves studiously resisting the ever-present temptation to bully, manipulate, and use fear, shame, insults, threats, or emotional outbursts in intellectual life. These low impulses are not unique to our modern era, but have been present from the time the first human ancestors shared words with one another.

[2] In the context of recent (January 2025) attempts at university reform by the Trump Administration in the United States, it is important to note that true reform cannot come from external changes alone such as funding incentives and executive orders, but must include the important dimension of internal work. Further, in order to be effective, the external reforms themselves must be multi-faceted in implementation rather than relying on a single administrative policy position, for example, eliminating DEI programs. External reforms must also emanate from all levels of university governance. The federal government is surely an important player in university reform, but so too is state government, boards of regents/directors, accrediting bodies, professional associations, alumni, industry, and other community stakeholders. Federal changes alone, without buy-in and deep coordination with these other administrative bodies, could prove ineffective or even counterproductive to true and lasting reform.

One can also see these tendencies *writ large* in young children. It is simply a bad intellectual habit we all must struggle with. As Plato (380 B.C.E./1987) illustrates with the character Thrasymachus in his *Republic*, we resort to intellectual force when we are imbalanced in our souls, guided by passions, have a character flaw or psychological defect of some kind, when we do not trust others, or when we are so fixated on a certain outcome in the world that we cannot delay gratification or discipline ourselves to do the requisite intellectual labor.

The danger is that action unguided by reason is misinformed; the exercise of ill-considered power is destructive. It is, therefore, incumbent upon members of the academic community to develop the intellectual virtues necessary to enable the ascendency of reason in their individual lives. Additionally, younger colleagues and students need good intellectual role models and a clear blueprint for how to properly engage in rational debate and inquiry. They will surely mimic our bad habits. We can easily imagine one of Professor Rodriguez' students (who actually did witness her outburst) behaving exactly as she did when later confronted in class or the residence hall by an interlocutor espousing a position with which they do not agree.

The second suggestion is to "do the work" described in Chap. 2 of addressing negative father, positive mother, and Prometheus complexes by dissolving projections, holding polarities, developing sufficient ego strength, and learning to integrate the multifaceted father, mother, and child archetypes into daily psychological functioning. One of the most important parts of this work involves building a psychic structure which will enable us to *hold opposites*, to keep in tension the ambivalent and paradoxical reality of archetypal life. This is done through the *transcendent function* and practicing the capacity to work with *symbols* (see Dillon, 2021). This is such an important step because the issues most academics care about, for example, economic justice, liberation, knowledge, truth, freedom, beauty, etc., are all complex and paradoxical wholes which cannot be understood in a simplistic and one-sided way.

External Solutions

Ellis (2020) has traced a decidedly ideological tilt in university faculty over the past 50 years. The 1969 Carnegie Commission on Higher Education survey of university faculty found that 45 percent of faculty had views they described as "left or liberal," 27 percent were "middle-of-the-road," and

28 percent were strongly or moderately "conservative." Depending upon how the data are gathered, by 2006 this breakdown shifts to 80 percent left or liberal, 11 percent moderate, and 9 percent strongly or moderately conservative. A left-right ratio of less than 2:1 in 1969 shifts to over 8:1 in fewer than 40 years. The ratio is more extreme in certain disciplines, with a left-right ratio of 4:1 in the professional schools, 9:1 in the hard sciences and mathematics, 17:1 in the humanities, and 21:1 in the social sciences (Ellis, 2020, p. 32). This tilt does not reflect ideological changes in the U.S. population at large (which in 2006 is roughly 19 percent liberal, 42 percent moderate, and 39 percent conservative), but is unique to the academy (Saad, 2023). This movement toward ideological uniformity correlates with increasing philosophical and methodological uniformity as well, so the problem is surely deeper than mere political outlook.

With all of the pressing demands for "diversity," it appears that when it comes to *thought*, modern universities are some of the least diverse institutions in the country. This is a real problem for a variety of reasons. Numerous studies have documented the errors that groups composed of too many like-minded people are prone to make (Janis, 1971). In my own discipline of psychology, Duarte, et al. (2014) present data showing that decreased political diversity in psychology has led to less reliable research over time. In the investigation of truth, there are massive benefits of having opposing views throughout the process. Further, ideological uniformity creates social and cultural norms which can transform an institution into something more like a club, sanctuary, or party headquarters than a community radically open to the investigation of reality and student development (Wexler, 1995). Therefore, the first external solution is that university administrators commit themselves to increasing viewpoint diversity in faculty hiring, if not to a left-right parity then at least to the 2:1 ratio which obtained a generation ago (see Zimmerman, 2012).

Over this same 50-year period of time, there has been an overall shift in the self-understanding of the purpose of the academy as a place primarily devoted to the investigation and teaching of truth, to an institution dedicated to "action" and "social change," a situation resembling the "sacred project" described by Smith (2014) in which universities,

> work to expose, protest, and end through social movements and state regulations and programs all human inequality, oppression, exploitation, suffering, injustice, poverty, discrimination, exclusion, hierarchy, and constraint of, by, and over other humans. (pp. 7–8)

There is surely nothing wrong with inspired political action and social change. The question is whether universities are particularly good at it, and whether doing this work impedes their larger mission. Universities are primarily *schools and laboratories*, places where scholars dispassionately build knowledge and help students learn. Constant demands for action and change (in an already determined philosophical direction) make that kind of work nearly impossible. So, the second external action requires universities to recalibrate their explicit and implicit missions to restore a vision of themselves as *avoiding the fray* of politics and social action (see Altschuler & Wippman, 2024). This is not because we do not like politics or lack the courage to take social action, but because impartiality helps students learn and scholars discover truth. Of course, this stance will be supremely difficult since there are real problems in the world which make all of us angry and which demand solutions. But the university cannot fulfill its primary mission if it is constantly dragged into this or that partisan cause. Schools and laboratories have a distinct contemplative function in society which needs to be protected and preserved by those who run and work in them.

As universities increasingly spend their time advancing justice and social change, it appears that students have not been learning much. As I document in another paper (Dillon, 2018), Arum and Roksa (2011, p. 35) present convincing data that almost half of undergraduates' skills in critical thinking, analytical reasoning, problem-solving, and writing show no statistically significant gains after four years of college. For the other half, gains are between 7 and 10 percentage points, depending on the dimension. What this means is that for almost half of all college students, four years of college has had no discernible academic impact on learning; for the other half, the impact is minimal. Derek Bok, who served as Harvard University president from 1971 to 1991, presents a similarly depressing picture of grade inflation and limited learning in college classrooms (Bok, 2006). This does not include additional learning losses associated with the recent Covid epidemic whose dimensions we are just now in the process of fully assessing (see Bryant, 2024; Hu, et al., 2024).

Increased pressure upon faculty to publish their research and get good student evaluations for tenure and promotion are surely factors which take energy away from teaching, but politicizing the classroom is another. To counter this tendency to ignore students' failure to learn, the third external solution involves implementing a rigorous regime of assessing standards of learning in students. Of course, there are dedicated offices of assessment on university campuses already, but they are hardly serious when it comes to ensuring student learning. Regional accrediting bodies also need to step up and exact severe penalties for failing to teach students, including not only loss of accreditation for the institution but refunding students their loans and tuition dollars when they graduate college without learning much of anything.

Most professions have guilds, societies, or licensing bodies responsible for articulating and maintaining high standards of competence and ethical conduct for their members. Lawyers have the Bar Association; doctors have the American Medical Association; public school teachers, mental health counselors, even real estate agents and cosmetologists have state-level boards of licensing and accreditation. What are the professional standards for the university teaching and research profession? Where is this information taught and presented to professors in training? Why are university professors exempt from a professional standards and licensing regime which obtains in nearly all other professions?

The present patchwork system of university/human resources professional conduct policies is not nearly comprehensive enough since it typically focuses only on egregious, often illegal conduct. It is also a bit like the fox guarding the proverbial henhouse. Imagine, for example, if each individual law firm was responsible for defining and policing the professional conduct of its own lawyers. This is the professional standards model currently in place for university professors. So, the fourth external prescription involves the establishment of an independent, national society of professional standards for university professors. Like doctors, lawyers, therapists, and public school teachers, these standards would be taught and practiced at the graduate school level. Professors would have to pass a licensing exam to work at any university, and would need to update their license every 5 or 10 years through continuing education. At the very minimum, these standards would mandate a practice of political impartiality in the classroom, and clearly articulate basic norms of intellectual discourse which would prohibit rhetorical tactics like the smear, name-calling, and *ad hominem* attack. Like a lawyer being brought before the bar for violating a client's confidentiality, there would be real sanctions for unprofessional behavior like calling students names or using the classroom for political indoctrination. In such a world, Professor Rodriguez could lose her license to teach at a university (permanently or for a fixed period of time) given her unprofessional behavior toward the students at their information table that day. More serious unprofessional and/or illegal conduct such as bribery, sexual harassment, or assault would obviously be included here as well (and is already part of the present system of professional standards on nearly all U.S. campuses).

This professional standards initiative will likely be opposed by many on the grounds that it violates "freedom of speech" or "academic freedom." This is not the case at all. Professors, like other professionals, are bound by codes of conduct which constrain the constitutional and legal rights they enjoy in other settings. This constraint is necessary for them to successfully perform the specialized institutional work they do, and to advance the larger mission of the university. Legal and professional freedom are thus two quite different things. A physician has a constitutional right to tell a woman he thinks she is attractive at a bar, but he is not free to do so in his role as a doctor during a physical exam. Telling him he is professionally barred from propositioning a woman in his office does not violate his "free speech." Similarly, a professor is free to go out into the street and call people names or yell at others in their role as a U.S. citizen, but when they do so at school *in their role as a professor*, it is an entirely different matter.

Conclusion

This chapter has presented an argument that three complexes are largely responsible for many of the trends and problematic behaviors on today's campuses. Other analyses point to a different set of psychological factors, such as the popular use of a "helicopter" parenting style which causes a weak, safety-obsessed ego (Lukianoff & Haidt, 2018), or large-scale father absence which leads to iconoclasm and perpetual rebellion (Vitz, 2013), or widespread undiagnosed personality disorders which trigger unstable relationships and emotional volatility on campus (Rufo, 2023). Other accounts point to larger institutional, cultural, or religious factors. For example, Bloom (1987) and Ellis (2020) blame campus administrators who have repeatedly capitulated to immature faculty and student demands, which both reinforces and encourages even more dysfunctional behavior in the future. Pluckrose & Lindsay (2020) argue that disturbing campus trends are due to the misapplication of certain "critical" theories which mistakenly discern violence and oppression in any and all social and economic structures (see also Good, 2001). Beckeld (2022) contends that current campus theatrics are part of a trend called *oikophobia* which appears in later stages of all cultures in which community members develop a strong hatred of themselves and a valorization of "the Other." Bloom

(1992) and Voegelin (1997) point to religious factors such as the large-scale embrace of a modern form of ancient Gnosticism in which we desperately seek to escape from the limitations of embodied existence. Similarly, Jacobs (2017) points to the operation of an unconscious mythical substrate involving purity, defilement, and purgation.

These accounts are all valid as far as they go, and they help contribute to a greater understanding of our present cultural moment. At the same time, they do not directly attend to deeper dynamics of the *psychological complex*, which gives us a fuller account of the particular constellating topic issues (power and injustice) and explains the explosive energy which often animates these campus phenomena. It may be that parenting practices, family breakdown, administrative blunders, changing cultural patterns, and religious ideas cause complexes (or vice versa), but these factors alone do not fully attend to inner psychological and archetypal dynamics. We ignore the angry gods of the modern academy at our own peril.

Competing Interests The author has no conflicts of interest to declare that are relevant to the content of this chapter.

References

Alonso, J. (2023, April 13). Shouting down speakers who offend. *Inside Higher Ed*. https://www.insidehighered.com/news/students/free-speech/2023/04/13/shouting-down-speakers-who-offend

Altschuler, G., & Wippman, D. (2024). Should academic departments make political statements? *The Hill*. https://thehill.com/opinion/education/5058218-should-academic-departments-avoid-making-political-statements/

Arum, R., & Roksa, J. (2011). *Academically adrift: Limited learning on college campuses*. University of Chicago Press.

Beckeld, B. (2022). *Western self-contempt: Oikophobia in the decline of civilizations*. Northern Illinois University Press.

Belkin, D. (2023, March 31). Americans are losing faith in college education, WSJ-NORC poll finds. *The Wall Street Journal*. https://www.wsj.com/articles/americans-are-losing-faith-in-college-education-wsj-norc-poll-finds-3a836ce1

Bloom, A. (1987). *The closing of the American mind: How higher education has failed democracy and impoverished the souls of today's students*. Simon & Schuster.

Bloom, H. (1992). *The American religion: The emergence of the post-Christian nation*. Simon & Schuster.

Bodley, M. (2017, February 2). At Berkeley Yiannopoulos protest, $100,000 in damage, 1 arrest. *San Francisco Gate*. https://www.sfgate.com/crime/article/At-Berkeley-Yiannopoulos-protest-100-000-in-10905217.php

Bok, D. (2006). *Our underachieving colleges: A candid look at how much students learn and why they should be learning more*. Princeton University Press.

Bromwich, D. (1992). *Politics by other means: Higher education and group thinking*. Yale University Press.

Bryant, J. (2024, April 8). Pandemic learning loss: How COVID-19 academically impacted college students. *Best Colleges*. https://www.bestcolleges.com/research/pandemic-learning-loss/#:~:text=Despite%20a%20current%20lack%20of,and%20discomfort%20with%20classroom%20discussions

Butler, J. (2007). *Gender trouble: Feminism and the subversion of identity*. Routledge.

Camera, L. (2023, December 12). Poll: Americans have lost faith in university leaders. *U.S. News and World Report*. https://www.usnews.com/news/leaders/articles/2023-12-12/poll-americans-have-lost-faith-in-university-leaders

de Boer, F. (2023). *How elites ate the social justice movement*. Simon & Schuster.

de Man, P. (1979). *Allegories of reading*. Yale University Press.

Deresiewicz, W. (2014). *Excellent sheep: The miseducation of the American elite and the way to a meaningful life*. Free Press.

Dieckmann, H. (2014). *Complexes: Diagnosis and therapy in Analytical Psychology*. Chiron Publications. https://www.amazon.com/Complexes-Diagnosis-Therapy-Analytical-Psychology-book/dp/B00OYAGD2G/ref=sr_1_1?crid=CJPERN3AF8H2&keywords=complexes%3A+diagnosis&qid=1690461953&s=digital-text&sprefix=complexes+diagnosis%2Cdigital-text%2C89&sr=1-1

Dillon, J. (2018). A letter to a new faculty member: How to stay sane in the academy. *The Humanistic Psychologist, 46*(2), 147–158.

Dillon, J. J. (2021). Reassembling the real person: A Jungian and mythical–dramatistic approach to human development. *Journal of Humanistic Psychology, 61*(5), 786–805.

Dillon, J. J. (2022). *The joy of duty: Human happiness and ethical obligation*. Ethics International Press.

Duarte, J. L., Crawford, J. T., Stern, C., Haidt, J., Jussim, L., & Tetlock, P. E. (2014). Political diversity will improve social psychological science. *Behavioral and Brain Sciences, 38*. https://doi.org/10.1017/S0140525X14000430

Ellis, J. M. (2020). *The breakdown of higher education: How it happened, the damage it does, and what can be done*. Encounter Books.

Flaherty, C. (2022, May 23). Princeton fires professor for misconduct. *Inside Higher Ed*. https://www.insidehighered.com/news/2022/05/24/princeton-board-votes-fire-professor-misconduct

Foundation for Individual Rights and Expression. (2023). The academic mind in 2022: What faculty think about free expression and academic freedom on campus. *Foundation for Individual Rights and Expression*. https://www.thefire.org/research-learn/academic-mind-2022-what-faculty-think-about-free-expression-and-academic-freedom

Good, G. (2001). *Humanism betrayed: Theory, ideology and culture in the contemporary university*. McGill-Queen's University Press.

Griffin, A. (2023, May 22). NYC college professor Shellyne Rodriguez cursed out anti-abortion students tabling at school. *New York Post*. https://nypost.com/2023/05/22/nyc-hunter-college-professor-cursed-out-anti-abortion-students-tabling-at-school/

Hu, K., Godfrey, K., Ren, Q., Wang, S., Yang, X., & Li, Q. (2024). The impact of the COVID-19 pandemic on college students in USA: Two years later. *Psychiatry Research*. https://doi.org/10.1016/j.psychres.2024.116082

Jackson, A. (2016, July 28). 'Disinvitations' for college speakers are on the rise – Here's a list of people turned away this year. *Business Insider*. https://www.businessinsider.com/list-of-disinvited-speakers-at-colleges-2016-7

Jacobi, J. (1959). *Complex/archetype/symbol in the psychology of C. G. Jung*. (R. Manheim, Trans.). Princeton University Press.

Jacobs, A. (2017). Wokeness and myth on campus. *The New Atlantis, 53*, 33–44.

Janis, I. L. (1971). Groupthink. *Psychology Today, 5*(6), 43–46.

Jaschik, S. (2017, March 5). The aftermath at Middlebury. *Inside Higher Ed*. https://www.insidehighered.com/news/2017/03/06/middlebury-engages-soul-searching-after-speech-shouted-down-and-professor-attacked

Jung, C. G. (1967). Symbols of the mother and of rebirth (R. F. C. Hull, Trans.). In H. Read et al. (Eds.), *The collected works of C. G. Jung: Vol. 5. Symbols of transformation* (pp. 207–273). Princeton University Press. (Original work published 1952).

Jung, C. G. (1969a). A review of the complex theory (G. Adler, & R.F.C. Hull, Trans.). In G. Adler & R. F. C. Hull (Eds.), *The collected works of C. G. Jung: Vol. 8. Structure & dynamics of the psyche* (2nd ed., pp. 92–104). Princeton University Press. (Original work published 1934).

Jung, C. G. (1969b). Concerning rebirth (R.F.C. Hull, Trans.). In H. Read, M. Fordham, & G. Adler (Eds.), *The collected works of C.G. Jung: Vol. 9 (part 1). Archetypes and the collective unconscious* (2nd ed., pp. 112–147). Princeton University Press. (Original work published 1939).

Jung, C. G. (1969c). On psychic energy (G. Adler, & R.F.C. Hull, Trans.). In G. Adler & R. F. C. Hull (Eds.), *The collected works of C.G. Jung: Vol. 8. Structure & dynamics of the psyche* (2nd ed., pp. 3–66). Princeton University Press. (Original work published 1928).

Jung, C. G. (1969d). On the psychology of the trickster-figure (R.F.C. Hull, Trans.). In H. Read, M. Fordham, & G. Adler (Eds.), *The collected works of C.G. Jung: Vol. 9 (part 1). The archetypes and the collective unconscious* (2nd ed., pp. 255–272). Princeton University Press. (Original work published 1954).

Jung, C. G. (1969e). Psychological aspects of the mother archetype (R.F.C. Hull, Trans.). In H. Read, M. Fordham, & G. Adler (Eds.), *The collected works of C.G. Jung: Vol. 9 (part 1). The archetypes and the collective unconscious* (2nd ed., pp. 73–110). Princeton University Press. (Original work published 1938).

Jung, C. G. (1969f). The phenomenology of the spirit in fairy tales (R. F. C. Hull, Trans.). In H. Read et al. (Eds.), *The Collected works of C. G. Jung: Vol. 9 (part 1). Archetypes and the Collective Unconscious* (2nd ed., pp. 207–254). Princeton University Press. (Original work published 1948).

Jung, C. G. (1969g). The psychology of the child archetype (R.F.C Hull, Trans.). In H. Read, M. Fordham, G. Adler, & W. McGuire (Eds.), *The collected Works of C.G. Jung: Vol. 9 (part 1). The archetypes and the collective unconscious* (2nd ed., pp. 151–203). Princeton University Press. (Original work published 1940).

Jung, C. G. (1970). Wotan (R. F. C. Hull, Trans.). In H. Read et al. (Eds.), *The collected works of C. G. Jung: Vol. 10. Civilization in transition* (2nd ed., pp. 179–193). Princeton University Press. (Original work published 1936).

Jung, C. G. (1973). On the doctrine of complexes. In H. Read et al. (Eds.), *The collected works of C. G. Jung: Vol. 2. Experimental researches* (pp. 598–604). Princeton University Press. (Original work published 1913).

Jung, C. G. (1989). The significance of the father in the destiny of the individual (G. Adler, & R.F.C Hull, Trans.). In G. Adler & R. F. C. Hull (Eds.), *The collected works of C.G. Jung: Vol. 4. Freud and psychoanalysis* (pp. 302–323). Princeton University Press. (Original work published 1909).

Lind, M. (2023, July 31). The culture of transgression. *Tablet*. https://www.tabletmag.com/sections/news/articles/culture-of-transgression

Lukianoff, G., & Haidt, J. (2018). *The coddling of the American mind: How good intentions and bad ideas are setting up a generation for failure*. Penguin Press.

Lyotard, J. F. (1984). *The postmodern condition: A report on knowledge* (G. Bennington & B. Massouri, Trans.). University of Minnesota Press.

Patel, V. (2023, March 13). UPenn accuses a law professor of racist statements: Should she be fired? *The New York Times*. https://www.nytimes.com/2023/03/13/us/upenn-law-professor-racism-freedom-speech.html

Plato. (1987). *The republic* (D. Lee, Trans.). Penguin Classics. (Original work published 380 B.C.E.)

Pluckrose, H., & Lindsay, J. (2020). *Cynical theories: How activist scholarship made everything about race, gender, and identity – And why this harms everybody*. Pitchstone Publishing.

Rufo, C.F. (2023, September 23). The cluster b society. *City Journal*. https://www.city-journal.org/article/the-cluster-b-society

Saad, L. (2023, July 6). Historically low faith in U.S. institutions continues. *Gallup*. https://news.gallup.com/poll/508169/historically-low-faith-institutions-continues.aspx

Shalit, E. (2002). *The complex: Path of transformation from archetype to ego.* Inner City Books.

Shibley, R. (2016, September 30). New video of last year's Yale Halloween costume confrontation emerges. *Foundation for Individual Rights and Expression.* https://www.thefire.org/news/new-video-last-years-yale-halloween-costume-confrontation-emerges

Smith, C. (2014). *The sacred project of American sociology.* Oxford University Press.

Stripling, J. (2023, June 21). The professor is canceled: Now what? *The Washington Post.* https://www.washingtonpost.com/education/2023/06/21/college-professors-fired-cancel-culture/

Vitz, P. C. (2013). *Faith of the fatherless: The psychology of atheism.* Ignatius Press.

Voegelin, E. (1997). *Science, politics and Gnosticism: Two essays.* Gateway Editions.

von Franz, M. L., & Boa, F. (1994). *The way of the dream: Conversations on Jungian dream interpretation with Marie-Louise von Franz.* Shambala.

Watkins, J. (2021, October 22). Building a 'robust free expression culture on campus.' *The James G. Martin Center for Academic Renewal.* https://www.jamesgmartin.center/2021/10/building-a-robust-free-expression-culture-on-campus/

Wexler, M. N. (1995). Expanding the groupthink explanation to the study of contemporary cultures. *Cultic Studies Journal, 12*(1), 49–71.

Wilson, W., & Link, A. S. (1966). *The papers of Woodrow Wilson, volume 19.* Princeton University Press.

Young, S. (2006). *Designer evolution: A transhumanist manifesto.* Prometheus Books.

Zimmerman, J. (2012, December 13). U.S. colleges need affirmative action for conservative professors. *The Christian Science Monitor.* https://www.csmonitor.com/Commentary/Opinion/2012/1213/US-colleges-need-affirmative-action-for-conservative-professors

CHAPTER 12

Implications of the Work, Remaining Questions, and Directions for the Future

James J. Dillon

Complex and Archetype attempts to preserve and stretch Jung's work to address the needs and questions of our time. Through theoretical chapters and case analyses, we show that Jung's concept of the complex remains relevant as a model of the psyche, functioning as a generative basis for addressing critical issues pertaining to archetype theory and the continued development of a Jungian psycho-social studies. We approach the archetype through the complex. And we approach the complex through everyday social and interpersonal life.

Part I (Chaps. 2, 3, and 4) focuses mainly on Jung's concept of *complexes* as the region where the psyche and the social intersect. Jung (1934/1969a) describes complexes as the "via regia to the unconscious" (p. 101). As we follow this royal road, we are inevitably led to the *archetypes.* Though these archetypes are veiled by our personal experiences, trauma history, language, and cultural background, each complex contains one or more archetypes—numinous images with the power to animate or possess. The chapters in Part I delve into the deeper meaning and developmental significance of complexes by examining the common contexts in which they emerge: the therapeutic and personal growth context, modern

J. J. Dillon (✉)
School of Social Sciences, University of West Georgia, Carrollton, GA, USA

J. J. Dillon (ed.), *Complex and Archetype*,
https://doi.org/10.1007/978-3-032-02609-5_12

science and society, and the field of psychology. The chapters in Part I help us appreciate a number of key points and raise important questions which should be addressed in future research.

Dillon's work in Chap. 2 illustrates what psychology misses when it ignores the dynamic interplay between psychic experience and social life, and how properly understanding the nature and function of the complexes opens the only real productive avenue for growth and development. Remaining questions involve examining the unique ways in which other dominant models in psychology, such as the biological/neurological and computer models, similarly downplay or ignore the role of the unconscious. Further study is also needed to examine the particular foundational myths behind each of these models.

Steder's work in Chap. 3 establishes the importance of complexes in the domain of personal growth by illustrating how the personification of complexes can facilitate self-knowledge. It shows how interaction with such complexes constellates an unconscious intrusion or disruption of various personal beings with whom we can communicate in a process which can reveal our identity and values, increase the awareness of our potential, and provide us with new ideas and practical actions which will help advance personal growth. Many questions remain. First, can all complexes be personified? Can every complex facilitate self-knowledge? Do personified complexes communicate in different ways with different people? Do different personified complexes communicate with the same person in different ways? Are there certain conditions or situations, such as depression or anxiety, which are more conducive to complex personification compared to others? Conversely, are there certain conditions or situations, such as relationship troubles, which are less conducive to complex personification? Are there certain personality types who are better able to personify and dialogue with imaginal material than others? Is psychological disturbance a prerequisite to the facilitation of self-knowledge through complex personification, or can complexes manifest in less stressful contexts? These questions can be addressed with future research by closely analyzing various domains in which complexes tend to manifest such as therapy, developmental transition, personal relationships, and political entrenchment.

Swogger's work in Chap. 4 assesses the current scientific standing of complexes and archetypes and shows that the Pauli-Jung conjecture is the model most capable of accounting for the complexity of complexes and archetypes. This finding suggests a reevaluation of Roesler's (2022) prominent social-constructivist critique of Jung's archetype theory which does not adequately take the Pauli-Jung conjecture into account. It also calls for historical research into the factors shaping Jung's thinking on the matter of the specific nature of the archetypes. One particularly intriguing future direction lies in the domain of psycho-social studies. This would include such analyses as some of those forwarded here in which underlying archetypal dynamics are explored for their acausal but meaningfully related connection to current socio-cultural themes.

Part II presents a series of case analyses which explore the way complexes and archetypes emerge across various aspects of personal and social life: popular culture, video games, romantic relationships, parenting, pet ownership, the campus culture wars, and the everyday challenges and routines of daily life. Each chapter uncovers practical insights about how to effectively engage with the feeling-tones, dreams, and images within the complexes as they manifest in our daily experiences, unlocking the guidance, depth, vibrancy, and energy that arise from the archetypes hidden within them.

Cochran's work in Chap. 5 explores contemporary expressions of archetypes, using examples of the *Lover* and *Creator*. It introduces the notion of a "pop-culture pantheon" which consists of the constellation of prominent cultural figures who come to influence and characterize distinguishable eras. Cochran argues that the emergence of contemporary archetypal expressions is in response to the needs and desires of both the collective unconscious and collective consciousness. Future research might include taking inventory of which figures from the pop culture pantheon characterize particular eras in order to both understand the cultural context and examine the popularity of particular archetypes as a method for analyzing collective representation and/or compensation. This can be done by applying the method Cochran offers which provides easily accessible means to substantiate claims of synchronicity and cultural relevance, blending quantitative and qualitative methodologies.

Grann's work in Chap. 6 explores how the contemporary medium of video gaming can provide meaningful engagement with Jungian archetypal characters and imagery through gameplay and imaginative immersion. While Grann focused on *The Legend of Zelda* franchise, it is not the only video game which can invite archetypal engagement or inspire self-development. Future research is needed to explore other games, whether stand-alone or a series, to investigate similar or novel archetypal dynamics. In addition, it will be important to track the psychological implications of the inevitable changes to the video game medium which will surely take place in the future.

Stover's work in Chap. 7 explores a population known as "Romantics" and how their quest to find a soulmate informs their path toward individuation. Embedded within this exploration of a Romantic's quest to find their beloved, Stover reimagines Jung's notion of marriage as a psychological relationship, identifies key archetypes involved in romantic love, and details the common experiences Romantics confront when seeking a soulmate (i.e., "the one," synchronicity and fated encounters, and heartbreak). There are several remaining questions for future research inspired by this chapter. For example, Stover frames the search for romantic love as being a path toward individuation. However, future research is needed to investigate the psychological prerequisites for being able to accomplish this task in the first place. Further, more research is needed to articulate various archetypal pairings on the path to finding romantic love (e.g., child looking for mother/father rather than a spouse) and ways mythology can help clarify and inform the plight of the Romantic.

Swogger's work in Chap. 8 returns to the root of Jung's writing to reveal the anima/animus as representing, most fundamentally, the relationship to one's unconscious. The personification of this relationship arises in compensatory response to a psychic imbalance. Sticking close to this description helps to guard against the tendency to conflate inner and outer worlds. More research from clinicians is needed to clarify the various ways in which anima and animus figures appear in therapy, and how they are shaped by the changing social conditions since Jung's time. This chapter also opens possibilities for future studies in literary analysis and the psychological humanities broadly.

Stover and Dillon in Chap. 9 explore the role that having (or not having) children plays in the process of individuation. They discuss the various ways that being a parent can facilitate individuation but also explore how these same complexes can be worked through for those who fall under the growing trend of choosing to remain childless. They provide several examples of "alternative children" which allow for the complexes to be brought forth and facilitate individuation. Future research is needed to explore the ways in which one's personal complexes related to parenting might interfere with their ability to decide about whether to become a parent or not, and how to identify these potential manifestations. Further, future research should examine how different materializations of "alternative children"—being a teacher, playing an active role as an aunt/uncle, working on an important creative project, becoming a leader of an organization, gardening/farming—allow the complexes to be revealed and productively integrated.

Rich's work in Chap. 10 considers the many ways archetypal material is expressed in the lived world through various forms of sacred practice. He provides examples of sacred practice which include: the sacred in the ordinary, the way sacred places promote and enhance sacred practices, traditional religious practice, and esoteric or non-traditional spiritual practices which have developed since the mid-nineteenth century. Future research is needed to explore the connection between the "New Age" movement of the 60s, 70s, and 80s and new sacred practices emerging in the contemporary West. This work will provide important insights on how energy from the collective unconscious continues to manifest in the world of lived experience through sacred practice guided by the archetype of the Self.

Dillon's work in Chap. 11 provides a Jungian psycho-social analysis of the tumultuous changes in university culture since the early 2000s. He shows how the modern academy in the United States is currently "possessed" by the repressed chthonic Mother within the positive mother complex; the judging, exacting Father within the negative father complex; and the *furor paedogogicus* (Jung 1940/1969b, p. 175) within the Prometheus complex. He catalogues the damage such possession causes and presents various internal and external solutions for addressing this situation. Future research is needed to determine if there are different types of campus possession in Europe and other parts of the world, and even if the different types of higher education institutions involve different kinds of psychological one-sidedness and archetypal possession. Future work will also be needed to provide practical strategies to university reformers to enable them to tackle the Herculean problems related to lack of viewpoint diversity in faculty hiring, the large-scale rejection of the idea that universities primarily exist to search for truth, and the declining ability of both faculty and students alike to disagree in a constructive fashion.

In drawing this volume to a close, I return to the "keyhole moments" discussed by Kevin Lu in his Foreword. Recall, these are moments or objects chosen as a starting point to investigate wider trends and patterns. He writes, "they serve as a springboard to asking more in-depth and complex questions, but also occasions to appreciate and understand the interconnectedness of human activity and the relationships that bind individuals and communities together." In many ways, we can view the topics which separately gripped each author in this volume as keyhole moments. These seemingly discrete phenomena—the Covid-19 pandemic; university turmoil; the changing social landscape on marriage, gender, and children; the decline of traditional religious practice; the exploding popularity of video gaming; the rise of Kim Kardashian and Elon Musk as figures of cultural fascination; psychology's captivation with the ego complex and radical social construction, as well as its struggle provide an adequate theoretical account of complexes and archetypes—have been springboards for our group to ask deep questions together, and using Jung's powerful concepts of complex and archetype as a guide, to appreciate the interconnectedness of human activity and the relationships that bind individuals together into communities. It was no accident that this group of researchers came together as it did in 2018. We hope this volume is an initial step toward teasing out the deeper meanings behind these moments, and an inspiration for others to explore related meaningful connections in the future.

Competing Interests The author has no conflicts of interest to declare that are relevant to the content of this chapter.

References

Jung, C. G. (1969a). A review of the complex theory (G. Adler, & R. F. C. Hull, Trans.). In G. Adler & R. F. C. Hull (Eds.), *The collected works of C. G. Jung: Vol. 8. Structure & dynamics of the psyche* (2nd ed., pp. 92–104). Princeton University Press. (Original work published 1934).

Jung, C. G. (1969b). The psychology of the child archetype (R.F.C Hull, Trans.). In H. Read, M. Fordham, G. Adler, & W. McGuire (Eds.), *The collected works of C.G. Jung: Vol. 9 (part 1). The archetypes and the collective unconscious* (2nd ed., pp. 151–203). Princeton University Press. (Original work published 1940).

Roesler, C. (2022). *Development of a reconceptualization of archetype theory: Report to the IAAP.* International Association for Analytical Psychology. https://iaap.org/wp-content/uploads/2023/04/Report-Archetype-Theory-Roesler-1-3.pdf

Index[1]

[1] Note: Page numbers followed by 'n' refer to notes.

J. J. Dillon (ed.), *Complex and Archetype*,
https://doi.org/10.1007/978-3-032-02609-5

GPSR Compliance
The European Union's (EU) General Product Safety Regulation (GPSR) is a set of rules that requires consumer products to be safe and our obligations to ensure this.

If you have any concerns about our products, you can contact us on

ProductSafety@springernature.com

In case Publisher is established outside the EU, the EU authorized representative is:

Springer Nature Customer Service Center GmbH
Europaplatz 3
69115 Heidelberg, Germany

www.ingramcontent.com/pod-product-compliance
Lightning Source LLC
Chambersburg PA
CBHW070748080926
51093CB00004B/244
* 9 7 8 3 0 3 2 0 2 6 0 8 8 *